Women's Work

Work

CHOICE, CHANCE OR SOCIALIZATION?

Nancy Johnson Smith and Sylva K. Leduc

**Insights from psychologists
and other researchers**

Detselig Enterprises Ltd.

Canadian Cataloguing in Publication Data

Smith , Nancy Johnson
Women's work

Includes bibliographical references.
ISBN 1-55059-046-4

1. Women—Interviews. 2. Women—Employment.
3. Women—Social conditions. I. Leduc, Sylva K.
II. Title.

HD6053.S64 1992	305.43	C92-091656-2

Detselig Enterprises Ltd.
Suite 210 1220 Kensington Rd. N.W.
Calgary, Alberta
T2N 3P5

Detselig Enterprises Ltd. appreciates the financial support for its 1992 publishing program from Canada Council and Alberta Foundation for the Arts.

Printed in Canada   SAN 115-0324   ISBN 1-55059-046-4

Contents

Section One : The Shaping of Women's Vocational Interests and Choices

Section Two : Women's Vocational Interests—Trends and the Status Quo

Section Three : Special Issues

Section Four : Where do We Go in the Future?

Acknowledgments

We are indebted to the many people who helped us over the project's almost two years of development. Most gratifying was the unselfish willingness of each of the people we approached for interviews to donate their time and expertise to the project. Drs. Duane Brown, John Holland and Donald Super generously gave time to discussing the book and suggesting potential interviewees with one of the authors by telephone and at the annual convention of the American Association for Counseling and Development (AACD) at Reno Nevada, April 21-24, 1991. Dr. Kris Magnusson of the University of Calgary's Educational Psychology Department and staff members of the Ontario Institute for Studies in Education (OISE) contributed invaluable insights into the issues. And we want to thank Pat Henderson of the City of Calgary for her very useful briefing on employment equity.

We also want to thank the Alberta Foundation for the Literary Arts for its grant to support author Smith during the writing of this book. And without the generous support of Warner Woodley and Mainstream Access Corporation this project would never have been completed. In particular, we want to acknowledge Mainstream administrative staff, especially Trina Laroche, Liz Hammond and Laurie Glasser for their patience and endurance in transcribing what may have seemed to be a never ending stream of interview tapes. As well, author and consultant George Melnyk, psychologist Dr. Maria Eriksen and career consultants Barbara Philpot (chartered psychologist) and Fran Kimmel have earned our enduring gratitude for timely contributions to the project.

We also truly thank our husbands, Derald Smith and Van Lawson, for their support and understanding during the long months when we were totally immersed in the project.

Finally, we thank our respective parents for their lifelong, loving encouragement.

Introduction

Women's Voices on Women's Choices

Both men and women grow up in ghettos. Male ghettos and female ghettos.
So they don't get the experience [that would expose them to the full range of
career options].
—John Holland, Ph.D., personal communication, April 23, 1991, American
Counselling and Development Assoc. Annual General Meeting, Reno, Nevada

Why this Book

We live in tough economic times, when most women as well as men have to toil at jobs outside the home in order to survive. In both the U.S.[1] and Canada[2], women are almost half the workforce. In fact, three-quarters of the women in the prime child bearing and rearing years of 25 to 44 are employed.

What these numbers mean is that for the majority of North American women today, choosing and competing to stay in an occupation is a major life responsibility, which entails juggling a desire for family and friends, a decent income and job satisfaction. However, no longer is it automatically acceptable for women to slot themselves into stereotypically female jobs. Increasingly, we are expected to consider the full range of career options, from full-time homemaker to nontraditional careers[3] such as engineer.

But there is a hitch to these new freedoms. The workplace is still set up primarily to meet the traditional needs of men. And often women are caught in a crossfire of socialized expectations—to be aggressively successful yet still play the traditional nurturing female role. To resolve such apparent contradictions, most of us need all the facts we can gather to sort out our options. And that is true no matter whether we are choosing our first job, rethinking our initial choice at mid-career or reentering the job market after work as a homemaker. We need to understand why we are interested in certain employment fields. What social forces compel

---

1 U.S. Bureau of the Census, (1991). *Statistical Abstract of the United States, 1991:111th Edition.* Washington, DC.
2 Statistics Canada (1992). *The 1992 Canada Yearbook, 125th Edition*, Ottawa.
3 Where nontraditional is defined as those fields where less than 35 to 30 percent of the workforce have traditionally been female. Personal communication, S. Kahn, UBC, October 9, 1991.

us? How much do our supposed choices reflect lack of experience and opportunity? What have we been told women are supposed to do? Do we even know what obstacles we face as women in a given field? To summarize, is our chosen occupation the result of chance, *informed* choice or socialization?

And even if we happen to be experienced career counsellors trying to help others make these decisions, our fast-paced lives and the demands of clients often mean little time to keep up with the burgeoning amount of information in our field. Counsellors too need ready access to new ideas and developments.

One source of help for all of us in exploring career choice more knowledgeably, whether we are making decisions for ourselves or helping others, is the experience of professionals who have spent a lifetime analyzing occupational issues, and whose own lives serve as road maps to job market survival. In short, we all benefit by more access to educated inspiration. Of course, many excellent guidebooks, texts and courses on career choice are already available. Yet what we also need to see distilled into print are the personal concerns and views of experts.

The purpose of this book is to provide access to such wisdom, not from the cold, dry facts of scientific literature but from conversations with living people. As such, this project has been a very personal odyssey for the authors. Both of us have done our share of stumbling through difficult career choices in nontraditional fields. The occupations of Nancy Smith (shown on back cover on the left) have included high school biology teacher, university research associate in Environmental Science and science journalist. Sylva Leduc (shown on back cover on the right) worked as a quality control inspector in road construction before retraining in psychology as a career counsellor. Therefore, in large part, this project reflects our own need to understand (1) the factors that influence career choice in women (often outside our awareness) and (2) some sense of the steps we as women can take to ensure more fulfilling choices.

We also realize some women may feel there is too much pressure today to consider only nontraditional careers. But we hope that by understanding some of the forces shaping occupational interests and aspirations, people will feel freer to resist outside pressures and pursue their occupational dreams—whatever their direction. Donald Super in an interview with one of the authors expressed the problem the following way:[4]

> *I've had [women] students who shifted majors from science to social science or social service and some people look at that and feel that counselling took that woman out of a field into which she should have gone. The feminists feel we need her there. My reaction as a counsellor has been that she needs self-fulfillment. She shouldn't be forced to go there because some other woman thinks she's letting her sex down. She shouldn't let herself down. And some women increasingly realize that. The pressure to go into a nontraditional occupation is being resisted more than before.*

---

4 Super, D., personal communication, April 24, 1991, American Counseling Association Annual General Meeting, Reno, Nevada.

Choosing Interviewees and Issues

After deciding the book's general focus, we next had to decide who to interview and on what topics. The problem was that, given more than two decades of rapid growth in this field, the literature was filled with authoritative voices and critical topics. Yet restrictions such as timing, page allowance and funding meant this book could only sample the issues and experts. As a result, we first selected a cross-section of the current issues based on a survey of the literature, the interests of our interviewees, the advice of career counsellors, and frankly, on the topics we wanted to learn more about ourselves. Then for each issue we chose an expert whose publications covered that topic prominently and who was available for a half-day interview within a five month window. In addition, we asked each person to make time to review her own chapter to ensure that the edited interview did not inadvertently misrepresent or eliminate important concepts. Of the eleven interviewees (two in one setting), seven are counselling psychologists. The others are a social psychologist, a sociologist, a biologist and a mathematician. All are women, although we did not initially choose this restriction. However, we found that most of the current work on women's careers is published by women and we feel the book benefits from a common female frame of reference.

General Organization of the Book

The book is divided into four sections, beginning with two overviews of the influences on women's occupational interests and choices. It then surveys the interest patterns that women over the last fifty years have expressed on one of the most commonly used vocational interest tests. The next section covers four specific issues or obstacles to women's pursuit of their desired occupation. (1) What happens on university campuses to quench a woman's passion for a career? (2) What special obstacles do gifted women encounter? (3) Why are there so few women in science and math-related careers? and (4) What health, safety and educational issues push women out of nontraditional jobs, particularly in the trades and technology? The last section includes three approaches to solving, or at least reducing, these difficulties. In conclusion, we summarize the common concerns and themes that emerge from the interviews and what these may mean for the lives of women in general.

Interview Format

Each of the ten interviews roughly followed a pre-agreed upon list of questions. But overall, the interviews covered the same core areas. Of course, having sources so expert and enthusiastic about their field often meant the discussions involved additional insights. First each interviewee told how she made her own career choices. Then she drew upon her own research plus general knowledge of her field to discuss a particular issue regarding women's vocational interests and choices. Most interviewees also described the kinds of research they thought needed more emphasis and the implications of their research for career counsellor practice. In closure, we asked each woman to extract from her experience final bits ["pearls"] of wisdom about career choice in general.

Although we have tried to edit the interviews to eliminate unnecessary technical detail, some is necessary to maintain the integrity of the discussions on research. To clarify these points and direct readers to more in-depth information, each chapter includes footnotes, the specific references brought up in the interview and a list of relevant publications and recommended readings. The chapters also include significant life events as identified by each interviewee.

We hope the following chapters will spark interest in reading more widely in this field. Most of all, we trust the passion our interviewees obviously feel for their work will inspire among our readers greater understanding, and thereby acceptance, of both their own and others' vocational aspirations and ambitions.

Section One

The Shaping of Women's Vocational Interests and Choices

Women are still socialized to be nice and pleasant, to go into the caring occupations. Even if they go into a competitive field, say a business or industrial field, they are so conditioned that they take on the more supportive roles, the administrative secretary rather than the manager. But they have more freedom now to aspire to and to move into the managerial roles and they do. Still there is the limitation as someone put in the title of a book, The Glass Ceiling—so high and no higher.

—Donald Super, personal communication, April 23, 1991.

For this section, we asked two counselling psychologists to provide an overview of the forces that too often limit women's career interests and choices. Each interviewee approaches the issue from a somewhat different perspective, drawing upon both her personal experiences and professional studies.

Helen Farmer of the University of Illinois focuses on how a woman's early environment and later social support affect her motivation to have a career and to be committed to it.

Helen Astin of the University of California at Los Angeles, who grew up in Greece, adds the fresh perspective of someone socialized outside the North American culture. Astin stresses the effect of institutional forces—such as laws, cultural values, educational systems and accepted concepts of the family—on women's career choices. Fortunately, changes in these institutions, she explains, can catalyze a woman's successful efforts to enter a career she had thought to be unattainable.

Chapter 1: The Influence of Early Environment and Ongoing
Social Support
Chapter 2: The Influence of Institutionalized Barriers

1

The Influence of Early Environment
and Ongoing Social Support

An interview with Helen Farmer, Ph.D., Professor of Counseling Psychology, University of Illinois.

Anyone watching Helen Farmer's eyes sparkle as she describes her research realizes she knows personally the benefits to be gained from the right career choice(s). During a four-hour interview on a rainy Ottawa summer afternoon, she also taught the authors a great deal about the obstacles women face from childhood on when choosing a vocation. One of the major obstacles, she suggested, involves unrealistic expectations placed on women today—to seamlessly mesh both a career and primary responsibility for nurturing a family while receiving little personal or institutional support.

Farmer's interest in the dilemmas facing career-oriented women germinated when her own dreams of being a minister lost out early in life to the Fifties' rigid image of a woman's proper role. For the next eleven years she raised three children and kept busy in a variety of temporary jobs, from teacher to newsletter editor. However, since reentering graduate school twenty-five years ago, she has made non-stop, award-winning contributions to career research. She has published over 100 major research articles, books and reports; received a full professorship; chaired major conferences; and as a Fellow of the American Psychological Association, earned, without question, her peers' respect.

Her latest contribution is a theoretical model of what motivates people to seek a career and then achieve in it. To develop her model she used data collected from a sample of women who have been studied from the age of 17 to 28 (see References: Farmer, 1985 and 1991). The goal of this ongoing project is to identify and track characteristics of these women's lives or selves that catalyze shifts in career aspirations, commitment to a career and the need to excel at whatever tasks they take on.

Albert Bandura's social learning theory, she says, strongly influenced her ideas. Bandura himself considers such psychological shifts and related behaviors to be derived from the interaction of three factors: (1) background or given influences such as gender, ethnicity and ability (2) psychological or personal self-concept factors such as a person's attitudes, beliefs and previous experiences, and (3) environmental or social factors affecting the individual. In the following discussion Farmer shows how all these factors influence the development of women's career choices, including the impact on her own life.

The Evolution of a Behavioral Scientist

Smith: *In your research publications you talk about the importance of a person's family background and early experience in shaping career choices. How did your own early background direct you into counselling psychology and the study of women's career development?*

Farmer: Well, I chose a nontraditional career, the ministry, back in High School in the west end of Ottawa, and my role models were two men—the local minister and an air force chaplain who was very inspiring in his sermons. Also I read a romantic religious novel by a Canadian woman and I got this kind of feeling that theology was the queen of sciences. Which is the way it was described in medieval times, when there was no technology. So when people would ask me "Don't you want to get married and have children?" I said, "Sure, I want to do both." But in their minds at that time, you couldn't have both a career and children. If you wanted to be a masculine something or other, then that was your life and you couldn't be a woman. So I went to Queen's University in Canada where there is a seminary.

How I ended up majoring in honors psychology was by chance. I was getting an A in introductory psychology and the instructor came along while I was walking through the quadrangle one day, and tapped me on the shoulder and said, "Wouldn't you like to major in psychology?" I knew theology required a liberal arts background as a bachelors degree but which area didn't really matter. In fact, I loved philosophy, which is more closely linked to theology, but didn't do as well in it as I did in psychology. So I went and talked with her but I won't call her a role model. I think that Bandura is quite right. Role models must be persons you identify with. They can't be too remote. And she was very masculine and single. As a student at that time I did not identify with her. So she was not the reason I went into psychology.

Leduc: *Yet by going into psychology you still were meeting your career goals because you would be able to understand people better in order to help them.*

Farmer: Yes and when I did go to seminary in New York City I entered a field of psychiatry and religion—very popular in the fifties. It was just kind of emerging— where theologians were trying to translate their concepts into psychiatric concepts. So it was a nice match. Then I discovered something I should have known if I'd had a realistic counsellor—that I was not going to be eligible for a pulpit. Women ministers were given only little churches in the country or they ran the church school. They could be ordained, yes, but not preach or baptize. So I was ordained and married in 1955 and had my first son in 1956.

My interest in women's issues evolved also with my thesis in seminary, on the role of the professionally trained minister's wife. I read the literature at that time on women, including Helene Deutsch, the Harvard psychologist and Karen Horney from New York, one of the earliest reinterpreters of Freud for women. And exposure to that was very exciting, but also discouraging. The main, very important idea I got from Karen Horney was that women were people first and women second. Helene Deutsch, in contrast, believed to bring women back to health you had to help them accept dependence and domination by men rather than be equals. I thought this was a terrible idea. But Karen Horney was a positive role model. And there was also a woman professor at the seminary who was very much a role model. She combined what I called attributes of a woman with scholarship and professionalism, which was important to me.

Smith: *I am struck by something in what you're saying. Unlike most women, you seemed to have encountered only later in your life the idea that there could be obstacles to your career dreams.*

Farmer: That's right. I wasn't in Gottfredson's crunch [see Chapter 8 for description of concept]. So you're wondering why?

Leduc: *Was it the parental influence in your early environment?*

Farmer: Yes. My father had two daughters, but we were his sons. My summer cottage is on my great-grandfather's farm and we've had this farm since 1840, so our family had this rural influence. My father was a market gardener and grew fruit, vegetables and flowers. He taught us when we were little to do the work in the fields with him and when we were old enough, he paid us. So my summer job when I was about 12 to 16 was in the fields. My sister and I had the sense that we could do anything a man could do. And he bragged to the neighbors that we were better than any hired man. I'll bet that was a very important influence on me.

The second factor was that I was born in 1929, in the depression. The depression has been shown to have made women in general want to be economically independent. Our generation tended to feel we had to earn our living—which is a current emphasis as well because of divorce and so many single heads of households. It's also a feminist principle I believe in. But it had this other source in the depression. Perhaps not for upper- or middle-class families, but for lower middle-class families like us. So my experience as a woman had some unique dimensions. Growing up in the Depression is typical of many women's early experience. The rural influence is not, neither is being treated as your father's son.

Lessons from Research

Leduc: *Why does there have to be a separate model for women's career choice and development? Is it that much more difficult or complicated for women than it is for men?*

Farmer: Yes it is, because of three major gender-related differences. The first is the interdependence between work and family roles. For most women. In fact that is the most salient difference. The second is their greater vulnerability to experience and environmental support, because girls don't get a clear message that you should have a career. The third difference has to do with women's lesser achievement career-wise over the lifetime. Now these three are all related. The interdependence leads to the lack of a clear message and the lack of a clear message leads to inhibition of all three types of career motivation—aspiration and commitment and mastery.

These differences don't all show up early, however. For example, we found in our own longitudinal study on aspiration no gender differences in high school—the girls were aspiring just as high as the boys and some even higher—and this finding has been found in a lot of other studies, for example, Carol Tittle in New York with her junior high students. And the Project Talent longitudinal study across the U.S. with thousands of kids in it. I would trust these data because these are large studies with representative samples. So when we get less achievement later in terms of graduate degrees, the salary earned, the levels of occupation entered, for women as compared for men, that's a serious gender difference, especially when we know aspiration and ability are equally high.

Smith: *Then something's happening when girls leave high school. Society must be doing something to them. I mean, they start off with the same ability, the same aspirations as boys. It's not because they don't want to have a career.*

Farmer: That's exactly right. We're finding that out more and more. For example, Johns Hopkins research on gender and math ability has looked at the top five percent of boys and girls in math scores and found differences for the sexes. But that difference is reduced in the more recent cohorts. And that's a hot topic. There's a wonderful book that came out in 1986 by Janet Shibley-Hyde and Marsha Linn which takes a closer look at math and science and gender differences. But as adults women find career choice a lot more confusing unless they've been prepared.

"Society doesn't yet expect women to have careers or work, but the support group for boys and men is automatic and internalized early."

Smith: *What's causing this confusion? In your model of women's career development, you comment that women are more sensitive to parental influence because of heavy socialization pressure. How does this affect girls and women?*

Farmer: You have to remember the difference in the social support for men's and women's careers. Society doesn't yet expect women to have careers or work, but the social support group for boys and men is automatic and internalized early. No matter what happens they have to be successful in work because the message is so pervasive. For women, however, it's a mixed picture. Some get support for careers—"you know you're very good at this, you ought to try it," or "you'll need it for security." But the real message is that work is only a failsafe and not essential. Work has a make-money value not a self-actualization value. And we need to ask how clear their parental messages are. Is there is a clear message of "yes you can" instead of "yes, you can; no, you can't"? More women get that ambivalent latter message. Or else they get "you don't have to worry, you don't have to get As in math because you're going to go to college and meet somebody and get married." Therefore to have someone, a parent, teacher, counsellor, or aunt who believes it's important for you to be fully engaged in a career or work as well as raising a family is very critical for women and has more influence on them than on boys for career choice.

So it seems like Gottfredson, Super and Holland are right when they say that a lot of our interests and values are laid down early. But I disagree with them about how closed they are. I'm an optimist in the sense that I think that change can occur when a woman sees that possibility. Linda Gottfredson would be more realistic. She would just say it's very hard to reverse the past. But I think interests can develop later although the timing of their development is different in women, compared to men.

Leduc: *How important is social class background to motivation?*

Farmer: Much depends on parental values. You can have very poor parents—immigrants are a good example—who aspire to the best for their children. You have many doctors and lawyers coming out of immigrant families but the parents have established the base, working in restaurants or laundries. That would be an example where class has to be looked at in terms of values of parents for their children. And this fits into what I was saying about role models. The effect of the environment is more critical for girls in terms of role models.

Smith: *That explains why within a social economic class, some people do better than others. Maybe socioeconomic class is not even that useful to look at.*

Farmer: However, social status still is quite a powerful influence. It's not to be ignored. It's just not the only factor. You can't say because you come from a poor family, or from a wealthy family this is the kind of experience you'll have had. That may have had some influence but there's also the effect of role models, experience in school and social support. I think you can also have influential experiences in community groups, girl guides for example, and other extracurricular activities. Especially because you can meet a mentor—a leader or a friend—in those kinds of groups.

Leduc: *What happens if you don't have a suitable role model?*

Farmer: Well, people also choose their own environment and can influence what happens by selection. You can choose to say "the world has closed doors" or you can choose to say "Hey! I can get my toe in there and I'm going to go for it. I'm going to find a role model." That is risk taking and seeing opportunity.

Let me tell a story to illustrate this point. I finished my Ph.D. late, as I told you. I was in my forties. I was out at UCLA and they still had a nepotism rule in 1972 and they wouldn't hire me because my husband was already on faculty. So I went to work in a research corporation hoping later to move into academia. My husband was invited to go the University of Illinois. I said, "I'm not going, I have a good job here in Los Angeles." So he talked to the person interested in hiring him about what could I do at Illinois. Dual career couples are considered together now but weren't at that time. They worked out an arrangement whereby I would have a temporary appointment as a visiting assistant professor and then at the end of three years they would see whether they wanted to keep me. I got to teach one course and work on a research project. No security and the salary was about $10,000 less than what I was earning.

So I worked on my list of positives and negatives about the move. Then I went to Helen Astin, at UCLA. She was a kind of role model for me because she was a full professor at that time, though it was interesting that she was two years younger than me. Reentry women run into that. She'd come directly to UCLA as a full professor from a research corporation in Washington, where she'd been with her husband for maybe 15 years, because she had published a lot and done very well. She said, "Going to Illinois would be getting your toe in the door. You take the risk, it may not work out but it could, and that is what you want." So I took the risk, and it worked out. Women have to make active choices and need the necessary decision-making and problem-solving skills.

But what we're finding in high school now is, yes, young women expect to work, but more to increase their life style for a time and then quit, rather than thinking of work as an important part of my being, myself and my self-actualization. I was working very briefly this summer with the Counselling and Guidance Foundation of Canada, and talked to Mary Balanchuk (Professor, Counselling Psychology, Queen's University, Kingston, Ontario). She has a grant to develop video tapes for counselling young women and has done some surveys in high schools. What she found was that girls still expect to grow up and get married and be taken care of. This is just not realistic.

Freud had a very important insight—as Astin also has written—that the twin poles of mental health are love and work. But Astin also says, "Work is not essential." She believes there are a variety of other options that permit satisfaction of the need to contribute to society. This need can be satisfied through home and family still, in Astin's view. In Louise Fitzgerald's view it cannot. She suggests work is essential to the fully actualizing woman.

Leduc: *And work being defined as paid work.*

Farmer: Yes. Employed work, not volunteer. So Astin has a broader view of what important development for a woman can encompass today.

Smith: *Maybe their differences reflect their own early backgrounds? Whether or not there were other opportunities for self actualization which Astin's particular society in her youth approved of, for example, volunteer work? Now, perhaps our society is devaluing those options and you really can only get that kind of self actualization through work.*

Farmer: And by being recognized for your work in an equal way to men. Volunteers today are abused. When it comes to decision making they are left out and not given a real say in the critical moments. So, yes, I think we are all influenced by our backgrounds. Astin's childhood was in Greece where there was a civilization that had different options for giving meaning to a woman's life. I like to think there are still options here. But what Louise Fitzgerald is saying about the importance of paid work is very timely for our present environment. And will become so increasingly.

If you think of work in terms of productivity, contribution and well-being, then you see how important it is to mental health. Now I let my children grow up first. But I believe that spending 17 years between my first and second graduate degrees was not right. It would have been much better to have been doing family and career together. So I have a strong commitment to the parallel career-family approach.

Smith: *Do you think if you were to go back now and could rearrange your life, would you have taken that break?*

Farmer: I would not have taken that break. I found that as a young mother staying at home I got very depressed. Some young mothers enjoy that, but not me! So I think knowing yourself is important. I would recommend women think ahead about what it would be like staying at home with young children.

Leduc: *Do you then see a difference in the career pathing of women depending on whether they've had children or not.*

Farmer: Yes, women with children are more likely to have interrupted their careers or lowered their aspirations, gotten sidetracked, taken stop-gap kinds of things. Sociologists have done a lot of good work on working women, with and without children, and looked at paths to promotion and job entry. They find children reduce the likelihood of promotion and salary levels.

Smith: *Would you generally recommend that women do not plan to drop out to raise a family?*

Farmer: I would say for any woman who is strongly career committed, be cautious. I firmly believe that a lot of the time in child care and child rearing is functional, not what we call quality care, the creative good times. If you combine the two roles you'll probably give up a lot of leisure time—your leisure time will be your time with your child—but you'll be a lot more interesting person. A depressed mother is no good for a child. My kids blossomed when I went back to school—"See, there's mommy doing homework, we're doing homework"— and that was great. So it's really very important for young women to see as role models both women who stay home and those who don't. And then ask themselves,"Am I more this person, or am I that person?" But if women get the message that work is important for mental health and still choose to stay at home for two or three years, well, okay.

Smith: *Then if they do stay home and start to get depressed, they can say, "I have a right to be depressed" and not feel, "Oh, what's wrong with me, this is supposed to be the most wonderful thing in the world."*

Farmer: Yes, and not blame themselves, but see this as a typical thing that can happen.

Smith: *Then you're saying establishing a career identity is really much more important for women than it ever was, or it should be?*

Farmer: Yes, but as I said, women need help synchronizing the two roles of family and career. The tendency recently has been to devalue career counselling, to say it's not as important as treating other kinds of psychological problems. But I disagree. You have to help women realize early they need to plan ahead, not wait for opportunity to get them on the career road. I said that also back in '71 but it is increasingly important to have a course in high school that helps them see, "Yes, it's going to be very important to have the person I marry support who I want to be." For example, I do have a supportive husband, but neither of us understood what a dual career meant in the early years. So I stayed at home. Yet he was the one who urged me back to graduate school. When you don't have role models or patterns to follow—and dual career couples still have to forge their own patterns—you need to think early about the potential problems.

Smith: *You've been bringing up some of the social environmental factors that inhibit women's career and achievement motivation, such as the dual demands to marry and have a career. You've also mentioned factors promoting it, such as supportive role models. It sounds like early counselling, in particular, in these critical window periods of development, is essential to get women thinking in this direction.*

Farmer: Yes, without counselling, you'll be inhibited by double messages or lack of role models. Think of the wolf child who couldn't speak because he had no one to model himself after. There's also the negative, discouraging messages because you're a girl—more potent inhibitors than lack of money. Now ability is not an inhibitor because we can only do our best, but achievement is learned. There is the potential to be developed but you must be encouraged to bring out the best.

Carol Dweck's work on learned helplessness and attributions for failure applies here. What she found was that it's not only what a girl's parents may say (she doesn't need math) but little girls are expected to dress properly and be nice and polite and do everything the teacher says and then be ignored. Little boys are expected to be rowdy and not be motivated to do their homework, and be praised to the hilt when they do well. So she found you had a very different environment from the same teacher, same classroom, for girls and boys—environments very inhibiting to a woman's career development by denying her a sense of achievement and competency. It wasn't important if a girl got As in math and science. Therefore if she didn't get As she was ignored. If she was failing she wasn't helped to see she could do it. But teachers made sure boys were taught because they needed science and math to get into pre-med, physics and engineering.

Leduc: *So in math the boy who made a mistake would have been told, "No you're not quite right but here's how to do it." Yet a girl would have been told, "No, you're wrong." Then the teacher would have said, "Johnny, what do you think is the right answer?"*

Farmer: Yes, these studies showed that boys were given opportunities for learning experiences and encouragement. Girls were ignored. So your mediocre ability boy would end up doing better in math than your high ability girl because of this difference in how they were treated in school.

Smith: *This fits in with social learning theories about the origins of career interests, the interrelationship between being acknowledged for doing something well and becoming interested in it.*

Farmer: Yes, if you do something well and you're praised for it, you want to do it again and get that good feeling and that builds confidence in yourself and interest in that task.

Social Support and Mastery Motivation

Leduc: *How do the social influences we've talked about affect the development of all three specific types of career motivation?*

Farmer: First, let me define the terms. Mastery motivation is the motivation to achieve on a discrete small task—to earn an A, win a race. This requires the person who likes challenge and risk and is persistent to estimate the odds. High mastery-motivated people are realistic; they don't shoot for 10 per cent odds. They shoot for 50/50. But mastery motivation may be task-specific. You don't have a general personality tendency, you have it in related specific areas. So it might be games, public speaking, entertainment, sports, and in my case it was academics. School was my area. I liked it, people told me I did well and I wanted to keep doing well. But in games with other children I was awkward. I couldn't catch the ball. So I didn't care if I won at games because I wasn't good at it. Now these characteristics are laid down in early childhood, some even before you get to school.

Smith: *Is any of this inborn?*

Farmer: No, I think mastery is very much learned. In contrast, temperament is kind of a given, whether you're quick or slow, or optimistic or pessimistic. Of course, ability in some of the areas you feel motivated to achieve in, such as sports, can be influenced by your genetic heritage, so in terms of mastery that would be partly a given. But things such as liking challenge and risk taking and estimating odds seem to be built on a base of learned self-confidence and self-esteem.

Social class also influences mastery motivation. A lower class family where children are expected to bring themselves up doesn't provide this reinforcement for persistence or risk taking. The literature clearly demonstrates that mastery or need for achievement is weaker in families that don't encourage it. So middle-class families have an advantage. Upper-class women may also be less career minded—they may expect a life of leisure.

Leduc: *Isn't there more stereotyping in the lower class, though, in terms of role differentiation? Men don't help in the kitchen or otherwise help their wives, so mothers and women who work tend to carry the double load.*

Farmer: Yes and that's not true in the upper class. They are freer from that. However, roles are changing. Lucia Gilbert's work on dual career couples has found what she calls traditional, transitional and nontraditional husbands. The transitional ones are helping but not taking the primary responsibility in the home. The nontraditional ones are taking on equal responsibilities. And of course the traditional ones are neither helping nor taking responsibility. Within middle-class families she finds all of these types, but increasingly the nontraditional. In the lower class there is much less change.

Leduc: *Which makes it much more difficult to pursue a career when carrying that double load.*

Farmer: Yes, girls growing up in lower-class families may grow up expecting to work but not to have a career. They expect to support the family, if they are single or their husband is lazy, but they're less likely to think about "What is the greatest thing I can do," and then plan for and achieve that. They "flounder." Super used that term. They move along like a taxi driver from one cab to another, or wait on tables for a while. We can't characterize all lower-class families like that. As I said, the immigrant families are very highly motivated, but the typical lower class will have that expectation.

Such background factors contribute to mastery and affect a person's self-concept regarding the traits of self-reliance, instrumentality and competitiveness. Now the literature shows persistence and mastery are related to competitiveness in boys but not in girls. You can be highly mastery motivated but not want to beat others all the time because you can choose to win for yourself. So girls don't have to be competitive to be highly motivated. Instrumentality—taking the initiative to go after something, and self-reliance, not feeling dependent—those two characteristics are also related to mastery, as are persistence and risk taking.

On the other hand, fear of success and learned helplessness are negatives for mastery motivation. Horner's fear of success—masculine success—means you don't try or take a risk because you fear people won't think as highly of you, especially men. You'll lose sexual brownie points. And that's a socialized inhibition. A female boss is often pictured in the media as someone with dementia. Katharine Hepburn is a wonderful example. In her films she needed Helene Deutsch's dominant man to fulfill herself.

In turn, learned helplessness is a negative because it's experience with a repeated failure not followed by constructive help. For example, it's probably responsible for a lot of our female graduate students saying, "Well, I'm worried about statistics because I'm no good at math." We have a graduate record exam where the top out is 800 but a score of 600 is very good and that is our cutoff. Most of the students have achieved the cutoff. They could do anything they wanted in statistics! They may even have equal or better aptitude to the men who go into the field. But this fear of statistics can be reversed. And that's what a lot of the work in schools has done—help provide success in increments and the necessary support and teaching to overcome this characteristic.

Leduc: *And to reframe the woman's self-concept.*

Farmer: Yes, and then you also need encouragement and opportunities to try out a task. You can't master something that isn't there. Once it's set in a young child, mastery motivation is less likely to change as a result of later opportunities or social influence. For example, marriage doesn't have much effect since mastery is a short-range motivation to achieve and that can be satisfied by decorating, homemaking, a lot of different ways.

Social Support and Aspiration

Smith: *What about the other two types of motivation, career aspirations and career commitment? How are they susceptible to social influences?*

Farmer: Aspiration, as in Linda Gottfredson's model, is strongly affected by early socialization and background. But it can be changed positively later through opportunity in the schools. It's affected most by a person's perception of their ability. People are not always aware of what they can do. It has to be developed. So aspiration has an important potential for change. The problem for women is that the initial ability measurements made on them may have been based on biased tests not representing women's ability in a true fashion. For example, the whole business of women not being as good at spatial relationships which are supposed to be important for engineering. That's being challenged. Studies show test scores depend on how they're measured, because women are good at spatial relationships. If they're given familiar examples rather than questions oriented towards boys' experiences. If you give girls questions involving a recipe or cutting out a dress, which also involve spatial relationships, they do well.

Smith: *Do you still see a place for tests?*

Farmer: Yes I do. They can do harm or do wonderful good if they confirm or give a new sense of self that a person didn't have. "Gee I'm better than 99 percent of the people in this area and I didn't know that!" So a test will then enhance aspiration. One of the things I've found in counselling adult women is that they lack confidence. They say, "Can I do it? Give me an aptitude test so I'll find out". But you have to get a test that is not sex-biased.

Leduc: *Does marriage affect career aspiration?*

Farmer: If the husband is supportive and there isn't a handicapped child or some reason that makes the woman feel she needs to be at home then career aspiration is likely to be maintained. But we know getting equal time to devote to your career is rare rather than typical for women. On the other hand, having a transitional husband is becoming more typical, the one who says, "Yes, I want to support you but I still want my dinner on the table" or "Yes, I want to support you but when the kids are sick you go home." That affects aspiration because then you think, "I have to have a career that allows me to pull off these two things." Many women became teachers and nurses for a long time because they could get home at the same time as the children, and teachers had summer off with the kids. So unless you've got support or the money to hire a nanny you can have problems. Adequate spousal support is important for aspiration, but adequate child care is also important. And that's something the government, the community and employers can do something about. Sometimes the nanny costs as much as you might earn and some people will say it's silly to work. But it's not silly if you are strongly committed to a career and you are laying the foundation for it, building equity.

Leduc: *But what do you do if child care is not available and you're required to work overtime or travel? Do you say, "I can't take that job"?*

Smith: *And then people say that women are not as committed to their careers as much as men!*

Farmer: Yes, some women don't even get asked to travel or to take higher level jobs or work weekends because of these attitudes. So it's not just the spouse that's important but the employer's attitudes and willingness to provide support and opportunity.

Social Support and Commitment

Farmer: Similarly, lack of social support also affects career commitment—the kind of motivation having to do with long range commitment and planning. It's Donald Super's idea. He calls it Career Salience. That just means a career is the outstanding feature of your life. But how much it's in the foreground will change over time. It doesn't bother the person with a long-range life plan. You expect to play a lot of roles with different roles becoming more salient at different times —Super's Career-Life Rainbow. So for high school girls to see they can pull career and family off equally well and not have to compromise is important. Many couples now have this idea of the different timeclocks, the biological clock and the tenure clock. You plan ahead to do this in this decade, that in that decade. That's how career commitment is different from career aspiration, which is "I want to get to the moon but I don't know how."

Smith: *Do you think women still sense that, somehow, marriage is not under their control as much as it is for men? I mean, how are you going to know how much spousal support you'll have or when you'll have kids until you know who you are going to marry?*

Farmer: I think the concept of androgyny—being instrumental in relation to who you choose as a partner and when—is very important here rather than learned helplessness—waiting for someone to come to you. You can decide instead that

I'll get married at age thirty or within two or three years. So that expectation of having a choice could be laid down by high school teachers and parents.

Also, career commitment as well as aspiration is affected by home career conflict, as I see it, at two levels. One is a kind of role overload where you just feel wiped out trying to do everything and it's hard, but you can apply good planning rules, role negotiation and so forth, like Hall's work. But if you have conflict related to value differences, such as "I'll hurt my kids if I work too hard or if I'm not there when they get home from school or when they're sick or on weekends or need help with homework" and all of that, then you are torn. That's not role overload. That's a feeling you are doing something terrible to the kids or your husband or your family life! And that inhibits commitment because you're anxious and you're conflicted.

The helpful way to handle this is to surface those values, to ask, "What is it you believe?" And then to help the person sort out the values they want to adopt and the ones they have been socialized to believe in but which they don't really like. So it's not that you are going to throw all your values away because some are very important to you. But if you sort them out and then choose to work less, because you know how important it is for you to be there when the kids are one or two, then that reduces conflict and you're okay.

Leduc: *So the verbalization really helps, to actually say what you feel. And to discuss it with others—that it's okay to be feeling this way. It's a normal reaction.*

Farmer: Yes, and reducing role conflict also sometimes involves feeling comfortable about letting go of roles. For example, I'm a terrible cook and still have trouble with not being the hostess, but my husband has become the host and he is a great cook, makes great sauces. So that allows me to let go of that role, to say to people, "My husband is the cook." Another example—our students still believe it's important to their own child for them to be present all the time in those first three years. Yet research from two sources shows that "t'ain't necessarily so." In the kibbutz in Israel where children ate their meals with their biological parents but their caretakers were really others, the mental health and kinds of adjustments these children made were as good as those made by children raised by their fully biological parents. Another example is the work of Lois Hoffman, a Michigan sociologist, on the effects of working women on children. She's found that with continuous quality care, the development of the child is equally good whether the caretaker is the biological mother or a substitute during the early years. There is some interesting work that suggests, however, a possible difference between the reactions of boys and girls, although that research is still in the development stage.

Getting the Message Out

Smith: *Okay, so we've got to get the messages out to boys, don't we?*

Farmer: Exactly.

Leduc: *They've got to realize that the women they marry are going to be working.*

Farmer: And that she'll have a commitment to that career. It's not just to bring home a paycheque for better food or a bigger house. So you can see in health classes as well as career planning and social studies classes the kids can get engaged in dialogues and think about how men and women can both have a good life if this is the way they plan their future. I guess the earlier we get to men and boys the more change we're going to have. The more their expectations, their cognitive mind set about the way life for them should be, will be congruous with gender equity and mutual development and all those good things.

Lifetime Changes in Women's Career Interests

Smith: *What changes do you see in women's career motivation over their lifetime?*

Farmer: I think changes are most dramatic when children are no longer home and women return to work or school in their 40s and 50s. The most dramatic change we see which is not predictable, that is, not normative or traditional, is women going back to work in their 40s, 50s. And they still have 20 to 25 years to develop a career. I guess that's what I told myself at 36 when I went back to graduate school. So for women who haven't been on this parallel family/career track or the career-only track, they still have 25 years or more left and that's a major chunk of their life.

There was a very interesting project by Deanna Chitayat of Hofstra University to locate women in her area who had had some training in science but then dropped out—never had a job in science. She was able to offer them retraining in science with government funding so that they could become computer programers or engineers or whatever they were on track to do before the interruption. And it was a very successful program. I think of it as an example of deliberately produced developmental change. But the phenomenon of the woman returning to the workplace still is not large enough to call predictable or normative.

Smith: *Do you think it's now becoming large enough to call it predictable? Looking at friends of mine, there seems to be a real resurgence of going into the professions in the late 30s or 40s. Is it happening so quickly that statistics haven't caught up with it?*

Farmer: Well, I think today it's something like 53 percent of women with babies who work. So now the majority of women don't stop. Then the answer to your question is there is a significant trend among younger women—well, 47 percent still take an interruption—but the trend is not to interrupt and reenter later, but continue working.

Smith: *More women may be working uninterruptedly but I have the impression their real interests still don't emerge until later. Before that they have just been doing jobs. So much of this research seems to be shaped by the male model where your interests should have developed in your teens or early twenties.*

Farmer: Well, you're right. As I said, it's more complicated for women to be clear about their interests. But we know schools, parents, are not preparing girls to identify their interests early, not saying to them, "It's important for you to find meaning in life through career." No, they're just saying, "Now you can earn money and bring in an income. The intrinsic interest doesn't matter." But it does. One job I took during this 13 year period out of school—I had a lot of short-term jobs—was as editor at the National Council of Churches. I put out an ecumenical newsletter during the sixties. It was an exciting time—grappling with ideas and differences—and I was in charge of the newsletter. It should have been interesting. But I called that my prune job. I thought I was drying up.

Smith: *I bet you could do it really well. And people were saying "great, great job". She's balancing family and work. But you were still drying up.*

Farmer: Yes, I don't know why, but I said that's not for me. And it's not just ability. I was doing a competent job as an editor but not a self-fulfilling job. Then I went back to school. So there is this latent period and it sounds from your backgrounds, Sylva and Nancy, that you've both gone through many successive approximations to find your present career choices. Yet there's been some continuity. And that's true for me also. For example, I can trace back to my childhood—maybe I was ten or twelve—and I got such a kick out of helping somebody fix a bicycle. And being a counsellor fits that original interest in helping and also being a minister. I always liked to help people.

Leduc: *You were always thinking "help." My continuity has been being task-oriented, wanting to make it work.*

Smith: *I also was always curious—wondering what made things tick—and the problem of finding a role where I could apply that best. Now I know it's figuring out people, psychology.*

Farmer: So we've all shown some continuous interests. They just had to connect with the opportunities out there.

Smith: *Do you think this latency is visible in interests tests? Or do you think they miss interests in many young girls that won't emerge until their 30s or 40s?*

Farmer: Well, interest and ability tests at best predict thirty percent of the variability in people's eventual career choices. Seventy percent is unaccounted for. They're not very reliable and valid, although personality tests are much worse.

" . . . schools, parents, are not preparing girls to
identify their interests early, not saying to them 'it's
important for you to find meaning in life through a career.' "

Future Research Needs and Opportunities

Leduc: *What do think are the major gaps that are going to have to be filled in our knowledge of women's careers?*

Farmer: In terms of research gaps, I think it's very important to identify how opportunity in the present affects early childhood determinants—whether these things really hold you back as much as we thought or whether Astin is right and change in the opportunity structure has a major effect. And how do you encounter new opportunity? Do you bump into it? Or is there a way that agencies and government structures can increase the likelihood that people will find the opportunities and make the most of them?

We also need to know a lot more about immigrants, ethnic and socioeconomic differences and gay and lesbian lifestyles. All those factors affect career paths because these people have a lot of obstacles set in their paths that are different from mainstream obstacles. In my own longitudinal study I included what I hope was an adequate nationally representative Hispanic and Black group but what they're recommending now is oversampling of minorities in order to be able to say with confidence what's going on for them. You need roughly equal numbers of all groups so you can say something about them all.

I see a need for more interdisciplinary studies—sociology, anthropology, psychology. These fields have a lot to say to each other. Whereas psychology is looking more at the child through adolescence with some adult studies, sociology is looking at large groups and adult women. We need studies of both men and women, boys and girls, not just adults, because that's the only way we'll know what's unique about women's development. We need to know about returning women and their late blooming interests—all those things cloaked in mystery. We know they're happening, but not how or why. Plus we need more qualitative studies.

We also need to look at inhibitors of women's career development. How global economic changes will affect career opportunities. I don't know that it will actually appear in our lifetime but we could see some radical economic change in North America—we've been very affluent but it's a question whether we'll stay that way.

Smith: *So the structure of opportunity could be negative.*

Leduc: *Or positive. I'm thinking of Rosie the Riveter in World War Two.*

Farmer: Yes, the second world war brought women into prime roles from which they were excluded before. But war is different from depression or recession. Still, greater international collaboration could help if it required more trained workers. Then we would need to use all the resources of the country, including women.

Smith: *Maybe because women are less reticent about ongoing learning and education, they will be giving themselves the advantage by going back to school, while a lot of men will say, "No, I don't need anything else."*

Farmer: Yes, because it's a loss of face to say, "I'm not adequate." Some go back, but very few, much fewer than women.

Of course other facilitators would be changed attitudes of parents, counsellors and employers. We're looking toward to a future where men and women have a equal say in running the country. [The TV series] "Star Trek" could serve as the norm where women are doctors and scientists. That kind of expectation facilitates a real attitude change. And the media can be very important in making a difference. Plus a boost might come from new technology to make home care easier. Grocery stores are already selling more prepared foods, really good things, health conscious, so that's all supportive of women working.

Leduc: *Do you think eventually there will be some sort of consideration of the kind of career absences women have to experience? That's a very difficult question. I don't know if it's even fair to pose it to you.*

Farmer: Well, you may know that in academe, we've been discussing what is called a rollback in tenure, which gives a woman two more years to earn tenure. That's on target with what you are talking about. It's hotly debated. But it is already in place in California. Women now have nine years instead of seven and it's broadly interpreted so it might be granted because of an elder parent that you had to care for at home or a newborn child. Then rollback can apply to the father or mother. What we have in Illinois and several of our mid-western states is case-by-case decisions. Rollbacks are not automatic. We've been arguing to get it as automatic policy. So there is some support for the idea that because career development is more complex for women, they should be given longer to achieve equally. And if it's known such a policy exists, probably more women will try to combine family and career than do one track or the other.

In industry, I think, related to this kind of academic parental leave is the maternity leave. The idea behind it was that there would be no formal career interruptions for women so equity would be maintained. If you interrupt, people are back at the bottom. But there are still problems. My son is with a large accounting firm and he tells me they now start at the MBA level with equal numbers of men and women. But by the time they get to the manager level—which is their first cut—the number of women to men is only one to five, and at the partner level there are no women. So what's happening? Well, there seem to be attitudes like "Yes, you can have maternity leave but we're not going to give you this challenging client because it involves travel." Yet what also happens is that you actually have to develop your own client list to make manager or partner—so a woman is viewed as not able to develop a client portfolio as well. The gap is not due to any differences in skills. It's just that a woman has this other role and the company thinks she can't do both.

Perhaps some of these attitudes will change as more men take parental leave. Attitudes of employers have already changed with regard to mobility because of dual career couples. We've seen less expectation that men will make automatic career moves.

Smith: *I wonder, with so many dual career couples, what will happen to this idea that a man has to be gung-ho all the way from 18 on with his career. If men and women took turns with their career moves, if men could take time out to get recharged, isn't it possible that men's achievement across the lifespan on the* *average might still be just as high but they'd be a lot happier? Maybe in the long term dual careers are not a zero sum game. Everybody benefits.*

Farmer: Yes, it could be beneficial to both. It's like intermarriage. You get this new breed that seems to have more ideas or health or something than either of the parents. So the dual career likewise might produce something new and positive.

Advice to Counsellors

Leduc: *Do you have any specific advice for counsellors? How we can apply what you've said to help women reduce their inhibitions about reaching their full potential?*

Farmer: One thing to avoid is making the nontraditional seem best. Sometimes we tend to think or write that way. I'm sure I even teach that way and I have to bite my tongue. However, if you think you'll be most fulfilled as a nurse or teacher that's what you should be. That is, the counsellor should avoid not accepting a person's interest in a traditional career or in homemaking. Counsellors should also avoid predicting unrealistic consequences. When someone wants to be a minister as I did, my counsellor should have said, "Okay, did you know that there will be only one and a half percent women when you go to the seminary? Do you know they won't let you preach from a pulpit?" I didn't know that at all. I had to learn it. So not to predict those kinds of negative consequences is also doing a disservice to women.

Leduc: *Do counsellors have to have all this knowledge base in the first place? Or, because careers change so rapidly, should they recommend a person conduct research to find out if that occupation is a fit for them in fact?*

Farmer: Counsellors can't know everything. They need to suggest that clients get a realistic base by interviewing, observing, getting experience, part-time jobs, a lot of different ways. Somebody I recently counselled who wanted to be a doctor when she was a little girl told me she got experience volunteering in high school in a hospital. And found she couldn't stand the sight of blood! She knew then she didn't want to go into Medicine. But if she'd never had that experience she might have wasted time going through pre-med.

On the other hand, a counsellor shouldn't discourage interest in nontraditional areas. The point is to teach how to make wise choices and how to plan. A wise choice is an informed choice, when you know yourself and the world. Also avoid sexist language, sexist labels for occupations, sex-biased measures.

Leduc: *So what does a counsellor do with a client who comes in and says "give me the test—tell me what I will be!"?*

Farmer: Teach them there's no test magic. It may give them some information that's useful but it will not be the final answer. They're the most expert on themselves, not the test. One way you can get around that when you're testing is to give more than one test of the same construct. They'll all produce different results so the client will say, "What's going on here!". But it stimulates their thinking and they do learn a little bit. It takes the magic out of it.

Smith: *Do you think interest tests are more of a problem with young girls?*

Farmer: Oh yes! Because if the test takes a long time to develop and the norms are five, ten, twenty years old then the occupational status quo they're reflecting may no longer exist. So what have you got? You've got the results reflecting a picture of the way the world was and not the opportunity structure for women today. That's why American College Testing Corporation developed the UNIACT in the seventies with activity items that were both gender-fair and gender-neutral. It was an attempt to suggest scientific careers to women even if their scores were lower than those of men and women already in science. That's because women in science today are very exceptional. And yet more typical women could do well in science. Even with the UNIACT it seems to me you need to give more than one test.

Leduc: *Given all the factors inhibiting women's aspirations and interests before they even get near a test, I wonder whether interest tests are going to be very useful at all to counsellors.*

Farmer: Well, they have to be used in conjunction with what we're calling now life planning, not just career planning. There are some games that have been developed for high school students where you plan your life and you learn the consequences and you say, "Ooh, I don't want that." So you take another option to find out what will happen then. The game is teaching decision making, problem solving, anticipatory planning, and I think that's going to be very helpful for reducing this complexity, by getting girls to ask questions early. And helping them aspire to become fully persons.

Leduc: *So it's injecting realism instead of expecting to ride off with the white knight.*

Farmer: Yes, instead of going for the stars and ending up plunging in the ditch somewhere. No you don't want that. There has to be a realistic middle ground. So you want to give them the skills in planning and realistic information about themselves and about the world and life roles. You reduce this complexity and mystery and lack of information. That's hard for the counsellor, making it clear to the client that there's no absolute truth in this. See, there's a lot of fascination with tests. It's like tea leaf readings. If something matches your own self-image, you want to believe it. The bad things there are bothersome. So the use of tests is tricky but the guidelines that the US Department of Education came out with to reduce sex bias in interest testing suggest you begin by talking with the client about the effects of socialization. You open up their mind set first.

Leduc: *What about the differences in usefulness between self-administered and computer-scored interest tests?*

Farmer: Well, almost none of the tests that give computer printouts, such as the Strong and the Kuder, are intended to be used without a counsellor's help. They are not stand-alone. The Self Directed Search (SDS)—just computerized—is self-scoring and stand-alone. It has a booklet that talks about help with planning and what it means—works pretty well for the typical student.

Holland says only about 30 percent of people need more help than the SDS provides to figure out what it is they want in life and to do it. I don't know if that's true for women. I think he's got a male model going there, but he is suggesting that people are different in terms of the help they need with planning.

Smith: *Have you any final "pearls of wisdom" for anyone trying to understand how to make wise career choices, either for others or for themselves?*

Farmer: Know your interests, aptitudes and values relating to the major life roles. Do careful life planning, dual career planning, and think ahead and respond to life opportunities. My advice is to take calculated risks.

References and Recommended Readings

Astin, H.S. (1984). The meaning of work in women's lives: A sociopyschological model of career choice and work behavior. *The Counseling Psychologist, 12*, 117-126.

Bandura, A. (1977). Self-efficacy: Toward a unifying theory of behavioral change. *Psychological Review, 84*, 191-215.

Bandura, A. (1982). Self-efficacy theory in human agency. *American Psychologist, 37*, 122-147.

Bandura, A. (1986). *Social foundations of thought: A social-cognitive theory.* Englewood Cliffs, NJ: Prentice-Hall.

Deutsch, H. (1945). *The Psychology of Women: A psychoanalytic interpretation (Vol. 2)* New York: Grune & Stratton.

Dweck, C., Davidson, W., Nelson, S., & Enna, B.I.(1978). Sex Differences in learned helplessness: II. The contingencies of evaluative feedback in the classroom: An experimental analysis. *Developmental Psychology, 14*, 268-276.

Farmer, H. (1984). A shiny fresh minted penny. *The Counseling Psychologist, 12*, 141-144.

Farmer, H. (1985) A model of career and achievement motivation for females and males. *Journal of Counseling Psychology* (Monograph length), *32*(3), 363-390.

Farmer, H. (1987). Female motivation and achievement: Implications for intervention. In D. Kleiber & M. Maehr (Eds.), *Recent Advances in Motivation and Achievement: Vol V* (pp. 51-97). Greenwich, CT: JAI Press.

Farmer, H. (1987). A Multivariate Model for explaining gender differences in career and achievement motivation. *Educational Researcher, 16*(2), 5-9.

Farmer, H. (1988). Predicting who our future scientists and mathematicians will be. *Behavioral and Brain Sciences, 11*(2).

Farmer, H. (1990). A home-career conflict measure. In C. Beere (Ed.), *Gender roles: A handbook of tests and measures.* Westport, CT: Greenwood Press.

Farmer, H., Vispoel, W. & Maehr, M. (1991). Achievement contexts: Effect on achievement values and causal attributions controlling for gender, race, SES and age. *Journal of Educational Research, 84*(1), 26-38.

Fitzgerald, L.F. (1986). Career counseling women: Principles, problems, and practice. In Z. Leibowitz & D. Lee (Eds.), *Adult career development.* Washington, DC: National Vocational Guidance Association.

Fitzgerald, L.F., & Betz, N.E. (1984). Astin's model in theory and practice: A technical and philosophical critique. *The Counseling Psychologist, 12*, 134-138.

Gilbert, L.A. (1984). Comments on the meaning of work in women's lives. *The Counseling Psychologist, 12*, 129-130.

Hall, F.E. & Hall, D.T. (1978). Dual careers—How do couples and companies cope with the problems? *Organizational Dynamics, 6*, 57-77.

Hoffman, L.W. (1979). Maternal employment. *American Psychologist, 34*, 859-865.

Holland, J.L. (1985). *Making vocational choices* (2nd ed.). New York: Prentice-Hall.

Raymond, J. (1974). *Unisex Interest Inventory* (UNIACT): American College Testing Program.

Shibley-Hyde, J., & Linn, M. (1986). *The psychology of gender: Advances through meta-analysis*. Baltimore, MY: The Johns Hopkins University Press.

Super, D. (1957). *The psychology of careers*. NY: Harper & Row.

Super, D.E. (1980). A Life-Span, Life-Space Approach to Career Development. *Journal of Vocational Behavior, 16*, 282-298.

Super, D.E. (1983) Assessment in Career Guidance: Toward Truly Developmental Counseling. *Personnel and Guidance Journal, 61*, 555-562.

Tipping, L. & Farmer, H. (1991). A home-career conflict measure: Career counseling implications. *Measurement and Evaluation in Counseling and Development, 24*(3), 111-118

Tittle, C.K. (1982). Career Counseling in Contemporary U.S. High Schools: An addendum to Rehberg and Hotchkiss. *Educational Researcher, 11*, 12-18.

Significant Events in the Life of Helen Farmer

1929	Year born
1952	B.A. Psychology, Queens University, Ontario, Canada.
1955	B.D. Psychiatry and Religion, Union Theological Seminary, NYC. Married Dr. James A. Farmer, Jr.
1956	Birth of first child, James S. Farmer
1957	Birth of second child, David S. Farmer, deceased
1958	Birth of third child, Paul A. Farmer
1966	Returned to graduate school
1969	M.A. Counseling Psychology, Teachers College, Columbia University, NYC
1970	First publication: Home-career conflict reduction and the level of career interest in women. *Journal of Counseling Psychology, 17*, 228-232.
1972	Ph.D. Counselling Psychology, University of California, Los Angeles (UCLA)
1974	Visiting Assistant Professor, University of Illinois
1977	First book: *New career options for women: A counselor's sourcebook.* NY: Human Sciences Press.
1977/78/80	Teacher of the Year Award, University of Illinois
1982	Birth of first grandchild, Jamie Farmer
1983	Who's Who of American Women & Who's Who in the Midwest
1984	Fellow, American Psychological Association, Division 17,35
1985	Landmark publication: Model of career and achievement motivation for women and men. *Journal of Counseling Psychology, 32*, 363-390.
1987	Professor, University of Illinois
1991	National Science Foundation Grant: Factors related to persistence and non-persistence of women in math, science and technology: A longitudinal study.

2

The Influence of Institutionalized Barriers

An interview with Helen S. Astin, Ph.D., Professor of Higher Education, Associate Director of the Higher Education Research Institute and former Director of the Center for the Study of Women, University of California, Los Angeles.

Like Helen Farmer in the previous chapter, Helen Astin believes in the value of women taking a few risks when planning their careers. In fact, it is only through co-operation and risk-taking, says Astin, that women can challenge the social institutions barring the expression of their career interests and dreams. And that optimistic credo shines through all of Astin's work; even the art collection in her campus office is a testimonial to her faith in the talent of women. Her commitment to women was evident also in the warm reception she gave the authors, complete with coffee and cookies and assistance while we visited Los Angeles.

What fuels her passion, as she describes it, are the sex role stereotypes she faced growing up in Greece and during her early professional career. However, these obstacles also fired her curiosity. "How do some women transcend gender stereotypes," she asked herself, "and go on to accomplishments that are highly nontraditional for women?" Eventually Astin began her own extensive research into the issue, resulting in the 1984 publication of her sociopsychological model of career choice and work behavior: *The Meaning of Work in Women's Lives.* In this model, developed at the invitation of the Committee on Women of Division 17 (Counseling Psychology), American Psychological Association, she set out her theories of how changes in what she labelled "the structure of opportunity" lead to modifications in people's work expectations, shaped initially by sex role socialization and early perceptions of their work world opportunities. Astin's more recent contribution to our understanding of women's careers is her book, co-authored with Carole Leland, *Women of Influence, Women of Vision*. In this she traces the struggles and contributions of three generations of U.S. women leaders and the new vision of a collaborative, more caring leadership they have created.

For this interview, Astin presents good news. Although socialization itself may not have changed dramatically, social, technological and economic forces are creating new opportunities for women's skills and career interests to thrive. To demonstrate this, she surveys some of the recent changes in our institutions, laws, concepts of the family and the functioning of the workplace.

Staying True to One's Deepest Interests

Leduc: *Could you give us an idea of how you first became interested in studying women's careers?*

Astin: To start with, I was interested in career development even as an adolescent. I was reading about how people choose careers and how important work is in peoples lives when I was 15 years old. Don't ask me why, or where it came from. My father was a civil engineer, my brother was in medical school, my mother never worked. And I didn't have anybody around me from whom that interest could have come. It was from somewhere within me but not at a conscious level, just an intellectual area I resonated with.

But thinking back I can understand it. I've always had a lot of very strong intellectual interests but because I lived in Greece, my parents, even though they were very supportive, thought that any of the careers I wanted to pursue weren't possible for me as a woman. Adherence to sex role stereotypes was much, much stronger in Greece than in this country. So when I made my first choice, architecture, my father said, "Yes, you have the brains for it, you're very good in mathematics and interested in design and space but forget it. You'd be the only woman in an all male world." Then I said, "Okay, I'll become a physicist. I'll do research and teach." And I started preparing to take the exam to enter university in that field. But again I was told my choice was not exactly the right career for a woman. Finally my parents suggested elementary school teaching as something a woman can do and have to fall back on. And that's exactly what I settled on, even though I was an outstanding student and my teachers had a lot of aspirations for me. So even though at the time I had no labels for what was happening to me, in a sense I was already experiencing how barriers in the structure of opportunity prevent us from pursuing our own interests and passion.

Then, after high school I entered a normal school, or teacher's college. My parents had told me I could go out of the country for a year to do some post-graduate work. That was a real incentive, the carrot. What they had in mind was Switzerland or France, somewhere nearby, but I'd already made the choice to come to the United States. So I said "fine" and started exploring what I needed to do to get to this country and the kinds of fellowships I'd require for support. I was very intrigued by the United States but I didn't speak a word of English when I got on the boat in 1951.

Smith: *You went straight into an American university where everything was in English?*

Astin: Yes, I came as a junior because I'd already had two years of teachers' school in Greece. And it was very tough. If I had to do it all over again, I might not do it that way—nothing like being naive and brave. I was sponsored by the Anglo-American Hellenic Bureau of Education, so at least I had somebody to greet me when I landed. And there were other students from the same bureau on the boat. I remember we talked of the Statue of Liberty and it was raining when we docked. You know how gloomy New York is in the rain. I started to cry and said, "What am I doing here!"

Smith: *Had you made any arrangements to learn English?*

Astin: What I did was register in English for foreign students the first semester. I decided to take also a difficult subject, biology, and a subject that I know something about, music—I'd already studied it in Greece. And I tell you it was very tough. I somaticized like you've never seen before. I got migraine headaches and broke out in boils all over my face. It was just a miserable time.

Leduc: *But you didn't go back to Greece?*

Astin: No. I was determined, boy, and I was also very poor because regulations at that time meant that all my family could get out of the country for my education was thirty-seven dollars. So I couldn't depend on them. But I had a fellowship. I also worked in the cafeteria for my board and baby-sat to make some spending money. Every summer I worked at two jobs. Those were hard years.

Leduc: *And when did you get married?*

Astin: 1956. As an undergraduate from 1951 to 1953 I was all alone. I did my Masters and then I was supposed to return to Greece. But my advisor said, "Since you're here why don't you get your Ph.D. first." And that made sense. He suggested I go into counselling psychology because in Greece I couldn't do anything with clinical psychology. Only psychiatrists had access to any clinical practice. Then I started my Ph.D. and met my husband. He was a classmate in counselling psychology and we married while still in school. Later after graduating in 1957, I, the typical good wife, followed wherever he went without any plans of my own, just going from state to state and city to city saying, "Here I am, I'm wonderful. Now take me in." And it was a real struggle for me. Very different standards were applied to the two of us. You know what employers said? "You've made too many changes. You don't look very stable." I replied, "You know what's interesting? My husband has made just as many changes but everybody says to him 'You must be wonderful because everybody wants you.'"

Smith: *Was there anyone in your circle of relatives or family friends who was in a nontraditional career while you were growing up? An aunt or anyone like that?*

Astin: No women other than my teachers in high school. The men were all very ambitious and high achieving, but not the women.

Leduc: *How did your family feel about what you were doing or now about what you've done?*

Astin: I had enormous support from my father and older brother to achieve. My mother couldn't have cared less. Her standards concerned how to become charming, how to entertain—all the social graces. But she also saw me as a strong and interesting person and I had a very good relationship with her. So growing up I'm glad I was able to develop my intellectual interests but also a lot of social skills through my interaction with her.

Smith: *Did she ever see you as unfeminine for having nontraditional interests?*

Astin: Well, in Greece, I chose to become very religious and joined a group, like many kids do here, sort of a Christian fundamentalist group. I read the Bible every day and went to confession and ran around the country helping the poor. Part of that movement's beliefs was also that we were not supposed to take care of our external bodies. No makeup, only long sleeves. Don't exhibit yourself. And my mother was very anxious about that. She thought it was wrong that I wasn't interested in high heels or clothes and things like that.

Leduc: *And therefore not marriageable.*

Astin: Exactly. She didn't say it in so many words, but I didn't meet her standards. Then when I came to this country, even though she was very proud of me, she used to write, "You know, you can collect all the degrees you want but without a family you're not a whole person." So all her messages said, "Everything you're doing is great, *but* . . ." Yet when she came here to visit me and I had the kids and was trying to work and balance everything she said, "What did you collect all these degrees for? To change diapers? Go out and work and hire somebody else to do the diapers."

But my American mother-in-law was very conflicted. She was a brilliant woman who never really fulfilled her own ambitions. She was a journalist but the minute she married she didn't do a thing and she felt I should've been home with the kids.

Smith: *Because your choices called into question her own?*

Astin: Right. So I had exactly opposite messages from the two important figures in my life, because my mother-in-law was very important in my life. But as I said, my brother and my father gave me a lot of reinforcement for my achievements in this country. There was never a question that I was doing the wrong thing once I did it. They were very proud. Which tells you something about the importance of support systems, role models, networks, all of these things we don't think about but which give us permission to try things, to be things.

Now to take my interest development a step further, what fascinates me is that for my honors thesis as a senior, I chose to look at women's career choices again. I remember being intrigued about why some women choose English and some Chemistry or Math. So I did five case studies of women and, being a psychology major, I gave them every test I could put my hands on. I also did in-depth interviews of how their families might have influenced their choices. But then for a number of years I disassociated myself from the field. Both my Masters thesis and my dissertation had nothing to do with career development. I only picked up this interest again when I found myself back in research in the mid-sixties.

Smith: *Do you think the Women's Movement influenced you?*

Astin: Yes, but the source of my interest was still very personal. I'd already experienced limitations as a child in what I wanted to do. The second phase of my interest in this field started in a similar way. I'd experienced a great deal of discrimination in the work place—again, so many limitations. My first job, by the way, was as a clinical psychologist at a hospital and all my work for two years was diagnosis and therapy. From there I moved to a clinic for epileptic children, again diagnostic work and treatment, as well as working with interns. I also taught at a small totally teaching-oriented college, so I never had a chance to do any research but found how much I loved teaching.

When we moved to Washington, D.C., in 1965, I presented myself to different universities to teach. They'd say, "You haven't published anything and if you don't publish right out of school you're not a good bet as a productive scholar." Nothing like using knowledge based totally on male behavior! So I couldn't get one teaching appointment but I got two research offers. Which is another madness in our society. Here I hadn't done research but I had fabulous offers to do research. Yet despite a lot of teaching experience I couldn't get a teaching job.

That, in some way, put the fire under me to explore how society limits women and how we can transcend those limitations. So I accepted the job as a research associate with the National Academy of Science on a very prestigious commission with twelve commissioners, all "Who's Who" in this country and all men. I was the only woman on staff in this tiny organization whose goal was to do a state-of-the-art assessment of human resource development and utilization in this country.

Again, let me stress the importance of networks as part of a person's structure of opportunity. I was asked to apply for this job through one of the commissioners who I knew more personally, a colleague of my husband. Also as it turned out the research director was unusual because he had such faith in people. When he interviewed me he said, "I'm taking a chance with you but come aboard." Then for two months we discussed the project with the commissioners and the word "woman" never came up although this was a national study of human resources.

One day, I said it doesn't make any sense. Women are half the talent pool yet nobody cares about them. So I asked why. The first response was that, really, we weren't attending to women because so many marry and drop out of the labor force. Then I said, "We don't know that. Has anyone studied how extensively highly educated women utilize their talents?" And they said, "No, you're right." My director said, "You're interested in it, do it." That's what started my true research agenda—career development with a focus on women.

Smith: *So if you hadn't been hired, they might have chosen a man and this core research might never have been initiated.*

Astin: Or I might have gone some other direction myself, because as I said, my graduate research was clinical. My Ph.D. dissertation in 1957 on empathy was very promising and involved a measure assessing empathy situationally. To this day it's still cited so I could have moved deeper into that topic. But circumstances drew me back to my underlying interest, which was always about women's lives and how they decide to pursue their own interests and how they progress in both education and the work place.

Influences on Women's Career Choices and Work Behavior

Leduc: *We've learned how deeply rooted your interest in women's work is and how it was definitely affected by opportunity. Can you give us a general overview of your model of career choice and work behavior, particularly the role of the structure of opportunity?*

Astin: Let me say first some of my colleagues are upset with me that I haven't done anything with my model since I wrote it. But when I reread and reflect on it, I don't feel it's aged by any means. It's what I call a sociopsychological model and incorporates the interactive effects of four constructs, or factors—motivation, sex-role socialization, the structure of opportunity and work expectations.

The psychological part of the model involves recognizing in ourselves certain psychological constructs, which can also be influenced by outside events. These include our interests, passions and intellectual abilities. And of course motivation, which I made a big issue in my model because there's something that drives all of us to work. Work fulfills certain very important needs in us. The second part of the model is all these social factors outside ourselves which have an impact on our work expectations, including sex role-socialization and the structure of opportunity.

I should give you a sense first of why I felt it was so important to focus on motivation. The first question I raised in the model was why are we all driven to work? I introduced the idea of three major elements motivating us. I wanted to go beyond the idea of working to make our daily bread or to meet survival needs, the first motivator. So in 1967 my students and I did a small project to see how young children develop concepts of work. We found the first concept children have of work is playing, the most existential level where it doesn't serve any instrumental needs. That gave me the idea of the pleasure principal, the second motivator—that by being active in work we feel alive and have a sense of creativity, mastery and playfulness. Finally I introduced the third motivator which work satisfies—contributing to society. People need to relate to others. A sense of contribution is a way of making that connection.

Another idea in my theory was the need to expand the concept of work. Motivated by my feminist notions of valuing women's work in settings beyond paid employment, I wanted to introduce the idea that work encompasses other activities such as volunteer and family work.

The next idea which fascinated me is sex segregation in the workplace. From the literature and my own work I realized the importance of socialization. Very early we're taught the norms of gender-appropriate tasks and interests. And my model shows how this socialization takes place in different settings—the family, school, work after school—before children even begin to think about career choices. That influence in turn encourages us to engage more and more in gender-typed activities. We do them, get reinforced, sharpen those skills and eventually develop a gender-differentiated set of interests and competencies which leads to different career choices. Later, our interests shift under the influence of changes in the structure of opportunity.

Leduc: *What specific factors are included in the structure of opportunity?*

Astin: The structure of opportunity incorporates social forces and structures that prevent or enable us to pursue our passions, work-wise or whatever. Specific elements come from my personal experiences, but also from theoretical notions I'd been exposed to before I developed the model. Over the years I'd observed technological, historical and social developments like the Women's Movement opening up opportunities for women. I saw women's aspirations changing. Looking closely, I also saw that sex-role socialization had not changed dramatically. This suggested how strongly the structure of opportunity affects the way we perceive ourselves, our options and the kinds of career moves we make.

Smith: *So really, you took the opposite tack to Gottfredson's ideas that the early circumscription of women's aspirations is hard to change. You're saying you can change a lot later.*

Astin: Yes, I feel very strongly about the power of the structure of opportunity to transcend early socialization and enable us to overcome barriers. We know people change both careers and themselves. Why? What makes this evolution possible? The answer is that as society and opportunities change, people begin to experiment. The effect of opportunity is very powerful.

As I first set out my model in 1984, the critical elements of the structure of opportunity included job distribution, the sex typing of jobs, overt sex discrimination, job requirements and how they are articulated and perceived by the sexes, the general economy, family structure and reproductive technology. Then in 1990, given additional societal change, I added more elements, including the changing nature of work due to workplace technologies. I also added the action of role models and the notion of family-work interface, plus the implications of expanding educational opportunities and new forms of financial aid, child care and employee benefits. In addition we have begun to see the effect of changing social norms, network contacts, organizational modifications and the whole idea of reference groups. As a result of these forces we develop work expectations, that is, we evaluate ourselves and what's possible and develop a set of expectations of what we can do successfully. Based on this information we make a choice. But if the workplace changes later, we're led to make new choices.

We've chipped away a bit but the power is still with men. As long as we're a patriarchal society, traditional socialization will continue.

Gender Differences and Changes in Socialization

Leduc: *Have you seen much change in gender socialization itself?*

Astin: I haven't seen enough to account for the changes in women's aspirations and work behavior. This is what makes me think that the structure of opportunity is such a powerful construct. Probably most change has occurred because more mothers have entered the work place, so their children are growing up with less structured gender roles. Of course the children's caretakers are still other women— nannies, grandmothers. Child care centres are primarily operated by women and this may reinforce old roles. That's why I say we've not been able to change socialization as dramatically as I'd like. And I don't think it's going to happen in my time, because I think patriarchy is still well and alive. We've chipped away a bit but the power is still with men. As long as we're a patriarchal society, traditional socialization will continue.

Let me say here that some of the new research on women bothers me. For example, Gilligan's work. On the one hand I like her ideas about another voice in women and the importance of expanding our conceptions of acceptable ways of thinking. On the other hand the notion that men and women think differently orients us back again to gender-appropriate roles and behaviors. Maybe there are two voices and, indeed, women may prefer to use one voice more. But they have that second voice. Women have their caring *and* their fairness and justice voice. Women have a wide range of qualities, many perhaps demonstrated only in a given situation. Unfortunately the way Gilligan's research has been used exaggerates gender differences and that's regressive.

In our recent book on leadership people kept trying to force me to state the gender differences. I say we never meant the book to compare men and women. Comparisons make people defensive rather than helping them overcome their differences. Instead, we did it to learn from women, to expand the possibilities of acceptable behavior for us all.

Smith: *I'd like to ask you about internal barriers that result from socialization. What's the impact of lack of self-esteem?*

Astin: That's an important question becuase to this day I see women underrating themselves. It just happened to me, which is interesting because my self-esteem is pretty good. Recently, we rated ourselves on a number of qualities having to do with leadership and management for a workshop. Then we had our superior, subordinates and peers rate us. Do you know on every item I underrated myself compared to the rating given me by the other group's ratings, by quite a difference. It upset me, because this is something I keep telling other people not to do. Afterwards a trained person debriefed us. Her interpretation was I do so many different things that I never feel I do them all well. So the problem involves the fact that I'm over-extended and have high standards. I wonder if that doesn't affect other women, too, because we balance many more balls than men do.

Changes in the Workplace

Leduc: *In your theory, does the workplace change first or do people's needs change and that promotes change at work?*

Astin: An important question. At first my model was pretty linear but it's become more interactional at every level. To some extent the workplace first changed because of demands for more diverse types of labor. As a result women began to raise their aspirations and enter more fields. Then we recognized the negative effect of home responsibilities on working women and the need to adapt to these demands. That's what I mean by interaction.

Women are saying, "If you want my talent, accommodate me." And organizations are saying, "Yes, I will invest in training but I don't want you to leave because of home responsibilities. Let me think of ways to make it possible to meet all your needs." So companies came up with the idea of cafeteria benefits. Instead of offering only a fixed benefits package, they say, "you can choose the individual benefits best for you at this stage of your life." Take the benefits right now in child care or later in retirement or whatever. It's an exciting notion with a lot of potential to break down barriers. It's organizational use is growing, but we've not really done the research to demonstrate who's choosing it or what the benefits are.

However, flex time and job sharing are the most interesting concepts in workplace change and the most difficult to implement. Let me give an example. I'm the director of the Center for the Study of Women, an organized research unit here at UCLA. When we founded the centre six years ago we believed strongly in restructuring organizations so women could cope with both work and family responsibilities. So we instituted job sharing. It has worked but with some problems for full-time staff. I'm a strong promoter of the idea yet I find it makes my work much more complicated as a supervisor. What happens is when I need something the person who can give it to me may not be at work. I had to make up this chart with the names, phone numbers and the date and hours that each person is working. Now every time I want to reach somebody I check the chart.

Smith: *And if you're bothered, someone who's not committed to helping women could really be upset.*

Astin: Exactly. Now I reflected on the problem a lot. It's difficult because we're functioning as a feminist organization within a patriarchal organization with its own bureaucracy. In a sense the university puts pressure on me which I pass on to those working for me. I feel frustrated if somebody asks me to do something and the person who can help isn't available. But if the whole organization had a different, more flexible approach then I don't think it would be as difficult.

On the other hand, how else do we change unless we start experimenting with alternative arrangements? I'm very outspoken on this issue. If we feel the only way women can actualize their work needs and interests is to change organizational structures and the way we think of success or careers, we have to lead the way ourselves. If organizations led by women don't model it how can we expect others to try?

But what's also happening, which is unfortunate in many ways, is that women are leaving the corporate world to start their own businesses. I spent last week at a workshop for executive women and a large number of these women said, "I'm thinking of leaving my organization. I'm at a point where the only way to go is up the ladder. But I don't want to play men's games. So either I stay on as a loser who won't accept promotions or I leave."

I pointed out that by leaving they weren't changing what bothered them. What they needed to do was to think about restructuring their participation. We talked about horizontal rather than vertical movement, about expanding their jobs in innovative ways so they could contribute to the organization in their preferred direction. Many of the women were excited about this possibility. Not knowing their organizations I couldn't offer specific solutions but I counselled them to explore this approach. By staying, they have a chance to change organizations.

Another interesting discussion at this workshop had to do with restructuring the workplace in general. One woman said, "You know, the cultural norm at my company says you have to work twelve hours a day. We all stay till eight or nine o' clock just pushing paper around and resenting it. Nobody dares leave because he or she would look not serious or committed enough. I really don't know what to do about it." So I said, "Why don't you get together a group of your peers, maybe include some trusted superiors, and discuss it. You alone can't leave early but a group can challenge the whole notion." So she's going to try it.

Again, this problem concerned the structure of opportunity—how do we change the organization of work and the way organizations function. In researching our leadership book we found such changes took place by first identifying the problem and then getting like-minded people to work together to make the change. If a group in your organization collectively says, "it ain't working any more," your boss will listen because a smart boss doesn't like to alienate good people.

Leduc: *How do we collectively change employers' attitudes to see women as equally committed to their careers as men?*

Astin: I know people say male workers are committed and always available but that's not true. Let me tell you what I've found. A friend of mine had a biopsy and was told it would take ten days to get the results. My brother, a physician, told me why it can take so long. The results may suggest surgery and the doctor may want to go on vacation or to a conference. The delay provides an excuse not to operate immediately. So men manage to take time off too.

In fact, in one of my own studies I asked how much time academic men and women took off for health or other reasons. There was no difference. Yet we still conclude when a woman takes time out for the family she's not as committed to work, whereas we never think twice about the man going away to a conference although it may be an excuse to have a little holiday. We take equal time off but for different reasons.

Toward Equal Parenting

Leduc: *What can we do to change this double standard?*

Astin: The problem is we've not encouraged men to take time off for parenting. If more men participated in child-rearing we could transcend our differential expectations and attributions of commitment for men and women. I feel strongly about supporting men in this, a change which well might appear deviant at first.

The question is how can we do this—free men to make some of these choices? What works and doesn't work and under what conditions? I think the more men take responsibility for parenting, the more norms will change. This is the interaction I see between what we do as individuals and the changes occurring in the structure of opportunity that benefit us all. I'm taking a social activist role here. And maybe counsellors are the best ones to help people feel okay about these new directions.

Leduc: *Do you think women have to push men into more parental activity or is it a latent interest that could be brought out?*

Astin: Well it's an interesting question—how do we help men feel okay about participating more? We have to consider the external demands they face—what does it mean as a man to call in and say, "I'm not coming to work today because I'm taking care of the kids." A lot of work has to be done in organizations to accept this kind of behavior from men. A woman may try pushing her man to take on child care but it's part of a larger social issue.

Smith: *What's going to be the driving force behind these changes?*

Astin: Women are still the child-bearers, although they're the majority of college students and potential new workforce members. So out of necessity work place practices and expectations for both men and women will have to change.

Smith: *But we hear a lot of controversy about the inadequacy of child care for working mothers. Are major changes needed in funding for day care centres for example, to make life easier for two-career parents?*

Astin: Definitely. We're not even close to providing adequate daycare. The question is, would people opt for day care at the work place or somewhere else? To my knowledge, most people opt for day care nearby because then parents can spend time with the child over the lunch hour. The extent to which institutions will be willing to provide that flexibility is another issue. Let me give you an example. UCLA says in order to provide day care we need space and other things which aren't cost effective. But, again, my sense is that more women become part of this institution at every level, we'll be forced to make such changes, to insure that people are satisfied and productive.

Leduc: *Which really is cost effective, but measured in a different way.*

Astin: Yes. Some members of the corporate world have set up daycare. Their primary motive was to make life easier for their employees so they'd be more productive but on-site day care also improves how employees feel about themselves and their families. So both employer and worker benefit.

Changes in the Academic
Structure of Opportunity

Leduc: *How are women doing in the academic workplace?*

Astin: If you don't publish you don't really move. Women publish more than they used to and I interpret that as being a consequence of changes in the structure of opportunity—more journals established for women to publish in and a switch to anonymous reviewing of both scientific papers in journals and research grant applications. And if you compare highly productive men and women, although the women pre-tenure have a little lower productivity they're more productive than men after tenure.

Smith: *You're saying women get going later?*

Astin: Yes, and eventually exceed the men in productivity. Most would say that with tenure people publish less but both men and women continue to be productive, women more so. My own work shows productivity has more to do with when people finish their degrees, not with age. I would venture to say you'd find older people just as creative.

Smith: *You've written quite a bit about changes needed in educational institutions. What's your opinion about mandatory math in high school?*

Astin: Actually I proposed that in a paper years ago when it was a bit of a heresy. Women opt out of math early, which makes it difficult for them to go on into science later. I said, we require all kinds of other courses, why not a fixed number of math and science courses for both men and women? People got very upset and said any time you make requirements it rigidifies the system. But I think if you not only required more math but taught it differently it would attract more women. The facts show that inherently women are no less interested in math or science. Women don't continue because of all the other messages. As a matter of fact equal numbers of men and women major in math but women teach math and men become theoretical mathematicians.

Leduc: *Doesn't that mean math taught at university remains male-biased?*

Astin: Fortunately the gender-balance of those earning the doctorate is changing dramatically. The proportion of men has stabilized but the proportion of women has increased and continues to increase. The growth has occurred more in the traditional disciplines but also in the nontraditional.

Smith: *But are enough women learning the right skills?*

Astin: I'll tell you. Right now the debate is about our falling behind in science and technology. Currently more women and minorities are in college and since traditionally these populations haven't pursued science and engineering, the question is what can we do? Well, what we can do is find ways of teaching or practicing science that will encourage more women to become scientists—to really de-sex science. And if we don't make it possible for them to be trained in these fields we're going to lose out as a society. I'm working on a National Science Foundation-funded project right now to look at the factors governing the accessibility of science and persistence of people within it. We're doing large surveys and institutional case studies to get a sense of how science at the institutional level discourages women and minorities from participating.

Leduc: *Do you see that science follows the male model?*

Astin: Very much the male model, and unless we start doing it differently, we're in trouble. I find science to be very dualistic, very authoritarian. My scientist colleagues will be very upset with me for saying this but one of my students looked at the beliefs, attitudes and values of faculty scientists as well as faculty in other fields and he found scientists to be very conservative and more likely to hold racist and sexist attitudes. So what message are they giving our women and minority students? We can't afford to hire only the token woman physicist or chemist any more because we have to create a climate to bring in more women students. If we bring more women in we have to find mechanisms to keep them there. There's a lot of work to be done but at least we're beginning to chip open the structure of opportunity. And as new groups enter, the field gradually transforms.

Thank God for new legislation. Law is a powerful way to help eliminate discrimination.

Key Structural Changes
that Benefit Women

Smith: *Within the structure of opportunity what changes have overall had the most influence on women's lives?*

Astin: Let me say thank God for new legislation. Law is a powerful way to help eliminate discrimination. Other changes have come about through new reproductive technology. Now women can postpone marriage, and child bearing. Our perception of the family has changed a lot. We don't think of "family" strictly as a nuclear family model with an instrumental man who goes out and brings home the bread and an expressive woman who stays home and takes care of the children. And the more we expand the notion of a family the more we provide opportunities to rethink how work and family can interface.

Leduc: *Do we need more change in our legal systems?*

Astin: Yes. For example, the U.S. has legislation on sexual harassment but we've not been able to implement it. I think our guidelines are still confusing and people don't know how to use the legal system. At UCLA if somebody alleges sexual harassment we don't know what happens after the complaint is filed. So I've asked the university senate to state, without naming names, the kinds of allegations made and their resolution. This way other women would know what happens and some men could wise up.

Given the power of the law, we also need more women in political office. That's where we should put our money next. I like the expression "EMILY'S LIST," Early Money Is Like Yeast, a female metaphor of the first order. It's also the name of the U.S. organization that finances women Democrats aspiring for office. It means just as a pinch of yeast results in dough expanding, money given to women planning to run for office pays off for all in the long term.

Within the work place, technology has made important changes in job requirements and structure. Take fax machines. My husband can do all of his work at home by writing something, then faxing it to his assistant to correct and fax back. Working at home expands the ways we can handle other responsibilities, such as taking care of older parents or children.

Opportunities for women in the workplace have also come about through changes in the demographics of education, the fact that women are now more than a third of Ph.D.s and close to fifty percent of law and medical students. We did that through legislation, by saying institutions couldn't discriminate on the basis of sex, by providing more opportunities for women to finance their education and by ending age discrimination.

What worries me today is the economy. On one hand a depressed economy makes us regress. All of a sudden we say, "You know a man really has to be there for his family. So if it's one job and two applicants maybe we should give it to the man because with a job he's more likely to stick around when the wife gets pregnant and has to stay home for a while." In a sense we regress to sex role stereotypes.

On the plus side, a depressed economy hoping to flourish again needs all its educated people. As more women are educated, they're the prime labor pool. From research we know in crises people tend to transcend sex-role stereotypes. In all countries historians record over and over again examples of women moving into the labor market during wars. And with floods or other kinds of local crises, traditional sex roles are put aside and everybody is considered a resource capable of doing whatever has to be done. I hate to say we need crises to keep chipping away at stereotypes but we know that's the case.

Leduc: *So the positive side of a recession is that employers will tend to look more at a person's talent, not their gender.*

Astin: This is what I'm forecasting. We're in an economic crisis, so we're going to look for talent, and not worry whether it's male or female.

Smith: *But couldn't some people be so desperate to get or hang onto jobs that they'll network together to shut women out? The old boys network in action.*

Astin: That happened in the past because men and women were differentially trained. The man tended to be more educated so he'd choose to go out and work because he'd have access to better jobs and salary. And in a sense the woman would get penalized even further. Now as women become equals and even surpass men in training and skills this is no longer the case. I can foresee a future where spouses say, "Of the two of us, who should be the chief bread winner?" And it will be the better-educated woman who's in a position of strength.

Smith: *Sounds like a cause for optimism if society is really going to need more women in the workforce, and if the fact that more women will be there will, in turn, force change.*

Astin: There's no question about it as far as I'm concerned. That's where counsellors come in, to help women through this transition.

Leduc: *What do you think right now is the key factor still holding women back from their most appropriate career direction?*

Astin: I don't believe women are being held back the way we used to be. Women today have wonderful dreams. The question is how do we help realize those dreams? What's the responsibility of counsellors, professors, parents, the extended family, all of women's significant others, including boyfriends?

We're seeing another gender-linked change that we could put under the structure of opportunity. Our institute has been monitoring changes in college students for over twenty-five years so we have a wealth of data. We're finding more and more men saying that raising a family is an important life goal, whereas women are showing increases in work and achievement, so I see a greater rapprochement between men and women about the importance of family and work. This suggests raising a family will be more of a partnership in the future.

Smith: *How does the structure of opportunity compare in North America with that in other parts of the world, for example in Europe? Are the same kind of changes occurring there?*

Astin: I'm most familiar with Greece because I was asked to do a study there. Dramatic changes in that country have benefitted women again, starting with legislation. That's why the Equal Rights Amendment would've been so important. In Greece I saw the power of legislative change. Formerly they had an archaic, though unpracticed, family law. Because it was so terrible, changing it brought women's problems out in the open and shook people up—they began to behave differently. It also encouraged women to stand up for their rights. Before they used manipulation. Now they say, "I don't have to manipulate, the law protects me."

New Research Directions

Leduc: *What research do we still need to do before we really understand how women are influenced by the structure of opportunity?*

Astin: First of all we have to become more creative with the way we do research. I feel we need new ways of collecting and analyzing data and representating that information to make it more powerful. For example, I'm thinking about different ways to represent my own data to take advantage of the power of the media and, boy, is that strong. In 1981 a journalist colleague of mine and I had a wonderful proposal for television, although it didn't see the light of day. We called it "Women's Eye View." It was going to interpret the news from a feminist perspective, including news that ordinarily never got aired.

Leduc: *Do you feel backlash prevents such a program from being accepted?*

Astin: I think it would be accepted right now, but it would need some energy behind it. The backlash definitely is there. My interpretation is we've really threatened the status quo and the men are starting to shake. They fear loss of power.

Then related to counselling we need to know more about how to help people see there's a world of opportunity to make connections and find like-minded people. Yesterday in my course on cognitive and personal development, we were talking about some of the things an administrator in the future might do to overcome the loneliness that such a high proportion of college students experience. Three-fourths of them say they feel very lonely. All of the work shows the best way for them to overcome loneliness is not by connecting to the family or finding a romantic relationship, but by making friends.

We also need more research about how women and men approach and organize their actual work tasks. Past research tells us differences exist between men and women regarding the dimensions of co-operativeness and competitiveness. For example, Jean Lipman-Blumen has collected data from all kinds of people of all ages and in all work settings on achieving styles and then juxtaposed them on transparencies to show how similar men and women are in all dimensions of achievement except in competitiveness and co-operativeness, no matter the setting.

To illustrate these differences, let me tell you my experience in an all-women Outward Bound program. The co-operation in problem solving was fascinating. One of us would say something and immediately another would add to her idea instead of saying, "No, I don't think it's going to work." We solved every problem faster than the allotted time. A woman taking notes on our progress had also observed teams of men and mixed teams of men and women grapple with identical problems. She told us the other teams never solved the problems because the men

would argue and try to one-up each other. By the time they'd all talked about their own ideas rather than building on the original, time had run out.

I'd loved to have videotaped that workshop as a demonstration of the power of team work in the workplace. We have to counter the false notion, any way we can, that women aren't as productive. Women still have to prove their worth over and over again and do twice as much to prove it. But everything we've learned about our survival as a society and as a world suggests we have to restructure the workplace in a co-operative direction, listening and building on each other's strengths, rather than arguing.

Counselling for Change

Leduc: *Given what we've just heard about the changing structure of opportunity, what do we say to younger women who are just beginning to make job choices?*

Astin: I'd advise them, if they want to be successful, to explore and develop as many competencies and skills as possible.

Another thing I'd do as a counsellor is work in groups of both men and women. I've found male and female college students communicate very little about how they see their respective family and workplace roles and their plans to combine them. They're coming from different perspectives. For example, some of our research asked men and women questions such as, "In your future, what kind of partner do you foresee in terms of education, career interests, etc.?" The next question was, "Once children arrive, what are your expectations and desires?"

What we found is that before any mention of children, both men and women said, "I want an educated and career committed partner." Once we asked, "What's going to happen after children?", the men were much more sex-role stereotypic. "I want my future partner to be at home taking care of the children. I think the children will suffer otherwise." But the women said, "I want to work and have an exciting life." The women were much more realistic about their future based on what the work world is like today. But men still haven't gotten the message that women are making different choices.

Smith: *What is the counsellor's role in warning women about the barriers, including men's attitudes, that they'll likely encounter? Should young women also be encouraged to think about solutions to propose to a future employer?*

Astin: Things are changing so fast that it's hard to advise about the future. I'd try to show people at any job or educational level how to empower themselves and identify the changes they can make right now to enlarge their own structure of opportunity. As I said earlier, what a person does to change her own opportunities makes it easier for other women. That in turn helps her to make more improvements in her life. Interaction again. And I think once people see they have the power to change their present environment, at school or wherever, the more they'll learn about making changes later on.

Really, I'm such an optimist about the possibility of changing the structure of opportunity. I'm also a believer in making your own realities. So many of us tend to look at the negative things about ourselves more than the positive. But I must caution people—if you feel negative about your chances in the workplace it's going to become a self-fulfilling process.

References and Recommended Readings

Astin, H.S. & Leland, C. (1991). *Women of influence, women of vision: A cross-generational study of leaders and social change.* Jossey-Bass: San Francisco.

Astin, H.S. (1984). The meaning of work in women's lives: A sociopsychological model of career choice and work behavior. *Counseling Psychologist, 12,* 117-126.

Astin, H. S. (1984). In appreciation of the richness of the commentaries. *Counseling Psychologist, 12*(4), 151-152.

Gilligan, C. (1982). In a different voice: Psychological theory and women's development. Cambridge, MA: Harvard University Press.

Gottfredson, L.S. (1981). Circumscription and compromise: A developmental theory of occupational aspirations. *Journal of Counseling Psychology Monograph, 28,* 545-579.

Lipman-Blumen, J. (1984). *Gender roles and power.* Inglewood Cliffs, N.J.: Prentice-Hall, Inc.

Significant Events in the Life of Helen Astin

1932	Born in Greece
1949	Graduated from high school
1951	Pedagogical Academy, Salonika, Greece Diploma - Elementary Education
1951	Arrived in New York
1953	B.A. Adelphi University
1954	M.S. Ohio University
1956	Married
1957	Ph.D. University of Maryland
1959 & 1961	Birth of children
1973	Professor of Higher Education, University of California, Los Angeles
1973	Associate Director, Higher Education Research Institute, Los Angeles
1976	Award for Outstanding Contribution to Research and Literature, National Association of Student Personnel Administrators
1977	(1) Fellow, American Psychological Association (2) Outstanding Book Award of Choice for *The Power of Protest* (3) Adelphi University of Alumni Association, Academy of Distinction
1985	Honorary Degree (Doctor of Humane Letters) Marymount Manhattan College
1986	Recipient of the Bread and Roses award of the Los Angeles Westside National Women's Political Caucus
1988	Distinguished Leader for Women in Psychology, Committee on Women in Psychology, American Psychological Association
1989	Honorary Degree (Doctor of Humane Letters) American College of Switzerland
1990	Acting Director, UCLA Center for the Study of Women
1991	*Women of Influence, Women of Vision: A Cross Generational Study of Leaders of Social Change*, San Francisco: Jossey-Bass Publishers

Section Two

Women's Vocational Interests—
Trends and the Status Quo

The effects of the social forces portrayed in Section One ultimately contribute to the distinct differences in the occupational interests and choices of men and women. But how different are they? To answer this question, Jo-Ida Hansen, director of the Center for Interest Measurement Research at the University of Minnesota, draws upon more than fifty years of information from the Strong Interest Inventory data bank to survey occupational interest trends of the last half century. She also discusses some of the strengths and limitations of using an interest test.

Chapter 3:   Messages from the Strong Interest Inventory

Messages from the Strong Interest
Inventory (SII)

An interview with Jo-Ida C. Hansen, Ph.D., Professor of Psychology: Director, Counseling Psychology Program and Director of the Center for Interest Measurement Research, University of Minnesota.

Despite the dramatic change discussed by Astin (see Chapter 2) in the career opportunities available to women, women and men in North America on the whole still demonstrate very different vocational interest patterns. Furthermore, these differences are found even within the same occupation. On average, men describe themselves as more mechanically inclined, women describe themselves as more nurturing and people-oriented. Overall, the genders still tend to be found in distinctly separate job categories.

Jo-Ida Hansen presented these conclusions as part of an overview on women's career interests which she gave to the authors one blustery winter afternoon, drawing upon the analyses that she and her colleagues have conducted on more than fifty years of information stored in the data bank of the Strong Interest Inventory. Unfortunately the building's balky temperature control had rendered her campus office that day almost as cold as the outside air. But Hansen's enthusiasm and thoughtful provision of a large pot of steaming coffee kept us both alert and fascinated.

Hansen developed her own interest in studying people's occupational interests when she was a graduate student, and later a colleague of, David Campbell. Campbell himself had been a student of E.K. Strong, who first published the inventory in 1927 as the Strong Vocational Interest Blank (SVIB). This inventory, also known as the Strong-Campbell Interest Inventory (SCII), remains the oldest career interest inventory still in use today and one of the most popular[1] in the hearts and budgets of vocational counsellors. Hansen collaborated with Campbell on the research in the 1970s-80s that led to a single form for both men and women and other revisions designed to eliminate sex bias. In turn, Hansen inherited from Campbell the demanding responsibility of directing the Strong's continued development. Yet despite her overflowing schedule she still insists on reserving time to promote equal opportunity in the workplace for other women.

The following interview focuses on the serendipitous development of Hansen's own career interests and her expert conclusions, plus studied speculations, comparing women's and men's occupational interests.

The Role of Chance in One Researcher's Career

Smith: *Looking back in your life, can you trace the threads of your present career? Have you always been interested in researching vocational interest tests?*

Hansen: In terms of my professional career, yes, that's been the major focus of my research. In terms of the source of that focus, well, as a counselling psychology graduate student at the University of Minnesota it's next to impossible not to be exposed to vocational psychology. That's really been historically the shining star of this particular graduate program. Minnesota was one of the first APA accredited programs in counselling psychology, springing largely from the efforts of the United States government to develop employment counselling after the Depression and again after World War Two when a lot of veterans were looking for work.

Smith: *And Strong himself chose this university to be the repository of his data.*

Hansen: Exactly, although he was at Stanford. During those early years it would have been people like Patterson, Williamson and John Darly and Lloyd Loftquist who provided leadership here. But E.K. Strong would come out occasionally during the summer to be a visiting faculty member. Minnesota was probably one of the few places early in Strong's career that really appreciated the work he was doing and embraced the use of his instrument. I think in some ways Stanford never really appreciated what a gem it had in Strong, whereas Minnesota had that applied orientation right from the beginning. So it's a given here that fairly early in students' graduate careers they're going to be exposed to vocational psychology and a bevy of assessment inventories along with psychometrics and statistical measurement.

---

1 J.C. Conoley & J.J. Kramer (Eds.). *The tenth mental measurements yearbook* (pp. 735-738). Lincoln, N.B.: Buros Institute of Mental Measurements.

Leduc: *So your professional socialization started early. But how did you become involved specifically with the Strong? Can you see the early threads of this focus or was it more an accident?*

Hansen: The actual stimulus was in fact happenstance. At the time I was a graduate student my incoming class was fairly large, probably about sixty. And the way they assigned us to advisors was simply to make up two lists of names in alphabetical order within their area, one of students and another of faculty and then just match them up. It wasn't really based on what the student's interest statement said or the professor's area of interest. Who we ended up with was by pure chance.

Smith: *That's a twist. The department used almost random assignment despite a reputation for taking interests seriously?*

Hansen: That's right. But they also said we could at any point change advisors, although they advised staying with the initial assignment for the first couple of quarters until we knew our way around the department, knew somebody available whose interests better matched our own. So there was flexibility over the long haul.

However, that particular year, 1969, the "Hs" were assigned to the "Cs" and I ended up as David Campbell's advisee. And that event interacted with the Women's Movement turning its attention about that time to interest inventories. By 1970-71 the Strong was under severe attack by a number of organizations across the country because of its separate men's and women's forms. And as advisors tend to do with their advisees, Campbell contacted me when he had some extra money and said, "Do you want to be my research assistant?" That occurred just before the outcry of test dissatisfaction so I was working with him when he became heavily involved in the revision producing the combined sex form.

Now even at that age I was enough of a feminist to think that revisions of that sort were very needed and fit nicely with my own beliefs about options for women and so on. But I can't say that without that serendipitous opportunity I would have gravitated towards interest measurements and career counselling. It's hard for me to predict where I would have ended up.

Smith: *I also wonder what would have happened to the Strong itself if you'd not been involved in its revision, or if you'd been male, but let's go back a little further. You came into graduate school planning to go into one-on-one counselling. Where did that goal come from?*

Hansen: Well, going back to the statement of interest I wrote for my application, I think it did suggest I was aiming to be more of a practitioner in a therapy type setting, or a counselling service. But at 21 when I went to graduate school directly from my undergraduate degree, which I also did here, I think my level of naivete was extraordinary. I thought that if anyone worked relatively hard and took advantage of opportunities, that other opportunities would naturally come along. But I think that naive trust helped me, because as a consequence my level of anxiety over career decisions—for example tenure— even after I was an assistant professor, was very low. And I think that made graduate school as well as being a new professional more fun for me than for some people now. I just wasn't wise enough then to know how hard it can be to start a career.

Also I think when I came into graduate school my knowledge of the breadth of the field of counselling was limited in spite of having been an undergraduate here. I'd never thought about teaching psychology as a profession, except that I had some notion that secondary or primary school teaching was too traditional for me. And I didn't know much about the university's graduate program itself.

My undergraduate advisor was Lloyd Loftquist, but we met at the most once a quarter. And I remember asking him at some point about good places to apply for graduate school but his response only was, "Well if you suggest some places I think inappropriate, I'll let you know." But at some point he did say, "Minnesota is not all bad, we have a pretty good program here, you should think about applying." And that's what I did, at the last minute, but not because I really knew what the program involved.

However, it turned out, once I'd been accepted and looked more closely, that Minnesota matched my interests pretty well. It certainly had a good reputation and its financial offer I think was better than anywhere else. That was important too, because I wanted to be able to support myself. The one downside here was the weather. I really hate the cold. I grew up in North Dakota, I went to school in Minnesota. When I finished my Ph.D. I said, "I'm going where it's warmer, I'm getting out of the North." But here I still am.

Leduc: *I realize this is completely off topic yet I'm curious, did ever you learn to type?*

Hansen: No, never learned to type, I think out of some subconscious fear that if I did, that's what I would end up doing. I saw that happen even in graduate school. Many of the women students who could type ended up taking secretarial positions within programs to support themselves whereas if you couldn't type they'd scratch around and somehow find you a research assistant position.

Smith: *So, looking back, how does your experience with choosing a career fit in with the emphasis today on identifying interests, careful counselling and life planning?*

Hansen: Well, I think I just was stumbling along without a very broad perspective of the work world, although we can do some terrific case studies of people's career paths like mine that post hoc seem to make sense. To give you an example from my life, my mother got her degree here too, in Medical Technology, and at some point went through career counselling. So of course as good mothers do she wanted to pass on her experience and said to me, "Well, I remember taking these tests when I was a student and they really helped me make my career decisions. Why don't you look into that?" So I trundled off to the student counselling service and said, "Give me the tests which will tell me what I want to do." And I can remember telling the counsellor there all these lofty academic goals—"Well I don't know what I want to do it in, but I know I want a Ph.D." The counsellor wrote all this down, taking me very seriously, and then gave me the Strong for women. I was supposed to come back a couple weeks later for the interpretation. However, I never did.

Later when I was a graduate student doing practicum at the counselling service, the staff said, "If you've ever been in to see a counsellor we can pull your file and see what's in it." So there was my Strong profile. And all I could think was that the counsellor had to have been so glad I didn't come back. Because here was this highly motivated young woman with this incredibly flat profile, absolutely no recognizable interest in anything except a modest score on physical education teaching. And I would have just scoffed at that suggestion—too unintellectual— and have concluded on the spot "This test isn't any good!"

That experience points out a couple of things. One is that, back when I took it, the instrument didn't have enough stuff on it, only the specific Occupational Scales, to be able to help people whose interests were not yet well defined. But since then, the added General Occupational Theme and Basic Interest Scales make a differentiation at a younger age. Which means a counsellor can look for a useful pattern on these newer scales for somebody whose interests are just starting to develop.

My experience also shows how good the Strong really is. It turns out, after all, that I've used the athletics interest that showed on the test. I've spent the last eleven years as Faculty Representative for Intercollegiate Athletics, serving as liaison between the administration and the athletic departments. I've always been a big sports fan at athletic events. In fact, I participate a lot. I think that illustrates how you can make sense out of the profile post hoc and that it measures more than career interests. In counselling, the test has more validity for individuals if you apply it to all life domains: recreational, living environment, career and so on. If you insist it reflects only career interests, people may say, "No, I wouldn't want to do that!" I certainly wouldn't have wanted to be a Phys. Ed. teacher, even retrospectively. But what I've done in terms of university service and involvement with athletics has been a lot of fun. The interest is there, but more avocational.

Smith: *I'm thinking about role models for you. Did the fact your mother had her degree influence your career at all?*

Hansen: Both of my parents had undergraduate degrees, and, yes, they were important models. Some of my earliest memories involve putting away silver dollars I received as gifts into my college fund. They just expected I would be successful and go to college. I also remember as a high school senior being surprised to discover that a lot of my friends were not going to college, because I assumed everybody had that goal. By the time I was a college freshmen I knew I would study for some sort of Ph.D. And I also knew I would have my family's support for as long as I wanted to stay in school. It would not be, "Get your bachelor's and be done with it."

Smith: *Did your mother work outside the home?*

Hansen: At a number of different things. When she finished college about the time of World War Two, she became involved with medical research projects in the state of Washington. Then my father was drafted out of college and ended down in Texas close to the war's end. So they married and she worked there, again in a medical laboratory. Then once he was out of the service my father decided to go to George Washington University in Washington D.C. to finish his undergraduate degree, so she worked in a couple of doctors' offices in that city. But very shortly after I was born—I was an only child—they moved back to North Dakota, where they'd both grown up, so my father could take over his family business, publishing the local newspaper. My Mom didn't work again until I think I was in grade school, then she started teaching microbiology and a lot of other laboratory courses for the nursing school at the local liberal arts college. After school I'd go there on the way home, and hang around the lab with her. I can remember going there on weekends when she would prepare cultures and get ready for classes.

Leduc: *So the idea of a university or college setting was never intimidating. Your mother liked what she did?*

Hansen: Yes, she did, but at some point she started another career writing about food for the newspaper. It started out with a column called the "Community Clearing House" and evolved into three pages a week of food recipes and travel. I mean, she has the wanderlust like no one else I know and has jaunted all over the world through her writing. Eventually she became affiliated with several national food writers' associations and her column was syndicated. So she's somebody in a relatively restricted environment, a community of sixteen thousand, who really made herself a nice professional life.

Leduc: *Did you ever write for your father's paper?*

Hansen: Well, my folks thought since I was in psychology, I should write an Ann Landers type column, which I never agreed to do, wisely. Even then I knew I was too empirical for such things. But as a graduate student, for three years I wrote a column about anything I felt like. Sometimes it covered my travels.

Leduc: *I imagine you've continued to travel?*

Hansen: Yes. And if I had more faith in mechanical vehicles and cold weather I would fly to the Pole on one of those champagne flights that swoop in and out. To stand with my toes on the shore of Point Barrow and see the ice cap out there two hundred yards away is just good for the soul and satisfies some need in me.

Women's Interest Patterns on the SII

Smith: *We can certainly see the threads of earlier socialization coming together in your career interests. Let's turn now to what your research says about women's interests in general. First, how do the interests of women and men compare?*

Hansen: Well, I've become more convinced over the years that there are still fairly large differences between the average profiles of men and women in terms of career interests. I used to think that if we looked beyond mean profiles, at Holland's structure of interests (see endnote 1), there'd be more similarity. We recently analyzed some data using the Women-in-General and the Men-in-General samples from the last revision of the Strong, 1985[2], using people 25 to 60, with a mean of about 38 across all the samples. Now these samples are carefully matched on occupational titles. For example, if there's one male nurse, there's one female nurse. If there's one female realtor, there's one male, and so on. Even with that careful design, the male data matches Holland's Hexagon (see endnote 1 for description) better than the female data. What we find for women's interests is more of a collapse of the Social interest across a number of different areas (Hanson, Collins, Swanson & Fouad in press).

Smith: *You mean, women tend to have strong Social interests, no matter what other area they're interested in?*

Hansen: Yes. If you think of Holland's Hexagon, the point for Social interests ends up drawn into the middle of the hexagon which suggests that it pervades the other five interest areas. The other interesting result was that Realistic and Investigative interests for women are not as well differentiated as for men— women tend to see the two interest areas as more related. They more loosely define these categories. I think that's reflected even when you look at the Holland codes for occupations used on the Strong. For example, when we measure the interests of people already working in a given occupation, for women more occupations show a combination of Realistic and Investigative interests, RI, as opposed to strictly Realistic or strictly Investigative interests.

And those two observations fit with what we know about the socialization of women. In many instances, women have had very few opportunities to go into either the Investigative, scientific work areas or the more Realistic, mechanically inclined areas, such as the trades. Women have probably not been socialized to think about these interest areas or identify their roles as well within the work world. Social interests, such as nurturance, sensitivity, warmth and emotional expressiveness, seem to be an underlying value for more women whatever their career interests and to pervade their approaches to problem solving and interacting with people. Whether that's innate or socialized, I don't know. But it's there.

Smith: *So women in general seem to have more developed Social interests and express them more in the work world. Did Social show up on your own profile?*

Hansen: No. I'm very much of an Investigative, Realistic type. Artistic would be my third interest area with Social very low, which is why I didn't end up being a therapist.

Leduc: *Where does Artistic fit in? You've written that men and women tend to have different levels of this type of interest too.*

2 Hansen, J.C., & Campbell, D.P. (1985). *Manual for the SVIB-SCII*: Strong-Campbell Interest Inventory, form T325 of the Strong Vocational Interest Blank (*4th Ed.*). Palo Alto, Calif.: Consulting Psychologists Press.
Hansen, J.C. (1984). *User's guide for the SVIB-SCII*: Strong-Campbell Interest Inventory, form T325 of the Strong Vocational Interest Blank (p. 26). Palo Alto, Calif: Consulting Psychologists Press.

Hansen: We certainly find that in terms of the mean profiles. The Realistic and the Artistic areas have the two largest mean score differences between males and females and, as you might expect, women tend to score higher on Artistic. But analyzing the structure of interest patterns—how the scores for the six interest types relate to each other—generally the way Artistic relates in females matches the way it does in males better than the mean profile might suggest.

Smith: *So on average, women express more interest in Artistic but less interest in Realistic activities. Your analysis also suggests that a woman with high Artistic interests is no more or less likely than a man with high Artistic interests to score high on any of the other five Holland interest types. That's in contrast to Investigative and Realistic interests which, in women, tend to occur together.*

Hansen: Exactly. It's really only the Social, Realistic and Investigative interests that stand out as relating differently to other interests for men and women.

Social interests, such as nurturance, sensitivity, warmth and emotional expressiveness, seem to be an underlying value for more women whatever their career interests.

Changes in Women's Occupational Interests

Leduc: *Has there been any change over the years in the interest patterns for men and women?*

Hansen: Well, it's not very often that people do something that becomes a definitive answer, but I think one paper we did comes close. Thanks to the archival data that both E.K. Strong and David Campbell kept over the approximately fifty years of research done with the Strong we were able to actually look at mean profiles of interests for men and women across four different decades, the 1930s, 1960s, 1970s and 1980s. We were able to do it both for the Men- and Women-in-General samples used in constructing the Strong scales as well as for six specific occupational groups—lawyers, fine artists, psychologists, life insurance agents, reporters and youth program directors.

What we essentially found was, much to my surprise, that the interests of women have hardly changed. On our General Occupational Theme and Basic Interest Scales (see endnote 2), if you look at the profile for Women-in-General in the thirties and compare that to what we found in 1985, they're almost identical. In fact, for both the Men-in-General and the Women-in-General samples the differences are so small that if you plot the profiles, the points practically land on top of each other.

I had thought, surely, there would be large changes across time, especially for the women, given fifteen years of the Women's Movement and so on. I just assumed that with increased opportunities there would be a different profile. What it says to me is that women have always had a wide range of interests. It's just that the opportunities haven't always been there for them to use the full realm of their interests, to get jobs in a variety of areas. And so we see more diversity in what women do now. But I think, had the opportunities been there, had Helen Astin's "social structure of opportunity" been more open to them back in the twenties and thirties, more women would have gone into a wider range of careers.

What makes these similarities more astounding was the fact that three different researchers collected the data with no real effort to replicate how the previous person did it. E.K. Strong's in-general samples would really not have been carefully selected in terms of a wide range of occupations or locations across the country because he used whoever was available around California. And in terms of occupational diversity his samples were probably quite restricted, especially for the women. Then when Campbell did his in-general sample collections in the sixties he would have selected a more national sample but at that time women were not employed in a wide variety of fields. So the occupations he was able to sample would have been fairly restricted.

When we look at interest patterns for a specific occupation the scores tend to differ more across the decades, but the overall pattern is very similar. So what was important to psychologists in terms of their interests back in the thirties would still be a high interest area now, and what they disliked back then they would still dislike, although the absolute levels would show some change between the decades. It's interesting that in the occupations, men actually had a greater tendency towards interest change over the 50 years than did women.

Leduc: *Less interested in some things, more interested in others but the relative rankings remain the same. So over the years there's been a stronger representation of women in Social areas and men in Realistic and Investigative.*

Hansen: Yes, the differences in interests of women and men continue to persist. Though a number of interest areas continue to exhibit large differences between women and men, the overall trend is a reduction in those differences.

What we find is change in the Enterprising area, which has increased somewhat over the decades for both women and men, particularly in law-politics and public speaking. But what's difficult to know is whether that just reflects a temporary infatuation with MBAs and those other Baby Boom characteristics or if it's a real change. When you think about today's emphasis on assertiveness and so on, it's hard to know if it's lasting or a phase society's going through. Overall, there also was a decrease in Conventional interests, that is, a drop in attention to detail among both genders.

Smith: *So you're saying the culture of the times generally influences interests.*

Hansen: Yes, and I can come up with some reasonable hypotheses for what society is going through right now that might be causing a little increase in those Enterprising scores.

Another example of change we found was an increase in the adventure score for men, but not women, between the 1930s and the 1960s. In the 1930s the scores for men and women were about the same but later the men's rose quite a bit. During the Depression people probably weren't responding positively to risk-taking. And we know that the Adventure scale on the Strong relates not just to physical but also to financial risk-taking and so on. So, we could say, again post hoc, possibly that score was depressed for men just after the Depression because of the economy. Then it recovered to what the norm for adventure probably is for men because we see that higher score both in the sixties and in the eighties.

One of the things relating to change that I was worried about, as the test constructor, concerned the age range in the criterion sample. Were we somehow jeopardizing the validity of the scales by including people nearing the end of their career? Could occupations so change that the interests of people hired today look very different from the interests of workers in the occupation for forty years? We did do one study of this, cross sectional, not longitudinal. It didn't cover the whole world of work but we selected a half dozen occupations, representing each of the six Holland types and essentially divided the criterion samples into three age groups, those who'd entered an occupation fairly recently, those who'd been there for ten or fifteen years and those approaching retirement. But then the profiles laid on top of each other. Again I was a bit surprised. I'd thought some change in the occupations would show up.

David Campbell did work in that area too. Some of his research involved a longitudinal study—working with bankers, I think—and he retested these people some thirty years later. Their interests had not changed. He did a study where he tested an initial sample and then went back and tested the person who'd taken the job of the person initially participating. Again they looked the same. So if there is one thing we know about interests, it's that they are incredibly stable both within an individual over time as well as within occupations and society in general. The interests of people in occupations generally don't change even though we might think the nature of the occupations is making a big shift.

Interests of Women and Men
in the Same Occupation

Smith: *You've written that the interest patterns of men and women within some occupations can be different on average. Pharmacy was an example. Is this fairly common?*

Hansen: Yes. Although it's not universally true, in those sex-stereotyped professions where there hasn't been any gender balance, the interest patterns of the sexes tend to differ more. For example, if we look at the score of female farmers on the male farmers' scale, a specific Occupational Scale, the women score very low compared to their male counterparts, suggesting there are still differences between men and women who go into farming in terms of their interest patterns. And if we take male beauticians, for example, and score them on the female beautician scale they score quite a bit lower than women would on that particular scale.

If we then look at mean profiles on the six General Occupational Themes we find almost the same differences between males and females within those nontraditional occupations as we do between Men- and Women-in-General. So for example, female veterinarians and engineers would score higher on the Realistic theme than Women-in-General, but they'd score lower than male veterinarians or male engineers, probably by the same amount as Women-in-General score lower than Men-in-General, five or six points.

What that says to me is that, where as people may really need to have some minimum ability to be successful within an occupation, we're not looking at some magic minimum of interest required to persist or succeed. So what we do is standardize scores by gender to provide people with a realistic estimate of whether their interests match the interests of their own sex in a particular occupation. At the same time we don't expect them to score at the other gender's level.

However, when roughly equal numbers of both sexes have been in an occupation for a long time the scores tend to be similar. If you look at male psychologists' scores on the female psychologists scale, and vice versa, their scores are much closer. Which means the interests of male and female psychologists are quite similar and probably we could use either scale for both.

Leduc: *But what happens as more women move into some of the nontraditional fields? Could this affect the difference between men's and women's scores in those occupations?*

Hansen: Well, I would assume, and I have been wrong before about change, that as men and women become more equally distributed in an occupation, the differences in their interests patterns will decrease. For example, as there are more women in drugstore pharmacy—that used to be rare, but now I see women working in those settings all the time—the profile for women pharmacists may well look different than it did in the past. The interest of the individual women in pharmacy may not change so much but the mean profile for them may change.

Smith: *I wonder if you might see changes in the men too because as the mixture of men and women in an occupation shifts the occupation itself may change and attract a different kind of man. Could the concept of what a physician or a pharmacist is shift as more women enter and their values become more prominent in the field?*

The first people who enter nontraditional occupations—the first female carpenters, the first female police officers, in other words the pioneers—tend to be different.

Hansen: Who knows what the truth will turn out to be. But as women come into an area that's been male dominated, I don't think the profile of that occupation's interests will change much. If it's been traditionally male I think it will still look traditionally male because what's likely to happen probably is the women are gradually going to look more traditionally male. If it's been traditionally female, the men coming into it will start to look more traditionally female.

Now there may be some anomalies when the occupation first opens to the opposite sex. One good example may be women in the trades—carpenters, plumbers, electricians. They have a fairly strong Investigative component in their interests whereas the men are Realistic through and through. But eventually the women also will come to look Realistic through and through, because those first women went in because of other traits in addition to Realistic interests. They're more willing to try new things and are challenged by the intellectual component of the job as well as by the physical skills. The first people who enter nontraditional occupations—the first female carpenters, the first female police officers, in other words the pioneers—tend to be different.

Likewise, when a new occupation defines itself the first folks in may look different and not provide the most reliable pattern. For example, the computer programmer scale on the Strong back in the sixties never seemed to work well when I used it with a college population because almost everybody scored high on it. Yet they'd say, "For heavens sake I'm not interested in that!" Well, it turns out what the scale probably was measuring wasn't an interest in being a computer programmer but sort of an academic orientation. The people who initially went into computer science were bright and willing to take some risks. After all, who knew where this new field was going to go? The computer programmer scale measures an interest in bachelor-level academics. And for a lot of young people that would be the only scale they'd score high on. They were flat-profiled people who were telling you they were in the right environment, but just needed some time to figure out and develop their interests.

So we probably need to check those scales more often for validity than the scales for psychologists, who've been around for years and where males and females already look pretty similar. One thing test developers need to worry about is doing periodic studies—if not full fledged revisions, at least spot checks—to make sure that such changes aren't happening. On one hand the overall stability our studies have shown so far reassures a researcher that the test doesn't need to be revised every year or maybe even every ten years. At the same time one can't become complacent.

Now, we don't have good cross-sectional data for all the decades for all the occupations, but we've looked again at between 20 or 30 across all of the Holland types—older occupations and the more established ones, but including some traditionally female and some traditionally male. And again we've seen that stability within the samples. What we wouldn't have seen yet, because not enough time has passed, is what happens to the interest patterns of the nontraditional sex cohort within the occupation over a long period of time.

Leduc: *What about engineering, medicine and law? There's been such a recent movement of females into those areas. Does what you say hold true for them too?*

Hansen: It seems to me that, again, based on the data that we have in those three areas, male and female interest patterns have looked more and more similar over the years. One of the frustrations with using any interest inventory clinically is that they're not precise enough to be able to differentiate specialties very well within an area, physicians for example. Efforts have been made to develop medical specialty scales but, by and large, they're not very useful. What you might find is that if you sampled female pediatricians, for example, versus male surgeons some differences would show on the Basic Interest Scales but if you looked at female and male surgeons they'd look very similar.

Then there are occupations where that hasn't been true and pharmacy again is a good example. I think it has to do with the early history of the occupation, with men and women going into such different areas. Historically women have tended to end up in a hospital pharmacy, or maybe a lab setting, and the men ended up in an enterprising setting doing all kinds of drug store management, marketing and personnel.

That split is reflected even now in pharmacy training. For example Minnesota's program in pharmacy has two tracks. One essentially gives a business degree along with pharmacy, which is on the male pharmacists' scale, the Investigative-Enterprising combination. The other track is much more research-oriented, more a pure Investigative, scientific track, closer to what is seen in female pharmacists.

Leduc: *But you also said that women generally score higher on Enterprising today so maybe that will affect the female pharmacist interest scores. They'll move more into management too.*

Hansen: Yes, I would assume that if, in ten or fifteen years, we were to sample female pharmacists again we would start to see some of that Enterprising interest emerging in part of their profile. But we have not in the past. So it's the kind of case where we say, "Well, in the past fifty years there haven't been appreciable changes we can identify but don't become so complacent that you never look again." There's still room for the gender patterns of interest to converge.

Leduc: *Do you also find other, more general differences between male and female patterns? For example, that women have more low, or flat, profiles than men?*

Hansen: No. Typically if we compare the average number of high scores for the males in a sample versus the number for females there'd be no significant difference. If we look at things like the validity of the scales predicting college major or occupational choice, the instrument actually works a little better for women than men, although it would not be a significant difference.

Using the SII in Counselling

Smith: *Some people have concerns that women on interest tests may appear more Social or less Realistic because they think it's the way they should answer. Have you ever had a counsellee come up after the test and say, "Look, I'm really interested in things but I answered another way, the way I think I should."?*

Hansen: No, I have actually never had anybody say that to me. I think it's hard for people to do that with the Strong. There are enough items and the method for constructing the occupational scales is complicated enough—involving both the likes as well as dislikes of the occupations—that I think scores are hard to fake. Somebody has to be pretty sophisticated to be able to look like a physician or a psychologist. They may be able to guess pretty well on the "likes" but usually they don't know the "dislikes." It's easier to fake the General Occupational Themes and Basic Interest Scales since their weighting schemes are more simple and obvious. So I might occasionally talk with clients who've managed to raise their scores in those areas but what I will find then is a discrepancy, if they really faked it, between the occupational part and the rest of the profile. And usually that's a startling enough contrast that they'll admit something like, "My father or mother was interested in these things so I thought I should say 'like' to those items too."

Now I have had people on occasion try to sabotage it by random responding and they're absolutely astounded when I sit down with them and say, "Well, this little index here suggests that you did not answer these items in the typical manner. How do you feel about having to do this inventory?"

Some of the worst horror stories I've heard about misuse of the Strong, for either women or men, involved clients who've said, "I had it interpreted and the counsellor told me this was my highest score and the **one** occupation I was suited for." No full profile interpretation! From the beginning a counsellor needs to set the scene for broad exploration and the understanding that career decisions should not be made in a vacuum. People really should be looking at their entire life plan. And as I mentioned before, the instrument can measure more than just vocational interests, and individuals looking at their scores should be considering the full range of their activities to judge how well the instrument is reflecting what they know about themselves.

Maybe the most important ingredients to focus on would be, of course, vocational decisions but also avocational decisions. For example, what kinds of people does the individual like to be around, whether in a personal, work or recreational context? For many it's the same but for others it's very different. Probably the other focus would be the work and living environment component that interest inventories occasionally pick up. Again for some, their life across all arenas is centred pretty much on the same environment, city or rural whatever, but for many it's quite differentiated. In Minnesota the prime example is that avocationally people go north for the weekend, up to Boundary Waters to their cabin, but they're very centred during their workweek right here in the city.

I think you can pick up pieces of that as you work through an inventory, probably getting the best information for those bits of exploration from the Basic Interest Scales. Compared to the Occupational Scales these probably have more of a tendency to change as a person's interests come and go. For example, if somebody suddenly develops an interest in public speaking, spends a lot of time at it, what we might find is that the score on the public speaking scale would go up. But what we then might also find as they acquire those skills is that it's no longer a passion and the score changes again. So we may find some real differences in the General Occupational Themes and Basic Interest Scales that reflect some preconceived notion. Perhaps the client says, "This is what I've been doing so this is how I should respond." Or maybe the person has a lack of knowledge about other possibilities or not enough experience.

Also, I think that taking an interest inventory ends up being a way for clients to structure their thinking about the world of work, to help them logically proceed from understanding themselves to finding out about occupations and understanding the world of work. I don't know that it ends up telling most people much that's a startling revelation. For an awful lot it will confirm what they already know and also give them some suggestions for new directions and for focused thinking. It's also a more or less efficient way for a counsellor to be able to understand the individual quickly and objectively.

Smith: *You're saying it's a two-way street—that the counsellee is learning something about herself and the world of work and that the counsellor is learning something about the counsellee.*

Hansen: Yes. What I try to do when I approach a profile interpretation is to have some hypotheses to offer clients about why they scored high or low. Then I ask the client to sort through them with the realization that only they can identify which hypotheses are true for them. And I suppose, if I were to approach this from the context of your readers who are parents or consumers of interest inventories, I would stress that career decision-making probably is best done in the context of individuals' entire life styles.

Research Needs with the SII

Leduc: *If you were given a few million dollars right now, what kinds of studies would you like to do using the Strong?*

Hansen: I think my biggest concern over the long haul is insuring that any occupational change in interests is not missed. So I suppose if I had a big pile of money I would go to some of those occupations we sampled back in the early seventies, probably starting with the occupations that have been nontraditional for one sex or the other—female veterinarians would be one example—and collect criterion samples again to insure that interests have been stable within those occupations.

I think what we would probably find at this point is that there are still large enough sex differences within these occupations that we couldn't do a completely combined sex profile. We might also find some responses have changed for the nontraditional sex that would warrant new Occupational Scales. But the General Occupational Themes and the Basic Interest Scales are good scales. They were standardized with new Men- and Women-in-General samples in '85 and we can feel fairly comfortable leaving those as they are for a time.

It might also be tempting to look again at the organization of the Basic Interest Scales for males and females according to the Holland type. There are probably more sophisticated statistical routines now to do a better job at analysis. The downside for that, of course, is that if there was a major upheaval in the way those scales are organized for either gender we would throw everybody's clinical wisdom out the window. Even when we moved the lawyers' scale from Enterprising to Artistic, that was incredibly disruptive for people. Typically researchers are much more willing to make changes than the clinicians using the test want or accept. So we have to be a little careful.

Smith: *Are there any studies you want to do regarding the usefulness of interest inventories with women?*

Hansen: One area needing more study, but this would be true for both women and men, is the effectiveness of interest inventories in stimulating actual career exploration as well as how well people remember what they've learned from their profiles. So far the results are discouraging. The studies we've done on the typical college student research population were not in the context of career development or counselling but strictly in terms of interest inventory administration and a fairly routine, one-hour group interpretation. What we were looking at really was the effect of the instrument without the counselling trappings.

Then in the follow-ups we did a year later to find out from students how much they remembered from the brief interpretation, most of them didn't even remember their results on the General Occupational Themes and of those that did remember, maybe half could tell with any accuracy whether they scored high, medium, or low anywhere across the profile. And that goes for Basic Interest Scales, Occupational Scales, and so on. The amount remembered was not impressive.

Leduc: *Did they remember what they came in for?*

Hansen: Not always. Some of them didn't even remember they were there—"Oh, did I do that?" I have to stress that's with the briefest of interpretations. But it's not unlike what happens in some real life situations. Then if we look at whether administering an inventory along with a brief interpretation stimulates any kind of career exploration, we find that it does seem to do a little something, as Holland found with the Self-Directed Search and A.R. Spokane found with a quasi meta-analysis of a number of different studies. But if we sort out the statistical from the psychological significance, it's not very big.

So the message is that we really need to have programs using tests as part of a larger program with more than just an interest inventory, probably also personality as well as some ability assessment and so on. And those need to be tailored to the particular population. So, for example, if you're working with university athletes, the particular program designed for them may look very different from one for high school students or for medical school students trying to decide on a specialty.

Smith: *Are women any more disadvantaged by inadequate counselling?*

Hansen: No. In terms of, again, the couple of studies we've done, which involved a marginal amount of interpretation, the women didn't look any less informed or remember any less than the men.

Leduc: *Any other studies you'd like to do?*

Hansen: If I had my pool of a few million dollars one other interesting project would be to carry out some longitudinal sampling and try a shotgun inquiry to see if one could come up with something to help predict at the first test, time one, which people were going to have stable interests. In the high school students we studied, the range of test-retest correlation was from zero to .99, a tremendous range, and in the college population the range was narrower but still quite broad. Probably the lowest was around .2 rather than zero. When we looked back at the demographic information we had on these people to see if we could figure out why some were stable and some not, we couldn't.

But Leona Tyler did an early longitudinal study from grade school on and although she laments in that particular reprint that her measures of interests were not very sophisticated, what she found essentially was that the best bet to have stable interests were people in science and math areas. It seems their interests develop or stabilize at a younger age than do the interests of people in other areas.

Leduc: *You're saying math and science interests solidify earlier. But what about young women who show a math and science interest in high school but don't go into those occupations. If their interests are stable, what's happening to dissuade so many from continuing?*

Hansen: Socialization kicks in. I guess I'd go back to maintaining that women have always had a breadth of interests, including science and math and that it's just been a case of other factors impeding their exploration or actualization. It's discouraging to hear that socialization against math and science is still so powerful. It just seems that the change in attitude should have happened by now. I do occasionally hear women say that because they did well in math and science that was the only thing they were allowed to consider, and so there is sort of a reversed resentment. But those are very individual cases.

The Future of Interest Testing

Smith: *Given today's tightening school budgets, how optimistic are you about seeing the use of interest tests improve in the future?*

Hansen: Certainly my guess would be that interest testing programs would be one of the things pretty easy for schools to cut. It's one very identifiable line item where administration can easily save dollars. However, I think an even larger concern over the long haul with potential for far-reaching social impact on the work force is simply people not being allowed to be where they belong, in terms of matching interests, needs and values with jobs.

Looking back, one of the things affecting my own career path was that I was certainly among first women with the notion she could pretty much do what she wanted. I can't remember ever thinking that I couldn't be a physician, for example, although at the time not a lot of women did go to medical school. So we've had twenty years for the most part where counsellors could say, "If you've got the ability, if you work hard, if you can figure out your interests there'll be a place for you." But we're entering an era now where interests are not necessarily going to be satisfied no matter how hard people work or how good they are. There are just not enough positions in some areas and as a result employers are going to be faced with dissatisfied employees on all different dimensions. No interest test is going to be able to solve that problem. It's just going to confirm that this person should be dissatisfied because her interests don't match her work environment.

Interest testing originally came about to meet the needs of educators primarily, because people were interested in human development but then very quickly industry realized that turnover could be reduced if people's interests matched what they were doing. But we may have reached a point in the economic cycle where the human development that we have luxuriated in over the last twenty years may be fast fading. If the available jobs continue to diminish, little upward mobility is going to exist, and that means lots of unhappy people.

I hear horror stories about people graduating from some of our best midwest liberal arts schools in economics or history and going a year without finding a job. They feel lucky to end up as hosts or hostesses for a Mexican restaurant with a chance to switch to waiting tables. So somebody from a high prestige school who spent a bucket of money getting educated becomes a waiter or waitress, and I just bet that's not where their measured interests are.

Not that data indicates simply being matched with interests guarantees satisfaction with a particular occupation, probably because satisfaction has to do with more than just the match of interests, although that's an important component. The client needs to be in the right value system and have appropriate needs satisfied, and there's probably some personality and ability dimensions which fit in there as well.

We're entering an era now where interests are not necessarily going to be satisfied no matter how hard people work or how good they are.

Smith: *So in the last twenty years there's been a massive commitment and funding for interest testing flowing out of this whole idea of personal growth. But there's no guarantee it will continue.*

Leduc: *Is it becoming more difficult also to get grants for research with the Strong?*

Hansen: Grants are a whole other thing. Public opinion is that publishers should support the research and so it's very difficult to get grants from the government or even private foundations. It would be nice to find funding for test construction and development but it's not easy even to find funding for basic research in interest measurement. We do a little better if we're trying to implement or evaluate particular programs. But when we look at the severe problems facing society, such as AIDS, I don't know that this work should be rated any more highly by funding agencies, because the dollars are limited.

Smith: *This leads to the final question—as they stand today, are interest tests such as the Strong fair to both sexes, however you want to define fair?*

Hansen: I would say that it's equally useful assuming there are gender-fair counsellors using it, which may be a dangerous assumption. The instrument offers adequate information for both sexes in the hands of skilled counsellors and counselling psychologists and can be used to maximize career choices for both.

Smith: *So you think the Strong is pretty good the way it is, if it's used properly.*

Hansen: [Laughs] Not that I have any biases!

Endnotes

1. Holland's Theory of Vocational Personalities and Work Environments

The theory of John L. Holland[3], professor emeritus of The Johns Hopkins University, has four main assumptions:

(1) All workers, in western culture at least, can be grouped into six basic personality types or combinations of these types: Realistic, Investigative, Artistic, Social, Enterprising and Conventional (see below for detail). Each of these categories reflects a separate pattern of interests, including typical hobbies, specific activities enjoyed doing at work and types of co-workers and physical work environments preferred.

Holland's Personality Types

Holland suggested these types can be organized in the shape of a hexagon in the R-I-A-S-E-C order, with types adjacent to one another on the hexagon more related than those diametrically opposed.

The types are as follow:

Realistic (R): a practical, mechanically-minded person, possibly lacking in social skills; includes the skilled trades, technical and some service occupations.

Investigative (I): a scientifically oriented, intellectual person, possibly lacking leadership ability; includes scientific and some technical occupations.

---

3 Holland, J.L. (1973). *Making vocational choices: A theory of careers*. Englewood Cliffs, N. J.: Prentice-Hall.

Artistic (A): an imaginative, creative person, possibly lacking clerical and practical skills; includes artistic, musical and literary occupations

Social (S): a people-oriented person with strong social skills; includes educational and social welfare occupations.

Enterprising (E): a person with leadership and sales skills; includes managerial and sales occupations.

Conventional (C): a person who likes orderly pursuits, possibly lacking artistic ability; includes office and clerical occupations.

(2) Work environments can also be divided into these six types.

(3) People search for environments that let them exercise their skills and abilities and express their attitudes and values.

(4) A person's behavior is determined by interaction between personality and the characteristics of his or her working environment, which in turn affects job performance, satisfaction and stability.

People are not rigidly classified by Holland's system. Instead they are characterized by degree of resemblance to one or more types, arranged in order of resemblance. This provides a three-letter code such as IAR, meaning that such a person is most similar to investigative, then to artistic, and still less to realistic people. To make it easier to find the occupations best matching a particular interest or personality type, Holland and his co-researchers also used their data to assign a comparable three-letter code to occupations listed in the *U.S. Dictionary of Occupational Titles* (DOT) and the *Canadian Classification and Dictionary of Occupations* (CCDO).

2. SII Scales[4]

The **General Occupational Themes** conform to Holland's six personality types, with each theme characterizing not only a type of person but also a type of working environment most congenial to that person.

Each theme is further divided into several **Basic Interest Scales** representing clusters of more closely related interests. For example, under the "Realistic" General Occupational Theme lie the scales of agriculture, nature, adventure, military activities and mechanical activities; under "Artistic" fall music, dramatics, art and writing. For all but five of these more basic scales, test-takers' scores are compared to scores of their own sex.

Occupational Scales are the most specific level. The 1985 SCII version carries 207 Occupational Scales representing 106 occupations. For each of 101 occupations there is both a scale based on a female-normed criterion sample and one based on a male-normed sample. A full 32 percent of the

---

4 Hansen, J.C., & Campbell, D.P. (1985). *Manual for the SVIB-SCII (4th Ed.)*. Palo Alto, Calif.: Consulting Psychologists Press.

scales or categories represent occupations with educational requirements less than a college degree, for example, bus driver, emergency medical technician and electrician.

References and Recommended Readings

Campbell, D.P. (1966). The stability of vocational interests within occupations over long time spans. *Personnel and Guidance Journal, 45,* 1012-1019.

Campbell, D.P. (1971). *Handbook for the Strong Vocational Interest Blank.* Stanford Calif.: Stanford University Press.

Campbell, D.P., Borgen, F.H., Eastes, S.H., Johansson, C. B., & Peterson, R.A. (1968). A set of basic interest scales for the Strong Vocational Interest Blank for Men. *Journal of Applied Psychology, 52,* 1-54.

Hansen, J.C., Collins, R., Swanson, J.L., & Fouad, N.A. (in press, 1992). Gender differences in the structure of interests. *Journal of Vocational Behavior.*

Hansen, J.C. & Tan, R.N. (in press, 1992). Concurrent validity of the 1985 Strong Interest Inventory for college major selection. *Measurement and Evaluation in Counseling and Development.*

Hansen, J.C. (1988). Changing interests of women: Myth or reality? *Applied Psychology: An International Review, 37*(2), 133-150.

Hansen, J.C. & Swanson, J.L. (1983). Stability of interests and the predictive and concurrent validity of the 1981 Strong-Campbell Interest Inventory for college majors. *Journal of Counseling Psychology, 30,*(2), 194-201.

Holland, J.L. (1966). *The psychology of vocational choice.* Waltham, Mass.: Blaisdell.

Holland, J.L. (1985). *Making vocational choices: A theory of vocational personalities & work environments.* Englewood Cliffs, N.J.: Prentice-Hall, Inc.

Randahl, G.J., Hansen, J.C., & Haverkamp, B.E. (in press, 1992). Instrumental behaviors following test administration and interpretation: Exploration validity of the Strong Interest Inventory. *Journal of Counseling and Development.*

Spokane, A.R. (1979). Occupational preference and the validity of the Strong-Campbell Interest Inventory for college women and men. *Journal of Counseling Psychology, 26,* 312-318.

Strong, E.K., Jr. (1955). *Vocational interests eighteen years after college.* Minneapolis: University of Minnesota Press.

Tyler, L.E. (1955). The development of "vocational interests": I. The organization of likes and dislikes in ten-year-old children. *Journal of Genetic Psychology, 86,* 33-44.

Significant Events in the Life of Jo-Ida Hansen

1969	B.A. Psychology (summa cum laude), University of Minnesota (U. of Minn.)
1971	M.A. Psychology, U. of Minn.
1972	First publication: *Journal of Vocational Behavior, 2* 479-493
1974	Ph.D. Psychology, U. of Minn. Assistant professor, U. of Minn. Director, Center for Interest Measurement Research (CIMR), U. of Minn.
1978	Associate professor, U. of Minn.
1981-Present	Faculty representative for Intercollegiate Athletics, U. of Minn.
1983	E.K. Strong Jr. Gold Medal Award Professor, U. of Minn.
1983-84	Chair, Big 10 Intercollegiate Athletic Conference
1984	Elected Fellow, American Psychological Association (APA), Division 17 (Counseling) Published *User's Guide to the SVIB-SCII*
1986	Elected Fellow, APA, Division 35 (Women)
1986,1990	Exemplary Practices Award, Association for Measurement and Evaluation in Counseling and Development
1987	Director, Couseling Psychology Program, U. of Minn.
1988	Published: Changing interests of women: myth or realtiy? *Applied Psychology* Elected Fellow, APA, Division 5 (Measurement)
1992	Invited participant, 38th Annual National Security Seminar, U.S. Army War College, Carlisle Barracks, PA Published: Gender differences in the structure of interests. *Journal of Vocational Behavior* President's Task Force on Gender Equity in Intercollegiate Athletics, U. of Minn.
1993	Editorial Board, *Journal of Counseling and Development*

Section Three

Special Issues

In the first interview of this section, which focuses on four, more specific issues regarding career choice, Nancy Betz of the University of Illinois describes women's all too typical experience in higher education. Even if a girl has decided by late adolescence that she is strongly interested in a nontraditional career, the way she is treated by peers and professors on campus can discourage her from following her dreams.

And if she is gifted, says Connie Hollinger of Cleveland State University, she encounters even more pressure, a crossfire of expectations that many find almost impossible to survive, according to the longitudinal study of gifted women, Project Choice. As a bright person she is expected to achieve but as a female she is still pressured to conform to the traditional image of the self-effacing, nurturing woman.

Given this stress on the bright female student and the societal factors discussed in Section One, it is not surprising, as Jacquelynne Eccles of the University of Colorado at Boulder notes, to find women's aspirations to enter the demanding fields of math and science to be eroded.

Finally, Montreal mathematician and consultant Lesley Lee and biologist Karen Messing of the University of Quebec discuss some of the barriers women face even if they retain their nontraditional interests, particularly in the trades and technology-related fields. Training, health and safety issues all contribute to the high attrition rates of women who choose to take on jobs in these areas.

4

The Invisible Woman: Effect of the Educational Environment on Women's Vocational Identity

An interview with Nancy E. Betz, Ph.D., Professor of Psychology, Ohio State University.

To feel invisible and alien—that's the fate of most women on university campuses, particularly in the nontraditional fields. Women are generally ignored by faculty and given no career direction by their families ("Do whatever will make you happy, dear"), yet at the same time are inundated by society's traditional messages about proper female roles and careers. Therefore it's probably no surprise that the result is a steady loss, for most women, of both their vocational aspirations and self-esteem.

These are some of the conclusions about women's academic experience drawn by Nancy Betz and other researchers within the general field of the career psychology of women (see chapter References). Betz's own scholarship in this field has been so varied and extensive that it has led to a series of milestone accomplishments, for example, her co-authorship of *The Career Psychology of Women* with Louise Fitzgerald, editorship of the *Journal of Vocational Behavior* and receipt of the John Holland Award for research in career and personality, given by Division 17 (Counseling Psychology) of the American Psychological Association.

For this book, however, Betz agreed to focus specifically on how seemingly innocent factors in the educational environment can combine to discourage even the most capable women from pursuing the vocational interests of their choice.

Although scheduling difficulties meant the interview had to be held by telephone, Betz easily communicated her authoritative command of the topic across the electronic distance.

In the interview, as follows, she first talks with feeling about her own experiences as a student. She then presents examples of campus conditions that make women in general feel like unwelcome foreigners and describes how these factors systematically restrict their options for careers. Betz concludes with ways that career counsellors, parents and individual students can counter such negative influences.

Growing up in the Driver's Seat

Smith: *We'd like to know more about your background. How did you get interested in women's careers, particularly the obstacles that women face in their education?*

Betz: Well, even though I was a girl I was always very strongly oriented towards math and science and actually not very great in the verbal arts. I started out as a pre-med major but eventually began getting discouraging messages about math and science-related careers. For example, I had a high school guidance counsellor tell me that if I became a physician I couldn't marry and have a home and family. That made me anxious because I thought I'd be a lonely old maid. Later in college my experience was the same as what most women go through, basically what Jo Freeman calls a "Null Environment", one that neither encourages nor discourages individuals—it simply ignores them. Which means that although I went to a very expensive, elite, liberal arts college I was pretty much ignored by the faculty, particularly those in the sciences most relevant to what I wanted to do, go to med school. At the same time I received very clear messages about what girls were and were not supposed to be from the society in which I was growing up. I learned that as a smart girl I was fighting an uphill battle in terms of having boys like me and that I shouldn't ever perform better than a boy.

Now my parents were wonderful but all they would tell me is "Just do what you want to do." And the point behind the concept of the null academic environment, which I'll say more about later, is that girls need more guidance than that when they're challenging nontraditional areas because meanwhile society is telling them to do traditionally female things. So just saying "do what you want to do" lets the traditional messages win.

Smith: *What kind of messages did you get from your peers, the boys and girls you went to school with?*

Betz: Well, by twelfth grade I was one of two or three girls left in math, chemistry and physics. I was viewed as a "brain" and the boys on the football team didn't want to date me, but as a sixteen-year-old I wanted to date those boys. I felt like an ugly duckling. I wanted to be liked by the boys as well as be smart, but it seemed in high school I couldn't have both. I now have learned that I can, but I didn't really get that message until graduate school when I was around a lot of smart boys who valued me.

Leduc: *Going back to the ugly duckling image, did your parents or relatives reinforce that at all? Did they expect you to be more feminine?*

Betz: No. My mother is a wonderful career-oriented woman, a psychologist, who didn't have many of the feminine arts. She didn't sew or cook much or know all about feminine dress and make-up. In high school I talked to her about feeling inadequate as a female and she said, "Well let's do something about it." She paid to send me, in essence, to a charm school eight hours every Saturday to learn the "feminine" arts of makeup, hair, nails and diet. My favorite class was "personality"! Its message was "Whoever you are doesn't matter. You have to develop the right personality." Looking back now I just have to laugh. I spent an hour every Saturday learning to have the right personality? But it wasn't my mother's idea, it was mine. My mother didn't want to do this but she thought, as a good mother, since she couldn't teach me the skills I wanted, maybe someone else could.

But I'm proud to say I flunked out. I was a charm school dropout at age sixteen because after about two months I realized this was the weirdest thing in the world. I wasn't like these other girls who were studying charm to be models and secretaries where they'd probably need, to put it bluntly, to get by on their physical appearance. I was headed towards higher education and eventually realized I was fine exactly the way I was. Still, for a long time I was very upset that I was not "five foot two and eyes of blue," like the song title, and a cheerleader so the boys would like me.

So that attitude really got in my way. But I don't blame it on my parents. I blame it on my peer socialization about what popular girls were like. Now all those popular girls are probably dowdy housewives with eight children. That's a generalization, but I'm much better off now than I would have been had I tried to live the life of a stereotypical female.

Smith: *Was your mother a role model?*

Betz: Yes. My parents were divorced when I was nine months old and my mother was a career woman from that point on. She was a wonderful role model, so in essence I've followed in her footsteps.

Leduc: *Did she feel pretty good about herself as a woman?*

Betz: No, she also didn't feel good about herself as a feminine woman, but gradually she learned she didn't have to be traditionally feminine to be valuable. We both had to learn that lesson.

Smith: *Are you an only child?*

Betz: I'm an only child from my mother. My father has three others. Two daughters and a son who's the youngest. But it was my mother and I, who let's say, grew up together.

Leduc: *What kind of contact did you have with your father while growing up?*

Betz: I spent every summer with my father and I have a very fine relationship with him and his wife of thirty-five years. My dad, by and large, has always treated me as sort of his first son. I was his first child. I was always oriented towards education so I was the ideal kid to take the role of a son. I was hard driving and achieving.

So when I would go to his home for the summer, he'd have a list of classical books and music I was to master. He's an attorney but his father was a math professor and he comes from a long line of educators. So scholarly achievement was important to him, and since I was a smart kid we got along well. He was always very, very nurturing of my educational goals. But he really had again that "Well, do what you want to do" approach.

Leduc: *Some of the other people we interviewed have also said they were treated as a son by their fathers. Sometimes that attitude was shown by doing carpentry with them and other kinds of physical activities. Was that an experience of your childhood as well?*

Betz: (laughs) My father would kill himself if he used a hammer. Neither of my parents have any manual dexterity, so my father didn't model the manly arts any better than my mother modeled the womanly arts. But they both modeled a value of higher education and achievement.

Smith: *On the other hand he didn't provide a role model indicating men were very different.*

Betz: No. Actually it's funny now because it's my younger sister, an architect, who does all the home repairs. My father waits for her to come home and she fixes everything. My father could not fix anything if it bit him. In a way I really didn't get a traditional socialization.

Leduc: *So when you say he treated you like a son would it be fair to say also that he expected you could do anything you wanted?*

Betz: Intellectually, that's right. I can give you a good example. When we were growing up he'd set up chess matches and other competitions between my brother and me, never the other girls. That's why I say I was his first son, mostly because I see the similarity in his treatment and aspirations for me and my brother and dissimilarity vis-à-vis the other two girls. Even though one of the girls is a civil engineer and landscape architect and, if anybody is able to do some masculine type things, she can. But because we come from this long line of educators, the scholarly life which I've led is what he really valued.

Smith: *I'm curious, though, about why you turned away from pre-med. What made you change your mind?*

Betz: It really was the culmination of a whole series of things in my college sophomore year. Until then I'd kept plugging along in my pre-med studies despite no support from the faculty and all these socialized messages that medicine was no occupation for a woman. But the precipitating event happened in my chemistry lab. My lab partner got too close to a Bunsen burner and her lab coat caught fire. Although our instructions were to pull the cord on the ceiling shower in such an emergency, all the socialized messages about girls' squeamishness in times of crisis or at the sight of blood instead took hold. Accordingly, I fainted, and that was the final straw. I was convinced I'd never have the stomach for medicine, and no one was around to tell me anything different. So I dropped my aspirations.

Another factor was that I only knew about exactly three careers—physician— which I'd always wanted to be, lawyer—my father's profession, and psychology—my mother's. Now I knew I didn't want to be a lawyer, so that left psychologist. Also I thought as a girl I should help people, if not as a doctor then as a psychologist. All those socialized messages again.

It did turn out to be a good choice, fortunately, but I regret that my range of choices was unnecessarily restricted by sex-role socialization. Also I was just dismally ignorant about any other careers and certainly could have used some good career counselling.

Leduc: *Did you ever make a conscious decision not to marry and have children when you knew you wanted to be an academic?*

Betz: I've never been strongly oriented towards children. And I'll tell you a story to illustrate my thinking. Because my mother and I were alone, I always got to ride in the front with her. Most kids ride in the back, right? I did not. I remember as early as age six saying to myself "Someday I'm going to be in that driver's seat and I'm not giving it up." Because I knew that any time I saw men and women together the men were in the driver's seat. So I said to myself, "Honey, you are getting into that driver's seat and never giving it up." I think that's a metaphor for my life—staying in the driver's seat. Now, I've contemplated marriage before but it just didn't feel right. So had I married I would've had children, but I didn't marry.

Leduc: *But you've still been a role model for students.*

Betz: I'm certainly a role model to many, many students today in terms of being a high achiever and a woman who's totally comfortable with statistics, math and technical things. I think that makes them feel more secure. Yet I've not combined marriage and children with a career, which means for some I don't think I've been an ideal role model. But I keep saying there are plenty of women on faculty who are married and have children. This is not something I do, nor do I really feel I should be expected to. They can't get everything they need from one role model.

The Null Environment for Women

Smith: *You've mentioned how the null academic environment, that is, being essentially ignored by your science professors, affected you in your education. We'd like you now to draw upon your own studies and others to tell us in more detail how this lack of support affects women.*

Betz: I'd first like to say the "null environment" is one of the most important concepts to help us understand why women don't achieve their goals. Nontraditional environments are tough no matter who you are. I mean, taking an advanced degree in the sciences or engineering is difficult for anyone. But men don't have to make it through school with no resources but their own, so why should women? Some women can make it on their own resources. No matter how unfriendly the environment, they persist. The problem I see is all those women for whom that's not enough. It reminds me of the old saying, "The world will be fair when mediocre women get the same breaks as mediocre men."

Let me describe a characteristic form of that lack of support involving faculty behavior. Professors generally are not that attentive to students of either sex. But men are less affected because they tend to come from external environments that reinforce their educational and career development more. They don't have a society telling them to go home, they'd be better off in traditionally female occupations. What they have is a society which in general reinforces their career plans. They also probably have a family, a girlfriend and friends who reinforce their goals, even if the professors are not doting over them. So the idea of a null academic environment is that women have a hundred voices telling them to do traditional things but little support helping them maintain nontraditional interests. Faced with this kind of opposition, most women can't do it alone.

Smith: *Do you think there are more opportunities, almost a tradition, for men to get together after classes and after work?*

Betz: Exactly. My favorite example is from a chemistry department. They hired five new assistant professors one year, four men and one woman. A friend of mine would see the four young men every Friday afternoon drinking in the faculty club, catching up on the week. Now this is a classic example of collegial support and information passing, passing on departmental gossip, wisdom, tips on survival in an academic environment. So one day my friend went up to them and said, "Why don't you invite the other member of your cohort, the new woman assistant professor?" Well, they just looked at her like she was from outer space. It had never occurred to them. That's illustrative of how this isolation happens.

Smith: *Is the barrier here a matter of sexual connotation? Do the men think if they invite this woman to join them she might somehow think they're interested in her sexually? Just as a woman doesn't quite dare offer to spend social time with a man because, in turn, it might indicate her sexual interest?*

Betz: Yes. There's the concept of sex salience developed by Cynthia Epstein. And it basically says that with women, their sexual role is much more important than their role as worker or student. But women's sexuality per se has no business in the work or school environment. Women are more than sex objects. So one of the songs I repeat over and over again is that men simply have got to view women as colleagues, as workers and as students. That other view is not only dehumanizing, it's juvenile! I don't have any tolerance for it. Let's be adults and view each other as something besides potential sleeping partners. Women do not go to work to go to bed, they go to work to work. And just as a man's marital status doesn't influence whether he's invited out by other men to have a drink, it shouldn't for women.

Smith: *Or you get comments such as, " What will their wives think if we invite you?"*

Betz: Which means that men have learned only four ways of relating to women—mother, wife, daughter and sexual partner. At work they put a female colleague into one of those categories but none of those respects a woman's role as worker. And of course there's the whole problem of sexual harassment. That's really not my area of research but I think that kind of thing is probably the most pervasive barrier to women with terribly dehumanizing effects.

Leduc: *So you're saying that women are going to continue to have problems feeling alienated until men learn healthier ways to relate to them in the educational system and workplace. But whose responsibility is it to change them, other men's, women's, or is it everyone's responsibility?*

Betz: When I go out lecturing I talk to both same and mixed sex groups about that, and I basically repeat to men what I just said to you. I charge each man with reeducating his fellow males. Let me give you a very good example from one university I know of. A university administrator came into a department to give a lecture on sexual harassment—what it was and how to avoid it. Well, two of the men sat in the back and giggled and whispered through the whole lecture, acting like eight-year olds. The department chair should have said something but, no, he sat there looking stupid until finally an untenured woman turned around and said, "Look, this is serious. I would appreciate it if you wouldn't talk until the speaker is through."

My point with this example is why did a woman have to confront this situation, especially an untenured woman? So that now she gets a reputation as a bitch and a harpy. One of the senior men there or the department chair should have said something. Another man communicates a lot to his male colleagues. I tell men "When you hear this stuff, don't wait for a woman to confront it. Dehumanizing people is not just a women's issue, it's everyone's issue."

The other way I like to communicate this message is to ask, "Do you stand by when racist comments are made?" Usually they say, "No." "Do you stand by when a fellow human being is being dehumanized?" Again they say, "No." Then I ask, "Why do you let a woman be dehumanized?" Of course the obvious answer they don't want to make is, "I don't think of a woman as a human being."

Another thing that's often said when you confront men is:"Well, that guy's too old to change. He's just a sexist old lech. So let him be." My response to that is, "Would you excuse racism because he's too old to change?" And the answer is usually, "No." So I view it as an issue of dehumanizing our fellow human beings, which

---

Men have learned only four ways of relating to women—mother, wife, daughter and sexual partner. At work they put a female colleague into one of those categories but none of those respects a woman's role as worker.

---

men have the responsibility to fight just as much as women. It is not a women's issue, it is a human issue.

Smith: *Does the null environment have a different effect on different age groups of women? So, in contrast to the young girl coming out of her family straight into university, can a woman who's had a chance to acquire some life experience, to test her wings, resist that negativity better?*

Betz: If that reentering or older woman does have a strong sense of self, then yes. I think your point is a good one. However, the reentry students I see are coming out of years as a homemaker and mother and they freak out when they get back into the academic whirlwind. They've lost their belief in themselves, and there's evidence that the self-esteem of housewives deteriorates steadily over time, whereas that of men and career women remains stable or continues to increase. So, yes, I think it depends on the experiences they've had in the interim. The women whose self esteem deteriorates are women in traditional roles.

Smith: *Then if women have been out there working at some job and taking care of themselves, they fare better.*

Betz: Much better, so it's not marriage per se. It's whether she's also been actively involved in the world outside the home. Women who've stayed home to raise their children tend to lose confidence in their ability to deal with the outside world, which makes sense.

Women in Higher Education: Forever Foreigners?

Smith: *What would be other specific examples of the obstacles women face in higher education? For example, how sex biased is the content of the text books we're using?*

Betz: The field I'm familiar most with is medical school education, which has been a terrible area for biased text books. My book, *The Career Psychology of Women*, has a chapter which goes at length into some of the studies on women in medical education. Until recently there were medical text books that talked about women being frigid and had pictures of naked women and sexist jokes, all assuming that the book's audience was all male and overlooking the fact that a female medical student is not pleased by jokes about her body. So medical school texts have tended to objectify women sexually just as much as society in general. And it's not all the medical schools. But many are the last bastions of sexist traditionality.

Smith: *Yes, part of my Ph.D. years ago involved medical school courses and I remember distinctly a sexist slide popping up in my anatomy course. But at the time I didn't dare protest. So have the text books improved?*

Betz: I think there's been a lot of improvement because of the attention on them. But I'm sure there's still a lot of sexism there, telling women in marriages to fake orgasms and all sorts of really sexually sexist stuff. So you can have an educational climate which conveys either overt hostility to women or simply ignores their existence, and I'm not sure which is worse. In neither case do women feel welcome. And although I can't tell you the extent to which this exists across disciplines, I do hear that women in the sciences and engineering still feel very unwanted.

I'll tell you one of the examples I've written about. I remember the discomforting experience of one young woman who went to study physics at a very well known university and upon first entering the department saw pictures of all the faculty and students on the bulletin board. And they were all white men. The sensation she felt, where it was obvious that everyone else was a white man, was of being a foreigner, an alien. I think that concept is a very good one. If I walked into a building in Japan I'd feel like a foreigner. Likewise, women feel like foreigners in traditionally male dominated areas, especially in the sciences and engineering.

Leduc: *What are the responses of foreigners or women in these roles?*

Betz: Certainly they don't feel as free to speak up in classes and as encouraged to seek mentors. They feel unwelcome. And anytime you're in a demanding educational environment which by its very nature has some discouraging elements, unless you get some active encouragement from your environment, you're inclined to say, "Just forget it." You drop out.

Smith: *What's the effect of this negative environment on the possibility of collegial friendships between men and women students?*

Betz: When a women is a token, one of just a very few women in an educational environment, the only friendship possibilities she has are with male students. Yet because she's sexualized, people assume they are dating. They view cross sex friendships as only romantic, which I think is absolutely absurd. I have the same message when I talk to groups of women professors. I tell them they need to seek support from the other women in their unit, certainly, but they also need to seek support from the men. Our friendships are so important to us. So men and women both have to get past the view of each other as only sex partners to a view of each other as friends and colleagues.

Smith: *So that you could casually ask a guy to join you for lunch without him thinking you have a sexual interest in him?*

Betz: Exactly. You do need him as a friend so there shouldn't be this assumption of ulterior sexual motive. I think that's one of the most archaic things in society. Now that doesn't mean you don't have a sexual relationship with a man at home, but at work you're friends. So your point is a good one.

Smith: *Do you think conditions are any better for women in same sex settings, educational or otherwise?*

Betz: Yes. There's much evidence that women in same-sex schools are vastly overrepresented among the higher achievers in society. Same-sex schools are really good for women because they can achieve to their hearts' content and boys aren't around to criticize. There's also evidence that women in mixed-sex groups will defer to a man whereas women in same-sex groups instead get a chance to exert their natural leadership qualities. If I had a daughter I would want her to go to a same-sex school.

Leduc: *I'd like to revisit for a moment the conditions for women working in nontraditional environments. I worked in construction as a quality control technician for a number of years. And the way I was able to be perceived as a "person" by the men was to change my dress style to very asexual. Also I changed my vocabulary to include more slang and profanity and it seemed like the more I swore the more I was accepted. I wonder if you've encountered that type of adaptation in other women, making themselves consciously more like the men? Also, I've attended some annual skits put on by medical students where the female students are just as derogatory as the men towards other women, especially female patients. Do minorities have to assume the personalities of the majority to survive?*

Betz: I guess the overriding concepts are, number one, that it's hard not to be sexist or racist in a sexist or racist society, and, number two, there are studies on minority groups which show exactly what you're saying, that they often adopt the characteristics of the majority group in an attempt to fit in. Which is really sad. But on the other hand I am to some extent a pragmatist. I would like to see society change so that wouldn't be necessary, but I also see the need for certain compromises in order to achieve your final goal. I think women do have to dress in a more neutral way in many environments. I'm not sure that I like the idea of having to adopt profanity but I've heard that too.

Leduc: *Again, it becomes a dehumanization process.*

Betz: Women internalize it. You're exactly right.

The "Inferiority Curriculum" and Other Barriers

Smith: *You were saying that part of the negative environment for women in education also involves factors such as the "inferiority curriculum," "stag effects" and putdowns. Could you explain these?*

Betz: The "inferiority curriculum" is what Jesse Bernard summarized as the effect of all of this negative stuff in our educational system, that no matter how strong a woman's self-esteem is when she comes in, the environment can beat her down. It takes an awfully strong young woman to not swallow some of that garbage. As I say, I was a gifted student in math and science but by college I was beginning to doubt that.

The "stag effect" is men's protection of their turf against the invasion of women. One good example was the four professors going out to drink and never inviting the woman. Another of my favorite examples involved another new female assistant professor. One of her male colleagues called her at home and said, "Hello can I speak to your husband?" He never really even greeted her. So Husband got on the phone and was invited to join the males for a golf game. What they didn't find out was that she's a good golfer and her husband a fairly shabby one. But do you think they asked her to play? Surely you jest!

Smith: *Her husband never thought of saying, "Actually the person you should be playing with is my wife"?*

Betz: I don't know her husband's response. I was so blown away by the fact that these men asked a man they didn't even know to play golf with them but never the woman who was their colleague. Actually the golf game is a classic example of the stag effect.

Some other examples I can think of, again mostly from the sciences, are the male professors and students who go out to lunch together or hiking and backpacking together. Or the male professor who invites some of the male graduate students over to his house but never the women. Of course the excuse is either the thought never crossed their minds or that old saw, "Well, what if her boyfriend or husband or people thought we were interested in her?" That's the stag effect, the boys hanging out together.

Smith: *What are the "putdowns" you write about as barriers?*

Betz: They're all the negative remarks about women and women's capabilities, the comments professors make. Those examples from medical school are putdowns. Some other examples would be male professors implying a woman is going to drop out or leave her career the minute she finds a man or asking how can that woman be serious if she's having a baby? Again these come from science, and engineering in particular. All are implications that women are not serious students, nor your best, and the minute they find a nice man they're going to drop out of school or their career. The idea is why would you want to put all this time and effort into a woman student when she's probably not going to have a long career? And this you hear over and over again.

Leduc: *Any change in the frequency of that over the last few years?*

Betz: I know that women students and faculty in the sciences and engineering still have a terrible time because, I assume, the attitudes of faculty are not changing that fast. Another problem is foreign teaching assistants (TAs) who come from countries where women are viewed as second class citizens. I don't want to stereotype any countries but the fact is some have a very, very narrow view of women. So when you have a TA who believes that women ought to be home having babies and barefoot, that TA is going to be very discouraging to women. And it's not just teaching assistants but foreign professors too.

Yet at the same time women in some of these countries do extremely well in math, and in fact the performance of Asian women on math tests is better than that of U.S. men. I always use that as my counter to people who talk about sex differences in math abilities. Sex differences in math abilities are not genetic or we would not see Japanese women blowing the top off the scores.

Leduc: *Why is this happening in those countries and not ours?*

Betz: Their culture certainly says that women are second class citizens but it also says that everybody in their culture is good in math and science, everybody should get higher education. Those cultures are marvelous in terms of their valuing higher education.

Smith: *They believe women can't do as well as men in many areas but math doesn't happen to be one of them?*

Betz: Yes. They have no doubts about women being good in math and science but there's also the belief that she'd better head home to take care of the husband and the children as soon as she develops her next chemical formula.

Staying in the Driver's Seat

Leduc: *How would you encourage other women to stay in the driver's seat of their lives and careers?*

Betz: I think you do it by encouraging their self-esteem, the idea that they can take care of themselves. Women are taught that men have to take care of them but that's not true. Women are perfectly capable of taking care of themselves. Another personal story. I spent Christmas a few years ago with my mother and two aunts, all of them divorced. On Christmas day we were having a picnic on the beach in Florida and when we got to the car to go home, the tire was flat.

Well, the aunt who owned the car was quite upset. She was convinced that AAA (American Automobile Association) would never come out on Christmas Day and that we'd be stuck at the beach until tomorrow. I said, "No, no. I'll fix the tire. Do you have a jack?" So I changed the tire, put the spare on and my aunt was so surprised. "Oh," she said, "my gosh, you young girls today are so competent." And I said, "No, you are just as capable of changing a tire as I am." So I showed her how and now she has a whole new outlook on her capacity to survive alone. Isn't that a neat story? And to think she thought we were doomed to spend the night on the beach because no man was around to change our tire.

Leduc: *It becomes a form of learned helplessness—like women saying they can't figure out this math stuff so they depend on their husbands. But once you know how to do it, it's such a simple act.*

Betz: Yes, and it changed her whole view, not only of me but of herself. So it's little things like that which begin to teach women they're competent and can be in control of their lives. And if you believe you can take care of yourself, you start doing it and do it well.

Smith: *How do we get these initial learning opportunities? Do we have to be exposed to an environment separate from men where we learn to do things on our own?*

Betz: You're right. A woman who stays in a traditional marriage, for example, may avoid learning she's truly competent. Of course, this is a big problem for women in battering relationships. They're so afraid they can't survive on their own that the better choice they feel is to stay and be beaten. It's what I call the "no option syndrome." She has no options because she feels she can't survive without him.

Women's Experiences in Higher Education: A Call for Change

Smith: *So what do we still need to learn to help women's career interests survive their education? If you were in charge of a large trust fund for research where would you put the money right now?*

Betz: The area I'm really interested in is the retention of women in nontraditional areas. Generally we don't know as much as we need about keeping women in both graduate and academic programs. We need to find out what it is that drives women out and then develop interventions to keep them in. How do we help women survive in a field they've chosen which has turned out to be discouraging? How do we enrich the educational environment for women? How do we counteract socialization—reeducate professors and administrators and educate men in general to view women as colleagues instead of sex objects?

Smith: *In one of your publications you also commented that women were in danger of being discriminated against by schools switching from high school grade point averages to SAT (Scholastic Aptitude Tests) scores for awarding scholarships. Do you want to comment on that?*

Betz: Because men have a small advantage on math, combined SATs, that is, combined verbal and math performance, will give men an advantage over women. But in fact women get better college grades than men with the same SAT scores. So the issue in the New York state schools is the overweighting of SATs versus high school grades which gives men the advantage in receiving scholarships. And that's been the source of a legal case against the State of New York.

Leduc: *Is that a trend in other states or systems, relying on single tests rather than overall performance?*

Betz: On the contrary, there are some very good schools which are now saying that high school grades are just as predictive, if not more predictive, of college performance than SATs. And if we are awarding scholarships based on how we predict the person will do in college, which is the criterion performance, then we really need to be looking at what best predicts that criterion. What you almost need is a handicapping system where you add fifty points to women's combined SATs so you'll end up with the same predicted collegiate GPA for both sexes. And, to the extent that men do better on quantitative GREs (Graduate Record Exams) you'll probably also find that college grades are more highly predictive of performance in graduate school.

In a way you can characterize women as grinds. They do their homework. So a woman with a given aptitude test score is much more likely to use those abilities. She goes home and studies, she goes to class. We see women do better in schools from the beginning.

Smith: *Not because we're any brighter, but we work harder?*

Betz: We use our brains better until we're discouraged from using them at all.

Smith: *Is there anything else from your research that would suggest the kind of improvements women should hope to see in their higher education?*

Betz: Well, people say that as more and more women enter the system they'll reach a critical mass, enough women to provide each other a support system. So getting a few more women into each scholastic environment is a very hoped for goal. But when you have only tokens you have to figure out creative ways of getting them together so that you still have the semblance of a support system. When I've worked with women on science faculties there's generally one woman per department. What we do to form a critical mass is bring all the women in the college together so the one woman per department still has support. But as more women enter at both the student and the professorial level, the environment itself becomes more friendly towards women. They survive better. So once you get more women you keep more women. It can be as self-fulfilling a prophesy as the discouragement of women.

Smith: *The benefit curve is not linear.*

Betz: No, it's not. You're right.

Leduc: *Is there anything the educational system is doing or should be doing to make it more possible for female students or staff to have children while their biological clock is still ticking?*

Betz: Organizations do need to be more sensitive to the fact that many people have families. At Ohio State, for example, we just instituted a time off the tenure clock for dependent care. What that means is either sex can apply to have an extra year to achieve tenure if they're responsible for any kind of dependent care, aging parents as well as a child. So that's one way of making the environment more humane. Also people with family responsibilities are helped by institutions having flexible work schedules and good child care facilities.

Ohio State has had an office for about five years which is charged with nothing but finding jobs for spouses. So when we hire Joe Smith from another university and Joe's wife is an academic, which in these days she may very well be, that office works on finding her a job. Or the reverse in the case of trying to hire a woman. But I don't know if it's that common elsewhere. So these are ways of acknowledging that people have spouses and children and if you want to recruit them you'd better help them with their families.

Smith: *What about accommodating the child bearing and rearing responsibilities of female graduate students? Such as letting them, without penalty, interrupt their program or delay taking orals?*

Betz: I think that would fall under the general category of dependent care policies, which apply to both women and men. There's no difference between a woman staying home to recover from childbirth and a man staying home to take care of the baby. Either situation pulls them out of the program for a period of time and that ought to be OK.

Leduc: *Are you seeing a trend toward accepting these multiple role demands?*

Betz: I think so. I certainly see many more women who are going about their business of having babies and just telling their male colleagues, "This is what I'm doing." Certainly there's still a lot of discomfort with that behavior, but things are improving a bit. Another trend is the dual career life style. Two thirds to three quarters of married couples already are dual career couples or at least will be in the future. So we really need to help them manage that life style.

Smith: *Do you think the young men you come in contact with are aware of this?*

Betz: There are studies suggesting that young men still want traditional wives and lifestyles yet young women want nontraditional husbands and egalitarian life styles. My comment is we're in trouble because what young men and women want is diametrically opposed and given the fact they're probably going to marry each other, we're going to need a lot of marriage counsellors. So when I teach men, I tell them if their wife has a good job and is happy in her career, that gives them the freedom to take a sabbatical or change careers. And all of a sudden they look at it quite differently.

Smith: *Are they aware of the other trade offs? If a wife is working at a career she may not be able to bake those cookies and clean?*

Betz: That's what they don't want to give up.

We're in trouble because what young men and women want is diametrically opposed and given the fact they're probably going to marry each other, we're going to need a lot of marriage counsellors.

Restoring Women's Options

Leduc: *You've written about counsellors' lack of information about women's careers. I think a lot of counsellors don't realize what you've just said, that women are undermined so they don't have free choices.*

Betz: Right. The whole concept of freedom and choice implies options. And so to talk about freedom of choice without viable options is silly. Women who don't think they can survive on their own and feel good about themselves have no option but to stay in unhealthy situations. So the whole idea of the null environment is that counsellors need to be option restorers. They don't make decisions for people but need to be aware constantly of how society deprives women of options and then be an active force in restoring them.

Smith: *Then if a girl indicates she wants to be a secretary because she didn't like sciences and math, for example, you can't take it at face value.*

Betz: No. If a girl comes in and says I want to be a secretary because I'm just not interested in math, I would say, "Talk to me about your experiences in school. Help me understand why you're not interested in math." Or, in another case, "Help me understand why you don't want to be a physician in spite of your very high aptitude test scores." It's not necessarily telling people what to do, but it's getting them to explore the barriers or the background experiences restricting them. Women in this society are systematically deprived of their career or personal life choices by sexism and stereotyping. And they're not even aware of it.

Smith: *Do you ever feel uncomfortable about women being almost over-encouraged to enter nontraditional careers?*

Betz: I feel like I'm restoring options, not necessarily saying that one option is better than the other. I'm only responding to what society says women should do and saying, "Yes, but I would like to add a few more choices." I don't believe that nursing or teaching are bad careers, but when they're the only options you've been taught are available, that's not right. Traditionally female careers don't pay much, let's face it. I don't care what women do but I think they deserve to be well paid and well respected if they use their abilities.

Leduc: *How do counsellors become more aware of all the options?*

Betz: A counsellor needs to believe that a woman can do any career and can survive on her own and be happy. But a lot of counsellors may be math anxious or believe women, including themselves, couldn't really survive on their own. And that attitude is going to be communicated to a client.

I once had a psychologist tell me that my mother must have lived a very lonely and unfulfilled life because she never married again after being divorced. My mother has lived a wonderfully rich life and I was really, really angry that this psychologist would have the nerve to say my mother couldn't be single and live a happy life. So that's illustrative of that kind of belief.

Smith: *Doesn't that suggest counsellors should do more self-exploration during training to know their biases?*

Betz: Oh yes, and to be taught about different lifestyles. I teach about all sorts of different life styles in my counselling women courses so that, hopefully, when those counsellors go into practice they'll know all lifestyles are viable.

Leduc: *What kind of questions should female students ask a counsellor to make sure those people are aware of the obstacles women face in the educational system?*

Betz: You could ask about their training in women's career development and general issues regarding counselling women. Did you have any course work in the psychology of women, counselling women or women in work? What do you know about the barriers to women's career development. If they mumble something meaningless, you know you have an ignoramus on your hands.

Leduc: *But those courses are still considered to be electives, not fundamental core counselling components. Do you see that changing?*

Betz: That really depends on changes on the accreditation guidelines. The APA guidelines now encourage the inclusion of course work in those areas but don't require it. I'm not on the accreditation committee, but the people who are need to be lobbied to make those courses required as part of an accredited program. I know questions related to the psychology of women are now included on the national state licensing exam in the U.S. Hopefully that trend will increase, but that will happen only when we get people on the examination committee who reflect those values. Change happens because somebody in power says the new way is better.

Hanging on to Your Own Career Options

Leduc: *What final wisdom could you give our readers to help them become more aware of how the educational system interferes with their freedom to choose a career?*

Betz: First, we all need to be aware of the ways in which society takes our options away and then try and restore them.

Smith: *What would you have parents do differently?*

Betz: I would teach parents that society is systematically removing their children's options, male as well as female. To counter that, they need to constantly ask a child, "What are you learning and how is it affecting you? Why are you not interested in this field? What are you learning in school about this topic?"

Smith: *What about individuals who think they've already made a career choice. Are there steps they can take to reexamine their choices, to make sure these aren't being distorted by their educational experiences?*

Betz: Students taking my classes learn a lot about reexamining their values and biases. If your readers can take Women's Studies, anything related to women's issues in general, that'll get them thinking about the effects of their own educational and social environments.

References and Recommended Readings

Bernard, J. (1972). *The future of marriage*. New York: Bantam.

Bernard, J. (1976) Where are we now? Some thoughts on the current scene. *Psychology of Women Quarterly, 1*, 21-37.

Betz, N.E. & Fitzgerald, L.F. (1987). *The career psychology of women*. Orlando, Florida: Academic Press, Inc.

Betz, N.E., & Hackett, G. (1981). The relationship of career-related self-efficacy expectations to perceived career options in college women and men. *Journal of Counseling Psychology, 28*, 399-410.

Betz, N.E., & Hackett, G. (1983). The relationship of mathematics self-efficacy expectations to the selection of science-based college majors. *Journal of Vocational Behavior, 23*, 329-345.

Betz, N.E. (In press). Sex and gender as individual differences variables: New concepts and findings. In R. Dawis and D. Lubinski (Eds.), *Assessing individual differences in human behavior: New concepts, methods, and findings*. Minneapolis: University of Minnesota Press.

Betz, N.E. (In press). The career psychology of women. In F. Denmark and M. Paludi (Eds.). *Handbook of the psychology of women*. New York: Greenwood Press.

Betz, N.E. (In press). *What stops women and minorities from choosing and completing majors in science and engineering*. Washington, D.C.: Federation of Behavioral, Psychological, and Cognitive Sciences.

Betz, N.E. (In press). Advances in career assessment. Invited chapter for S. Brown and R. Lent. (Eds.), *Handbook of Counseling Psychology* (2nd Edition). New York: Wiley.

Betz, N.E., & Hackett, G. (1986). Applications of self-efficacy theory to career development. *Journal of Social and Clinical Psychology, 4*, 279-289.

Betz, N.E. (1989). The null environment and women's career development. *The Counseling Psychologist, 17*, 136-144.

Brooks, L., & Betz, N.E. (1990). Expectancy theory as a predictor of women's career choices. *Journal of Counseling Psychology, 37*, 57-64.

Epstein, C.F. (1970a). Encountering the male establishment: Sex-status limits on women's careers in the professions. *American Journal of Sociology, 75*, 965-982.

Epstein, C.F. (1970b). *Woman's place*. Berkely, CA: University of California Press.

Epstein, C.F. (1971). Law partners and marital partners. *Human Relations, 24*, 549-564.

Epstein, C.F. (1976). Sex role stereotyping, occupations and social exchange. *Women's Studies, 3*, 185-194.

Freeman, J. (1975). How to discriminate against women without really trying. In J. Freeman (Ed.), *Women: A feminist perspective* (pp.194-208). Palo Alto, CA: Mayfield.

Hackett, G., & Betz, N.E. (1981). A Self-efficacy approach to the career development of women. *Journal of Vocational Behavior, 18*, 326-339.

Hackett, N., Betz, N., D'Halloran, M.S., & Romac, D.S. (1990). The effects of verbal and mathematics task performance on task and career self-efficacy and interest. Journal of Counseling Psychology, 37, 169-177.

Taylor, K.M., & Betz, N.E. (1983). Applications of self-efficacy theory to the understanding and treatment of career indecision. *Journal of Vocational Behavior, 22,* 63-81.

Walsh, W.B., & Betz, N.E. (1990). *Tests and assessment.* (2nd Edition). Englewood Cliffs, NJ: Prentice Hall.

Wohlgemuth, E., & Betz, N.E. (1991). Gender as a moderator of the relationships of stress and social support to physical health in college students. *Journal of Counseling Psychology,* 38, 366-374.

Significant Events in the Life of Nancy Betz

1949	Born in Kansas City, Missouri
1971	University of Minnesota, B.A. in Psychology Phi Beta Kappa, Summe Cum Laude
1972	Research Assistant, University of Minnesota
1973	First article published
1974-75	Instructor, Psychological Statistics, University of Minnesota
1976	University of Minnesota, Ph.D. in Psychology
1976-81	Assistant Professor, Department of Psychology, Ohio State University
1981-88	Associate Professor, Department of Psychology, Ohio State University
1982-84	Appointed Director of Counseling Psychology
1984-90	Editor, *Journal of Vocational Behavior*
1987	Co-authored, with Louise Fitzgerald, *The Career Psychology of Women*
1988-present	Professor, Department of Psychology, Ohio State University

Awards and Honors

John Holland Award for Research Integrating Career and Personality Psychology
Recipient of 1983 Alumni Distinguished Teaching Award, Ohio State University
Fellow, American Psychological Association, Division 17, 35
Fellow, American Psychological Society

5

Oh, To Be Young and Gifted: The Career Fallout

An interview with Constance L. Hollinger, Ph.D., Professor of Psychology and Co-ordinator of the School Psychology Program, Cleveland State University.

Gifted North American girls today, whatever their racial or cultural backgrounds, are caught in a crossfire of contrary expectations. That was the central message that Connie Hollinger shared with one of the authors from her research on career development in gifted and talented women. Sequestered in a quiet, wooded resort one Fall afternoon Hollinger, whose personal achievements mark her also as gifted, began the interview by describing the expectations for women permeating her own rural Pennsylvania childhood. With gratitude she described the strong female role models her family and education provided along with their lasting imprint: her undeniable passion for accomplishment paired with an equally undeniable compassion for those in need. As a result, Hollinger's career remains dedicated to helping women use their talents to the fullest and personally most satisfactory extent possible.

Much of what Hollinger has learned about the career choices of gifted girls and women stems from the masses of data generated by Project Choice, an experimental career development program involving approximately 300 gifted and talented female adolescents from six socioeconomically and culturally diverse schools: two all female private, two all female parochial and two co-ed public. Led by Lee Fleming, currently the director of Doctoral Studies in the College of Education at Cleveland State University, Hollinger and five other psychologists began the project in 1976 in two phases. First was a one-year career education/intervention program and second, a still ongoing longitudinal study following the lives of these women, now entering their early thirties. For fifteen years the researchers have documented their participants' career achievements and life choices and compared them to the women's own earlier expectations and aspirations, to societal norms in general and to the life achievements of gifted women in similar studies, including the pioneering work of Lewis Terman.

The following interview focuses on the insights gained from the above research and illustrates the career challenges today facing the gifted woman.

Retrospect: One Gifted Woman's Life

Smith: *You've been studying the development of career interests in gifted, talented women. Now you are obviously in this category. So looking back in your early life, do the things you've found out about these women apply to you too?*

Hollinger: Without a doubt. What we've seen consistently with the women we've studied has been the importance of socialization and I can certainly see a whole host of similarities with my own life. One of my earliest and clearest recollections for example, was when I was four or five. A seven-year-old girl, as big for her age as I was little, asked me what I wanted to be when I grew up. I told her, "I want to be a cowboy," and she said, "No, no, you can't be a cowboy. You have to be a cowgirl." But I said back, "Oh no I don't!" I knew they just sat in the wagon or waited back in the cabin and I wanted to **do**! Certainly my gender identity was firm. I knew I was a little girl. But in terms of a career, cowBOY was a career.

If I think about it now, I should have wanted to be a nurse or something a little more traditional. So where did that agency come from? Well, that's really clear. It was the socializers in my early environment, very strong women. My paternal grandmother was a determined, independent farm woman. And I had an aunt who did the absurd thing for her time, the early 1900s, of going to college and then working as an administrative assistant to the head of the Brethren Church in Chicago, travelling world-wide as a lifetime career. And she'd come home every year or two and take me to Chicago, New York City, Broadway, the Natural History Museums and the "Projects," low income housing for minorities. "Minority" wasn't even a concept where I grew up, rural Pennsylvania Dutch farm country, at that time 101% Republican. Few role models for that matter existed either. Most women stayed home or worked to enhance family income but not as a career. But I did have my aunt.

Choosing psychology as a career, however, was influenced by my mother, who was strong in a stereotypically feminine way. She seemed to defer to my father, depend on him. But if you looked closer, she was a determined, strong woman.

Smith: *What were your parents' primary occupations?*

Hollinger: Mother completed tenth grade, dad, high school. He worked his way up from driving a feed truck to managing a feed and grain company. Then when it burned, my Dad at 50 years of age decided to start his own business in the burned out property. He built a fine, successful business on the principles he believed in, like trusting people, offering value and customer service.

Smith: *Did your mother work?*

Hollinger: In the traditional way, complementing the family income. So my mother did not have a "career" per se but did work outside the home a number of years.

Smith: *But you had that exposure of women working outside the home in your background. What did your mother think about the role of women? Did she ever express that?*

Hollinger: Her perceptions, I would say, were quite stereotypic. About my aunt, for example,"she's just gallivanting all over the world and doesn't have a home or family and that's not quite right." Well I knew my aunt was a nice woman whom I loved very much so there was something there I didn't buy. The choices she made were different but they didn't appear to me to be at all wrong.

Smith: *What about your experience in school? Were there any messages there about being a woman?*

Hollinger: Very clearly. The key factors were the role models and mentoring I received in school. And the group of about 25 or 30 students who stayed in the same section as me all the way through junior and senior high school had a major impact. All the girls were driven achievers and you never covered up your paper to hide the high score you got on a physics test from the boys or whatever. Fear of failure, yes. I remember that clearly. But when I think of the "chilly climate phenomenon," the discouragement of girls' achievement by teachers, subtle and otherwise, that I hear gifted women and their parents describe going on today, I say my god! I really have no such recollection, even though I grew up in Amish country surrounded by fundamental religion and certainly stereotypic gender roles. So I really do think we had a kind of critical, anomalous mass in my school group countering these social forces. And we were also very social. I was into athletics, student government and the junior board of directors of the community recreation centre, so the message I received was you could be a woman and also achieve.

Smith: *That builds esteem. You had support from other girls, you got together and talked.*

Hollinger: You bet. And it wasn't even talking about possible flak for achieving. It didn't even occur to us.

Smith: *What about career aspirations? Did you talk about that?*

Hollinger: Now that's where the stereotypic socializers did get me. I knew I would go to college, because our whole section was going. But in 1967 the only options I saw were teacher or nurse, literally. My mother would have liked nursing, but not me. So that left teaching. I also had a number of very strong, competent women teachers throughout my high school years, which also helped enhance the attractiveness of a teaching career. We had confident women teachers in both traditional and nontraditional areas.

I also had to figure out my major and that's where the barriers came in. Out of all the kids in my section, I chose to compare myself to Peggy. Our school used alphabetical seating and she sat just ahead of me. It wasn't competition in a negative way at all. Peggy meant nothing by it, but every time our class papers were passed back she'd turn and say "dummy, you got only 98%." Of course she'd get 100%, or more from answering the bonus questions. So in comparison I knew I was dumb. Later, Peggy had her Ph.D. and a doctorate in veterinary medicine by age 25. I mean, she was bright!

Actually I'd felt dumb since first grade. I have the image of standing up in this reading group. I had to read a capital "W" and I blocked. I went home that first day and just knew I was flunking first grade. And I knew it was important to my grandmother that I did well. I had to face the fact that I wasn't going to pass first grade. And there were 11 more years of that fear of failure, wanting to succeed very badly, yet being ready to buy "oh, I'm going to fail."

Smith: *Did you feel that was due to the expectations of you because you were a woman? You were expected to be perfect, keep both a clean house and perfect grades? Or were the boys in your class feeling the same way?*

Hollinger: No, I don't think they were. However, I think my fear wasn't due to necessarily stereotypic female socialization but my own personal socialization. Certainly Peggy didn't worry about failing.

Smith: *How did this pressure affect your feelings toward your studies? Were you so worried about school you didn't develop outside interests?*

Hollinger: If anything I think I reacted in the opposite way. While I was neurotic about grades I got involved in everything, whether it was athletics, the pep club or editing the year book. In some ways that might have taken some pressure off.

Smith: *Especially if you had girlfriends who liked you, reassuring you that you were normal.*

Hollinger: Yes. There wasn't just the absence of discrimination, there was active support. Teachers encouraged our participation in science fairs, fossil hunts, trips to weather stations. Math and science in fact were the two areas I was most interested in. Looking back I've wondered, though, given the environment I grew up in, where was the passivity you'd expect? In physics or chem labs we girls certainly weren't sitting back taking notes while the boys conducted the experiments. I think the women in my group were agentic.

Smith: *So you were socialized by some unusual female peers for that day.*

Hollinger: And by teachers who took an interest in us and reinforced us for science fair projects. Really as I look back I was very fortunate, highly atypical. I never had any notion that I shouldn't do my absolute best, or that there would be some dire consequence to me as a woman for doing well.

Smith: *You didn't feel boys were supposed to do better in math?*

Hollinger: Absolutely not. Math was just a subject—of course you did well in it. Science I loved. So, no, there was no "girls shouldn't be doing this."

Smith: *Did your parents ever say anything about getting involved in more social activities? Anything like "It's all very nice that you get good grades but you should be dating more too."*

Hollinger: No. Maybe that's because I pre-empted them. As a member of the junior rec board which sponsored dances twice a week, I was always at the dances. The only thing I clearly remember was Mother making sure I knew she would not be happy if I got pregnant before I was married.

Smith: *What happened at university then? Did you discover unexpected limitations because you were female?*

Hollinger: Well, probably to the contrary. I went to a state school and majored in health and physical education because I was a good athlete. I thought I would be happy bouncing a basketball for the rest of my life. Teachers would say, "Connie, you're going to be bored," but at 17 you couldn't tell me that. I don't know how to say this delicately but I also found college a lot easier than high school. Without Peggy and the old competition. Even our former teachers still say, "You graduated with an atypical group of students," which of course I didn't know at the time. So college was quite a bit easier.

Then one night friends a year ahead of me were talking about student teaching and they said, "Why don't you come along with us? Hurry up and finish college." Which I did, finishing my undergraduate work in three years, working in the summer and also taking summer school just so I could student teach with my friends. This is not logical career decision-making, life work planning as I teach it. It was just a neat idea that somebody came up with on a Saturday night. In fact, neither my educational not my career pathway has been particularly linear.

But I don't want to make it sound like all I did was study. I partied, though not that much. And I didn't have to worry about rejection from boys because I was attached back home.

Smith: *Obviously your aspiration level had gone up. What was the trigger?*

Hollinger: Well, I lucked out. I had a very sharp lady as advisor to the high-school yearbook when I was editor-in-chief who knew that saying, "Connie, don't go into Phys. Ed." wouldn't work. Instead she shared Frankl's *Man's Search for Meaning* and other psychology books. So by senior year, for fun I was reading psychology, and chatting with her about what I found interesting. I think that was a major seed.

Smith: *She was exposing you to new ideas.*

Hollinger: And they were subtly presented. Because I was as stubborn an adolescent as they come. And though my college program had no electives, I was able to pass a proficiency test in Spanish to get a couple of electives. I'd liked general psychology. So for electives my last summer I chose abnormal and personality, taught by one excellent instructor.

Smith: *So now you were starting to think about something other than teaching physical education.*

Hollinger: Maybe. The competition from my college peers wasn't as strong. I was beginning to get a sense of doing pretty well. My GPA in college was higher than high school. But I was getting a little confused. I was doing better in physics and chemistry than athletics, my major. So I pursued information on exercise physiology for graduate school. Then I got a phone call from a faculty member at a liberal arts college asking me if I would apply for a position. Which I did, and they hired me.

Smith: *As a faculty member with only a bachelor's degree?*

Hollinger: Yes. It wasn't my mind, it was my body that they were after. I was rather good in field hockey and it turned out I had worked with one of the college's faculty members in summer hockey camp one year and she wanted me in her department. She had seen me coach. And as a former farm kid, it was probably not as scary as going off to study exercise physiology on the West Coast. So I graduated on a Friday night in August and by that next Monday had a full-time contract as an instructor, only 20 years of age.

Those were interesting years but they also solidified my interest in psychology. A coach's position attracts a lot of students seeking counselling. I had a young man come into my office on a bad acid trip. I'd have kids say "I'm pregnant. What do you think about abortion?" By that time I'd had enough psychology to know I didn't know enough to help although I certainly wanted to. And I also knew that to move through the ranks at the college level, I needed additional education. So I did the logical thing. There was a clinical psych program at Millersville State College, now Millersville University. I applied and was accepted for the clinical psychology masters program.

Smith: *Did you do your Ph.D. right off or did you work for a while?*

Hollinger: I kept working full-time, did the clinical M.A. program pretty full-time and completed a school psych specialization. See, I like going to school, that's fun. Then in my last year, one of the faculty members, Betty Finney—dynamite, strong, bright lady—cornered me and said, "I have a doctoral program just right for you—my alma mater, Case Western Reserve." I said, "No thanks." Because you could get tenure back at that time with a Masters degree. Well, Betty kept at it. And eventually, I said yes. Besides by this time I had coached my third season of swim team and I knew we were never going to beat Penn. State University.

Smith: *So you were against a ceiling and looking for fresh challenges.*

Hollinger: Absolutely. I tend to become bored with routine rather quickly and if someone says, "Connie, why don't you try?" Well, why not? So I came to Cleveland and finished my Ph.D. in two years. By that time I was involved in a number of projects so I stayed another three years as a senior research associate.

Smith: *I'm struck right now by all the women in your life. That's been a consistent theme all the way. It's been the women who have encouraged you. They have sought you out.*

Hollinger: Yes, the women have been there for me. Lee Fleming was my doctoral advisor and, without a doubt, I can attribute a significant proportion of anything positive about my life to her. At the end of my first semester Lee called and said, "Would you be interested in assisting in these projects?" So I started working with her. I remember she'd say, "Connie you're going to be evaluating the largest reading intervention program in the Cleveland public schools." My first reaction would be, "I don't know anything about evaluation." She'd say, "Yes, you do, now just go and do it." And there was just that unequivocal trust, handing me this big thing and saying, "I know you can carry it off."

Smith: *Did she leave you alone to figure out what to do or could you go to her for help?*

Hollinger: Oh, constantly. She was always accessible and not only for references. Brainstorming, encouraging, supporting—being there personally when I would get wound about a deadline or something not going right.

Smith: *Were there many women on faculty when you were doing your Ph.D.?*

Hollinger: We had four women in that department, all strong, well respected professionals but it was predominantly male. However, Lee was the chairperson. Women in power is not a foreign concept for me.

Smith: *Now that you've come so far, how do your parents feel? Are they surprised and pleased?*

Hollinger: Well my mother died in 1977 after a struggle with cancer for many years. But I can sum up her attitude probably with a story. When I defended my dissertation, I called home, and jokingly asked, "Does anyone want to talk to Doctor Hollinger?" She said, "No, but I'll talk to you." Certainly there was ambivalence there. I remember her saying to me also, "I am so tired of being Morgan's wife and Connie's mother." Oh, I heard the pain. And to this day when I think back about how well my mother could read people and their actions, I think she's still the best clinician I've ever known. A very bright lady in many ways, not so much academically, but in social intelligence and creativity. But that comment she made, that's a shame.

I think my Dad's proud of me. I have it on good authority. He was talking to my best friend who in turn told me, "You know, your dad is proud of you." Actually this last visit he did say it with the goodbye hugs. Certainly there was nothing ever from either parent that was obstructive. I had free rein all my life. So it's kind of a mixed bag. What's sort of sad is that they couldn't derive the kind of satisfaction some parents get from sharing their child's success. Cleveland State has a lot of first generation kids and, let me tell you, at graduation those parents, grandparents and aunts are so proud. "My kid went through college!" I wish my parents could have had some of that joy I see in other parents.

Project Choice

Smith: *How did Project Choice, your career development program for gifted, talented women, actually get its start?*

Hollinger: Again, this goes back to Lee Fleming. WEEA funding came along, the US Women's Educational Equity Act. Until that point my area of interest basically was self concept although my dissertation examined gender dependency, control ideology and classroom interaction. When Lee talked to me about working with her on a proposal, I thought, "Wait. I'm a sixties underdog. And we're going to apply for a lot of money to help the gifted? Why? They have it all going for them. Help somebody like me who is dumb, or help handicapped children."

Smith: *Because gifted girls were seen as "you guys get all the As and just have it all made. So what's your problem?"*

Hollinger: Exactly. That was my bias until I thought, "Now wait a minute, everyone thinks that way. And if they do, the gifted really are underdogs, because they are overlooked and expected to perform with no one tending their needs. Once I could break out from my own stereotypes, I was gung-ho to write the proposal, which was then funded. We pretested the girls in their sophomore year of high school in the spring of '77, and worked with them from the fall of '77 through the winter of '78. But we had information on them predating that—school records, standardized tests, that kind of thing, from freshman year and a talent inventory we created and gave in the fall of '76.

Project Choice itself was only 14-15 weeks long but we ran 16 groups a week, 15 kids each. During this time we tried several types of counselling intervention. We had weekly two-hour group sessions, as well as mentorships and role models, Sunday workshops on how to finance careers, talks by college representatives and so on. We even brought in their families and high school counsellors. It was a three-ring circus.

We learned that because of individual needs, different talent profiles and different backgrounds, you can't just point to a gifted woman and say, "Her problems are due to low self-esteem or fear of success." It's also perhaps that she doesn't have a role model, her two brothers will be sent to college first because "they'll be breadwinners," and she's black. All of these factors and more may be barriers to any individual. Now I don't want to make it sound like these women are burdened down by a truck load of barriers. But their needs aren't as simple as a little counselling to address a single internal barrier. It's much more complicated.

So we started with exploring life-work planning, gender socialization, the messages in their own family and society. Then we moved into the career arena with information labs because sometimes it was simply a matter of these young women not having much career information, like me at their age, seeing only nursing and teaching. And one cardinal principle we addressed, a little ahead of the Gottfredson model, was that once an occupation is eliminated as a possible choice, it's gone. To reverse that elimination process, we consciously would bring those choices back up, and ask girls to interview "x" number of women in careers that the girls themselves would **never consider.** Given that our commitment was to choice, we'd say, "Please look at the whole spectrum of career options."

Smith: *Did you compare their reactions to a group of gifted males?*

Hollinger: No, because the funding was earmarked for studying women. At the beginning of Project Choice I think we probably spent the first decade bemoaning the absence of a comparable male sample, except that now I see that the diversity within the gender is so extensive I can study it the rest of my life. I want to look at what makes a difference among these sub groups of gifted women in the sequencing and nature of their choices.

Attempts at Intervention

Smith: *Among your girls, what intervention worked best?*

Hollinger: The program had so many dimensions that it is difficult to say. There wasn't any agreement on the most effective aspect. Certainly you could rank order them but if you looked at the distribution, you'd find some girls hated, for example, the stuff on gender socialization. They weren't ready. Others loved it!

Smith: *Would it be better to have intervention earlier?*

Hollinger: Obviously I'd want to start any intervention in kindergarten or at least get schools to stop putting doctors' hats on boys' desks and nurses' hats on girls'. A number of folks in fact have questioned me: "You're intervening in adolescence and that's too late." Yes, I'd be first to want an equitable career development program in kindergarten but there are still needs that emerge later on and it isn't too late.

In adolescence, especially if you're gifted, you pay attention to what's most salient. A gifted girl is excited to go to college so she's concerned about financial aid and college selection but right now she also wants to go to the prom. And you want to talk to her about choosing a career? Later, later. But some of the girls in our program did turn around. Some did have their views significantly expanded and opened.

Smith: *Should a career course be mandatory then in college?*

Hollinger: I'd love to see it but I wouldn't mandate it. It's almost like freshman orientation courses, they're hated. I'd like it to be available when they're trying to make decisions.

Smith: *Is it important to reach parents too? I was thinking about PTA.*

Hollinger: Yes, as much so as reaching gifted males. Our parents responded very positively to the program, on the telephone, to the letters describing the program, but we weren't always communicating the same thing. While it was apparent that parents wanted their child in the program, it might be only so "she could find a job if her husband died."

Smith: *They didn't consider nourishing a woman's career interests important?*

Hollinger: Some parents did. We were in six schools, very socioeconomically and ethnically diverse. Many parents wanted their child to go as far as possible, to the Senate, if not the White House. I'm not saying all parents are the same.

Smith: *What was your role or roles in the Project?*

Hollinger: My role in the piece was project manager. Lee led it and was the most knowledgeable about gifted women and we had a team of women who, with the exception of me, were career achievers with a home and family. And really the strength of Project Choice came from bringing together six women who had worked at doing it all, achieving and also getting the little one to the pediatrician on time. It was a beautiful creative process, built week by week by this group coming together and brainstorming. It was a phenomenal experience. I was lucky to have had the opportunity.

Smith: *So again there is the importance of working with women.*

Hollinger: Well, we had some male students assisting with coding and other technical details but they didn't help define the program's issues. And when I look at the program in retrospect, there are so many things about it that were ahead of its time. We were already working with Super's ideas about life spheres back in '77. We told our participants, "When you make career decisions, consider all life's spheres. You don't have to use every talent in a career. If you're an athlete, for example, maybe you don't have to teach PE but play tennis as an avocation while pursuing your career as an engineer." The emphasis was on putting together a composite of all life roles as part and parcel of this decision-making process—an idea that I think flowed directly from the complex lives of those "superwomen" on the team.

Identifying the Gifted and Talented

Smith: *How did you actually select who was gifted and talented ?*

Hollinger: We drew on all the literature in setting our criteria so there were standard practice aspects of our definitions but we also tried to cast a broader net. Lee, whose professional career has focused on the gifted and talented, went beyond the federal definition. We included some categories in our identification procedures that were quite strange by the conventional limited definition. We had gifted homemakers, for example. If a kid by ninth grade wins the state bake-off contest we said, "That is gifted." Most of our folks were multiply talented, strong in other areas, perhaps math or science, but the opportunity was there to be selected on homemaking skills.

Leadership was another difficult talent to define. School records only capture what has been done within school, not outside. And we had young women who were certainly leaders out there in the community, from ethnic families, for example, where they might be in a leadership position. Or they might be in a performance group of skilled dancers but weren't athletes in school. By using a broader net we identified women who'd achieved in special skill areas.

Smith: *So they just had to receive an overall score contributed to by many talents?*

Hollinger: Each individual was rated on fourteen different talent dimensions. Our selection was not based on just straight intellectual or even academic ability like math precocity. For enterprising talent, for example, we tried to see if we could find the next "Donalda Trump," a girl who by the time she was a high school sophomore has already figured out how to run a business by getting 17 younger kids in the neighborhood to wash windows, walk the dog, whatever, for a quarter but charge clients two-fifty.

What's Special about Being Gifted?

Smith: *Once you'd selected them, what did you find that's special about these women? What is unique about their experience?*

Hollinger: Number one is being caught in a crossfire of messages. Gender and sex role stereotypes are there from day one, but as they are identified as gifted and talented they also become aware of all the expectations for the gifted. So from the gifted stereotypes they get the message they're supposed to achieve, but at the same time they get the cultural message it's not feminine. Then add in the occupational stereotypes. It's a three-way interaction and you end up feeling like the proverbial pinball in the pinball machine.

Smith: *So they don't know what's expected of them. It just doesn't make sense. Yet nobody seems to think they have a problem.*

Hollinger: And that's why these kids have a tendency to think they have to make an either-or choice, either career or family, because these are conflicting messages.

My own dilemma now is the definition of achievement. What is underachievement? What really is the realization of potential?

What Is "Achievement" Anyway?

Smith: *Your women are entering their thirties now. How bad has the fallout been on their lives so far from this message crossfire?*

Hollinger: Quite honestly, despite the contradictions in their lives, we feel our cohort has been doing quite well. But I need to back up now and say my own dilemma now is the definition of achievement. What is underachievement? What really is the realization of potential? Who defines it and against which standards?

Smith: *I guess I've heard of achievement as the popular ones of how much money you make and your occupational classification.*

Hollinger: And also your educational attainment. Those are the three traditional criteria. But if you look at any of the longitudinal studies on the gifted, what do

(handwritten margin note: "disagree somewhat")

they mean when they say people have realized their potential? Have they realized their potential for being kind, empathetic, nurturing? Jackie Eccles opened my eyes in the mid-eighties. For the first time I heard someone else clearly say, "Whoa, we have a stereotypic definition of achievement that flows from the patriarchal culture." And that way we end up asking questions such as "why don't women chose medicine or engineering?", a deficit model question, instead of asking why **did** they choose what they chose.

OK, maybe they chose nursing instead of medicine because of fear of success or low self-perceptions of ability or the other internal barriers we talk about. But it is also possible someone chooses nursing because they like direct patient contact, because they know they can comfort someone who is dying. What a talent! So it does not have to be the deficit internal barrier that determines choice.

For example, one of our project participants is in nursing. When we asked her to identify her three greatest achievements, she wrote, "I am perceived and recognized as being a compassionate and caring nurse." It was not that she became the floor supervisor. Now that would have been recognized as an achievement. She is not going to get awards for being compassionate. Yet for her that is an achievement. I happen to believe that too. But I am still in the midst of sorting out what is and what is not achievement.

Smith: *How does someone like your nurse feel about herself when she says, "This is what I have done best"? Does she have self-doubts from not having accomplished according to society's rules?*

Hollinger: Two aspects of our follow-up questionnaires indirectly address that. We checked on their ratings of life satisfaction in diverse areas—"How satisfied are you with your family or personal relationships, career, education?" We also asked, "If you had to do it over again, are there missed opportunities?" Very few cited anything they would do differently and the group as a whole is just quite satisfied with their lives, thank you, regardless if they are married, have children or are neurosurgeons!

Now in our sample many are in relationships, married or otherwise, but children are few and far between and these young women are turning thirty. It's not that they have stayed out of relationships as much as they have delayed starting families. We had to shift our definitions in the follow-up questionnaires so that "marital status" and "married" also meant "being in a relationship." One of our young women also caught an error and wrote back that under "relational status" we had listed "married" and right after that "children, yes or no." She said, "What is your perception! You don't have to be married to have children, you know." Bingo! And you think you're free of sexist assumptions.

Follow-up Results

Smith: *Has there been much career switching?*

Hollinger: Very much so, both in level and occupation. Changing Holland types and going from traditional to nontraditional and vice versa. We have a group who have already surpassed their adolescent aspirations, but some have not met these. A substantial proportion did not have a clear career focus at the beginning of the program and I am not sure how clear it was at the end. Yet they have focused now and are achieving.

Smith: *Is the trend to go more nontraditional?*

Hollinger: I would not know how to label that yet. I have not looked at that data carefully enough.

Smith: *What is going to happen to society if everyone goes nontraditional, ends up in medicine or engineering and no one is going into nursing and teaching?*

Hollinger: It means trouble.

Smith: *Another thing, you have only followed these women to about age of 30. But their life span extends another 40, 50 years. Don't they still have time to achieve a lot more?*

Hollinger: Exactly. Sears and Barbee followed up Terman's women when they were in their sixties and they do talk about missed opportunities. At 65, OK, I can genuinely talk about not going to medical school as a missed opportunity. But at 30 or 35, no, I don't know that a number of our folks who are married haven't decided to have children now and pursue graduate degrees later.

Smith: *Is there a way of asking what they plan to do with the rest of their lives?*

Hollinger: We have not specifically asked about conscious decisions of timing. I wish we had. My dream of all dreams would be to get funding for a Project Choice reunion, where there could be a lot more chance to talk. As it is, there is just a carload of incredibly rich data to analyze. For example, we have 1 800 "fear of success" protocols, although I know that construct has fallen out of favor. I have not had time to look at them but there is much to be learned from those protocols.

Smith: *That term, "fear of success," bothered me the first time I heard it.*

Hollinger: Well, I know where Horner was going and we did not stay long enough with it in my opinion. When we analyzed those protocols there were negative consequences of success for women in the stories our kids wrote, yes, but we also recognized that some included coping messages. Or the stories implied, yes, there were negative consequences but who cares! So embedded in those stories were not only the themes of negative consequences for succeeding, but messages about here's how I am dealing with it.

Lee and I looked at one kid's file the other day. She wrote three fear of success protocols that were frightening, bizarre. However, today she is a physician working on her second sub-specialty. I am saying, OK, in that sample maybe we saw not even coping behavior, but the developmental nature of adolescence.

Smith: *Or since you were working with the gifted and talented, their creative side said, "They want me to give them a story, so, boy, will I give them a good one."*

Hollinger: Exactly, I don't know. Certainly, fear of success was present using that measurement approach. But it has not stopped her!

Barriers to Success

Smith: *From your data, then, what are the basic obstacles to making appropriate career choices for gifted and talented women?*

Hollinger: The simplest answer for me is gender socialization starting from day one, whether the messages are from television or magazines, consistent or subtle, which sometimes is much more dangerous than the blatant. These messages tell young women not only what it means to be feminine, but, what is more scary for me from my own area of self-concept research, also what they should not be. For example, since agentic attributes are stereotypically masculine, young women are socialized so as NOT to be agentic, that is, take action on their own. Yet time and again, a sense of agency or instrumentality, which are the new names for the old PAQ masculinity scale, predicts social self-esteem, achieving one's occupational goals, educational confidence, life satisfaction, that sense of I am captain of my own fate.

I keep hearing stories of gifted adolescents or undergraduates and I think, "That could have happened back in the time of our project but, no, the professor couldn't have said that to you today. No, the kindergarten teacher couldn't have said that to your little girl today." A recent article by Reis and Callahan says it best, "Gifted girls, they've come a long way—or have they?" Well, look again. Nothing is more embedded in our culture than gender socialization and gender identity.

Smith: *It strikes me there can be an overall progressive trend but an individual girl's socialization could still be the same as it was thirty, forty years ago. So you really can't make assumptions about a gifted girl's background when you are trying to explain her difficulty in making an appropriate career choice.*

Hollinger: Maybe the general societal message is the significant message for one gifted woman. But for another what is important may be "Who am I in class with? What is my mother or father saying to me? What are all the relatives, the teachers saying?" You can think of it as concentric circles. The global societal message is the outermost. It might be significant for a few, but the immediate social network varies and some of the immediate networks of gifted women are still traditional.

Smith: *What is the biggest internal barrier?*

Hollinger: All of them! Lack of agency, lack of a sense of self-efficacy, fear of success, any of those internal barriers in the literature might be THE significant one for an individual.

Smith: *What about external? Has anything changed in the last ten, fifteen years to make it easier for gifted and talented women to find appropriate career choices?*

Hollinger: I feel the world has changed, yes. The first thing we are reaching is a critical mass of role models. You see women checking your oil at the gas station, and women physicians at your health care organizations, women on television, albeit perhaps in limited and sexist roles. However, gender stereotypes are very difficult to break. I remember the first woman physician I chose and went to. I was maybe twenty-one. I found myself questioning her then thought, "Wait a minute, if that had been a man I never would have doubted him. What am I doing?" Yet I'd have to admit this summer when our building was being renovated, one of the construction workers with all the tools and belts came into the ladies room. I did a double take because "he" was a woman. And that brings home how strong gender socialization and stereotypes are. Twenty-one years, the majority of which have been spent examining these issues, and I'm still not completely free of gender stereotypic perceptions!

Smith: *And if you stare and betray your feelings, how does she feel?*

Hollinger: That's right. So having a critical mass of women as role models and leaders in traditional masculine areas would be, in my mind, the number one change in external barriers. What I'm hoping is that you don't have to have 50 % male and 50% female engineers before it's no longer viewed by gifted women as a male domain. From a survival standpoint a critical mass in a given engineering class could be "I'm not the only woman in this room." But I don't know what that mass is, if it's four or five women or two really strong women.

What Still Needs to Change

Smith: *What still needs to be changed before gifted women are able to make their most appropriate career choices?*

Hollinger: The answer of course is everything. I don't know that I could think of one aspect of gender socialization, whether it's parenting or education, where I could sit back and say, for example, "Oh well, in schools of education we've trained teachers in gender equity for long enough that I can relax. They're not going to shuttle off Mary to the kitchen area of the kindergarten and Johnny over to the building blocks." So no matter what I look at in terms of external barriers, I don't see any place where I can say, "We've made it."

Smith: *Vigilance must be maintained.*

Hollinger: Exactly. We're aware of things like flex-time, job-sharing, paternity leaves, the essential nature of the need for available child care. But those concepts were around in the 70s. I haven't seen them mushroom. I certainly haven't seen a plethora of institutions and companies granting paternity leave. And if I hear one more time about all our social ills, the kids on drugs, the teen pregnancy, always paired with, "Well look at the realities. Mothers are working!" I say, "Fathers are working too."

But according to our girls in the pre-test questionnaire, "External barriers? There aren't any." No external barriers in the whole world. The world was their oyster. In follow-ups however, they have since encountered many of those barriers.

Smith: *I was thinking about a parallel here with the Soviet Union where demo-cratic forces pushed through changes and then there was this fear the whole thing would be lost. But it wasn't. Have we made enough changes regarding women's roles that we can't slide back? The Handmaid's Tale can't happen? Any answer is speculation, I realize.*

Hollinger: I'm pretty confident we can't slide back—but not completely. We've talked about seeing more career equity, and barriers preventing our gifted women from realizing their potential being removed. But on a broader scope there's the increase of violence toward women. Whether it's battered wives, whether it's rape. If those statistics weren't quite so frightening I'd be more confident.

Smith: *So a backlash is always hanging over our heads.*

Hollinger: What triggered that thought was your mentioning *The Handmaid's Tale*. Do I think that scenario is possible? No I don't. I believe there are enough women CEO's, enough women physicians, enough women lawyers to prevent that. God bless Sandra Day O'Connor. I'm hoping we've reached the critical mass. Would I put money on it? Some, but not all my life's savings. Anyone who has read Susan Faludi's *Backlash* will understand why I'm still so concerned.

Smith: *Then is society really beginning to take the talents and aspirations of gifted women more seriously?*

Hollinger: I think so. That's the optimistic part of me. The cynical part thinks, yes, but for reasons that aren't altruistic adherence to the principals of equity rather than economic. We can't afford to continue to waste 50% of our human resources, not if we're going to remain viable in a world market. I find it interesting that as the baby boomers approach the age where their health is going to begin to fail, an economic cost, we as a nation really get into fitness. That's an interesting coincidence. And we have these statistics that show by the year 2000 a large part of our labor force will be culturally diverse, black, Hispanic, oriental and so on. My, isn't it coincidental that now we're taking multicultural sensitivity seriously. Exxon needs good engineers, women or not. They need that profit at the bottom line.

Smith: *So the expectation is that a woman is going to work. But what about the expectation that it's for more than money? A lot of countries have women working outside the home but it's not the same thing as taking their careers seriously.*

Hollinger: I mean it specifically in terms of using their talent and ability. Otherwise we'll lose out in the computer industry. We've already been surpassed in the auto industry. I believe industry out there is looking for and encouraging talent.

Smith: *Then will young men have different expectations of their future spouses?*

Hollinger: Other than the work of Barbara Kerr—thank god, she worked with gifted men—I think that's one of the biggest gaps we have in research, a focus on gifted boys. Boys are still socialized with stereotypic gender role expectations and we're socializing and counselling gifted women in a whole different way. What does that mean? I worry that if both gifted males and females aren't travelling on a similar road, we'll have relational problems. Medical school faculty were more accepting of female medical students than male students.

On the pragmatic side, Gayle Sheehy in *Passages* suggested everyone should have a housewife. I'd love it. As I'm trying to schedule someone to clean my fireplace chimney before winter and do the furnace maintenance and I don't have a watch on because the battery died seven days ago, I understand men wanting a traditional wife in a traditional role.

Smith: *What do you think about the suggestion that girls be more instrumental in choosing spouses? Could that help gifted girls achieve? For example, finally you've got a free weekend and want to call up that guy and ask him to the movies rather than making yourself extra attractive and going by his office, in the hope he might ask you out. And if it's the weekend before your big report is due and you say "no," he'll assume you're not interested in him.*

Hollinger: It's an excellent point. Asking for instrumentality in the relational context. I like that concept but don't think I'm going to live long enough to see it. Although certainly younger women are more agentic in initiating phone calls so they're not home the whole week waiting for the phone to ring. I don't know about actively seeking a spouse as men do.

Smith: *Is it harder for gifted women to make a career choice because of their multiple abilities?*

Hollinger: It's not easy. Number one, the multiply-talented are drawn in multiple directions. Then we come along and tell them not only can you be anything you want as far as a career, you can be any kind of person. But how much do you sell androgyny to adolescents? They are trying to deal with the gender salience of adolescence, "Who am I in relationship to the opposite sex?" We come bouncing in saying, "Oh, let's be androgynous." We spent a lot of time debating that issue, because I really think a gifted woman still lives in and has to deal with multiple cultures. For example, when I go home to Pennsylvania to my dad's business—I am a kid again helping out in the store. And not coming from an academic family, I'm still asked to explain, "Now what is it you do exactly?"

Smith: *You tell them you teach.*

Hollinger: I just work at a school for big kids. But that is a simple situation to deal with compared to one where I would be going against strong ethnic, religious or other kinds of pressures. Some of our kids have said to us that resistance from family members has been a major barrier. What if I went home and my dad was angry with me, asking, "Why aren't you doing what you should be doing in life?" "You don't have six kids, what is wrong with you?" I think some of our gifted women may well encounter that.

Smith: *So socialization is very pervasive. Is it fair to ask if it's more from parents, more from the media or from some other source?*

Hollinger: No, I wouldn't pick on any one source. I think there's significant diversity both in parenting styles, teachers and so on. But I also wouldn't because my whole focus is on the individual's perception of their socialization. So if mother tells me "x" happened, it doesn't mean daughter perceives it the same way. There is the issue of perception, the issue of interpretation and then the issue of meaning. First, there are lots of things in our environment all the time we don't perceive. Then given what does come in, how do I interpret that? With Peggy I certainly interpreted the difference in our scores. It meant I was dumb. So you also have to factor in how the individual is processing whatever is out there.

Another thing we can't assume is who the significant others are in a person's life. In '78 Rosenburg said in his self-concept research that we can't assume a mother or a father is a significant other. Someone from Big Brothers or Big Sisters could be. The question is, "Who do I empower?" It's those persons' messages that will have impact. I could have had 12 years of very sexist teachers but what would be the effect if I didn't listen and didn't let their messages in?

Counselling Gifted Women

Smith: *Do you think that gifted, talented women can or should be counselled to make more nontraditional choices?*

Hollinger: In my mind that's quite simple. Yes, they can be counselled to pursue nontraditional careers. Taking your question literally, no, they shouldn't be. Counselling should remove the internal barriers thwarting a gifted woman's progress, yes, so she can make her own choice free, or as free as any of us can be, of gender socialization. But if she has been socialized in a very traditional way regarding what's important to her, and if her family of origin will give her flack for pursuing the nontraditional, then we have to look very carefully at what prices she would have to pay. I want to seek counselling for free choice. I don't think we can just become another social straight-jacket of "You shoulds." You are mathematically talented, therefore you should be an engineer, you must be a physician, you should be a statistician.

Obviously I have my own value hierarchy. I want to see gifted women talented in math and sciences pursuing those careers. But what's going to make this gifted woman happy with her life? Am I concerned most about societal loss of her potential? I think gifted women need a lot of support, counselling and encouragement. But I don't want to become another patriarch telling women yet again what they should do.

Smith: *How effective is direct intervention in turning interests around? Can you counsel girls into the nontraditional?*

Hollinger: For some it is possible. Again, this is not global evaluative data but rather the results of following "x" number of individuals in the project. A match with the right mentor at the right moment in the right area can change "I want to be a bookkeeper or a hairdresser" into "I want to be an engineer." It can happen. But I don't think we should force-funnel.

Smith: *What did you learn about counselling gifted women from your intervention steps?*

Hollinger: In the counselling process, looking at self-perception, we tried to break away attributes and careers from association with a specific gender. So that independence or decisiveness is not associated with only masculinity, for example. We'd try to get the girls to look at the possibility of manifesting different attributes in different life spheres. For example, I can be competitive as the devil in a tennis tournament, but in academia I try to avoid competition. Though I don't like to compete, I can if the environment triggers it. This way we were teaching them context specificity. You can be kind, gentle and nurturant and also be x, y and z, depending on the context. It is not either-or.

Gifted women themselves taught us that, when they balked at answering yes/no to the questions on our rating scales. I didn't hear them clearly at the time when they'd say, "Sometimes I am this way, and sometimes I am that way, how can I answer this?"

To take it another step, we'd say sometimes men cry and are giving and sometimes they make hard decisions in the board room, and women can too. It does not say anything about their masculinity, about your femininity. You can have a range of attributes. I don't think anyone in the project wanted to see those young women losing the best of what is stereotypically feminine. We just wanted them also to have flexibility. To know when to be assertive, *when* to be whatever. There are special skills all women as well as men need. I have seen it in myself in negotiating. Every time I'd interview for a job, they'd say "This is the salary." I'd say, "Oh, OK." Then I'd watch some younger folks come in and demand, "I want a course release to get my research started. I need this lab space." Things that never occurred to me to ask. I'd just take what was given and think "if I am a good girl they will give me more."

Two of my closest male friends when I was going through my doctoral work were industrial psychologists. I watched them as they negotiated. They'd say, "Of course you want me. Now what are you going to pay to get me? This is what I want, this is what I deserve." That's a very different attitude.

If you look at gender socialization globally, the message to gifted women is second class status.

Also there's the need to learn to prioritize. If the gifted woman values relationships but still wants to attain high career aspirations, I don't see any answer other than knowing how to organize, time-manage and all those kinds of things—unless you want to see the burnout of the super woman syndrome. I have seen some super women and I have marveled: cooking gourmet dinners every night, doing surgery at six a.m. and sewing their own clothes. Halloween costumes for the kids. I am in awe. But I don't think the majority of gifted women are going to do that. So I see a group of survival skills counsellors need to develop in girls.

Smith: *Are these skills that men are already taught in a way institutionalized by society? Or are we talking about supplementary skills that girls alone need to overcome additional barriers?*

Hollinger: I think more men have those skills, but they're not inborn. They have to pick them up somewhere. If you look at gender socialization globally, the message to gifted women is second class status, not the message the men receive. So, yes, men have a sense of entitlement and, not being so relationally oriented, it is a lot easier for them to say, "These are my career goals, honey. You coming along? Bring the kids." Or, "I don't have time to talk. I have this corporate report to do."

Future Research Needs and Opportunities

Smith: *We've discussed what is known about gifted women's needs. What are the major gaps in our knowledge about gifted women's career choices. What kind of research would you like to see funded?*

Hollinger: Number one, I would like to see a shift from *prediction* of career choice or change to *why* these choices are made. I think we've predicted and predicted in terms of achieving potential. Instead, we need to look at the differences in why they have chosen what they have chosen. Again going back to the within gender research approach.

Number two is more emphasis on development across the life span in general. We don't know much about the adult years and a lot of what we do is about adult males. I feel with our sample we're just on the brink as they enter their thirties. From the literature I can generate some hypotheses but I don't know what to predict, or why. There aren't that many longitudinal studies of gifted women.

Number three, I would like to see us focus on the effect of context, context, context. For example, whether it's the work environment or the people within the work environment that make a gifted woman NASA engineer feel she belongs. Context in terms of family too. How is her husband or partner reacting? How does her "significant other" facilitate, or obstruct, career development. We've not analyzed the data, but we asked a lot about responsibility for home/family chores. How much of a role does your husband play in getting chores done and how does he feel about it? Is he doing you a favor by taking the garbage out or the kids for two hours? Or is it a true partnership with equitable responsibility? We don't have that much research on gifted couples.

Also, how are kids reacting to mother continuing her education, her career? I don't think we know anything about that relational system. For example, one of our participants, not a happy camper at all, said, "Mother deserted and that's it." Another said, "Mom's back in school and that's great."

And to the extent that women are relationally oriented not just to kids and spouse but parents also, we need to understand the influence of that third relational system. I've seen a number of folks my age with pressure from both their husband's parents and their own—"Kids. When are you going to have kids?" We look at parents as significant others only until adulthood but they can remain influential factors. I know I tend to those familial connections and loyalties. They're more important to me than anything career-wise. That's my value hierarchy, which I like to think is a choice, not a function of gender socialization.

Advice to Counsellors

Smith: *From what you've learned, do you have practical suggestions for the teachers and counsellors of gifted and talented women? Any sage bits of advice?*

Hollinger: I guess my number one advice to counsellors in particular, teachers also, is examine carefully your own biases, stereotypes and expectations. How do you really feel about these gifted young women and men. Secondly, as I've learned the hard way, don't make assumptions about their perceptions of the world. Do a reality test. I can be working with a gifted young woman, everything feels like it's going along fine, she's focusing towards, say, medicine. She's talking about how it could be financed. Then she asks, "After my residency, how can I remain current for 18 years [until my kids are grown] before I can practice medicine?" And it hits me! I never tested what getting a medical degree meant to her, how she thought it would fit with the rest of her life. You and I know, you go to med school, get a degree and open a practice right away. But some women really don't know.

Advice for the Gifted Woman

Smith: *Are there messages from your research for gifted and talented women to use when considering a career?*

Hollinger: The first step is knowing yourself. Looking at your self-belief system, which includes values and interests and everything we carry inside our heads. Who am I, what am I interested in? Then look back for the source of validation. I believe this about myself. Why? Is this my own validation or did this come from my first grade teacher?

Then, to borrow from my mentor Betty Finney, pick your own judges.

Smith: *Pick people you respect, let them be your judge but don't let yourself be judged by everyone and anyone?*

Hollinger: That is my compromise. Not to be the independent loner who doesn't care what anyone thinks but selectively pick "judgments" from those you trust and, as Steinem suggests, trust your own inner self above all!

References and Recommended Readings

Atwood, M. (1985). *The handmaid's tale*. Toronto: McClelland & Stewart.

Belenky, M.F., Clinchy, B.M., Goldberger, N.R., Tarule, J.M. (1986). *Women's way of knowing: The development of self, voice & mind*. New York: Basic Books.

Eccles, J.E., Adler, T.F., Futterman R., Goff, S.B., Kaczala, C.M., Meece, J.I., & Midgley, C. (1983). Expectations, values, and academic behaviors. In J.T. Spence (Ed.), *Achievement and achievement motives* (pp. 75-145). San Francisco: Freemen.

Faludi, B. (1991). *Backlash: The undeclared war against American women*. New York: Crown.

Frankl, V.E. (1984). *Man's search for meaning*. New York: Washington Square Press.

Hollinger, C.L. (1991). Facilitating the career development of gifted young women. *Roeper Review, 13* (3), 132-136.

Hollinger, C.L. & Fleming, E.S. (1988). Gifted and talented young women: Antecedents and correlates of life satisfaction. *Gifted Child Quarterly, 32*(2), 254-259.

Horner, M.S. (1972). Toward an understanding of achievement-related conflicts in women. *Journal of Social Issues, 28*, 157-175.

Jordan, J.V., Kaplan, A.G., Miller, J.B., Stiver, I.P., & Surrey, J.L. (1991). *Women's growth in connection: Writings from the Stone Center*. New York: Guilford.

Josselson, R. (1987). *Finding herself: Pathways to identity development in women*. San Francisco: Jossey Bass.

Kerr, B.A. (1985). *Smart girls, gifted women*. Columbus, OH: Ohio Psychology Publishing.

Kerr, B.A., & Ghrist-Priebe, S.L. (1988). Intervention for multipotentiality: Effects of a career counseling laboratory for gifted high school students. *Journal of Counseling and Development, 66*, 366-369.

Noble, K.D. (1987). The dilemma of the gifted woman. *Psychology of Women Quarterly, 11*, 367-378.

Noble, K.D. (1989). Counseling gifted women: Becoming the heroes of our own stories. *Journal for the Education of the Gifted, 12(* 2), 131-141.

Noble, K.D. (1990). The female hero: A quest for healing and wholeness. *Women & Therapy, 9*(4), 3-18.

Reis, S.M. & Callahan, C.M. (1989). Gifted females: They've come a long way - or have they? *Journal for the Education of the Gifted, 12*(2), 99-117.

Rosenberg, M. (1979). *Conceiving the self*. New York: Basic Books.

Sears, P.S., & Barbee, A.H. (1977). Career and life satisfactions among Terman's gifted women. In J.C. Stanley, W.C. George & C.H. Solano (Eds.), *The gifted and the creative: A fifty year perspective*. Baltimore, MD: Johns Hopkins University Press.

Sheehy, G. (1974). *Passages: Predictable crises of adult life*. New York: Dutton.

Steinem, G. (1992) *Revolution from within: A book of self-esteem.* Toronto: Little, Brown and Co.

Terman, L.M., & Oden, M.H. (1959). *Genetic studies of genius: V. The gifted group at midlife.* Stanford, CA: Stanford University Press.

Significant Events in the Life of Connie Hollinger

1949	Year Born
1967	High School Graduation
1970	B.S., Health & Physical Education, East Stroudsburg State College, East Stroudsburg, Pennsylvania (summa cum laude)
1973	M.S., Clinical Psychology, Millersville State College, Millersville, Pennsylvania
1970-73	Instructor, Health & Physical Education, Elizabethtown College
1973-75	Graduate Assistant, Case Western University
1975	Ph.D., Educational Psychology, Case Western Reserve University, Cleveland, Ohio
1978-79	Assistant Professor in Psychology, Lake Erie College
1979-80	Interim Dean of Students, Lake Erie College
1980-81	Dean of Students, Lake Erie College
1981-Present	Co-ordinator of the School Psychology Program Assistant, Associate (1984) & Full Professor (1992) Psychology Department, Cleveland State University

Selected Honors/Recognition

A.H.S. Fellow Case Western Reserve University, 1974
Ohio Association for Gifted Children Award for Achievement
Commencement Speaker, Lake Erie College, June 1982
Yearbook Dedication, Lake Erie College
Certificate of Achievement, Ohio Association for Gifted Children
Certificate of Appreciation, Ohio Department of Education
Consultant, National Center for Research on the Gifted & Talented

6

Why So Few in Math and Science?

An interview with Jacquelynne Eccles, Ph.D., Professor of Psychology, University of Colorado, Boulder; and research scientist, University of Michigan.

Why do the educational and occupational paths of men and women diverge? And why, in particular, are there still so few women entering and persisting in math and science careers although their grades in related course work are better than men's? Jacquelynne Eccles gave the authors her insights into these critical issues one October afternoon at her Rocky mountainside Colorado home—while her four feline friends thoughtfully entertained her cat-loving guests with grand "jetes", microphone cord nibbling and wistful meows after tempory banishment outside.

Eccles' expertise in these issues has been firmly established by twenty years of extensive research. She and her colleagues have studied the social and motivational factors differentiating people's career aspirations, vocational and educational choices and avocational pursuits, such as sports participation. And they've concluded that people's achievement-related choices unconsciously or consciously are guided by two general factors: their expectations for success in an occupational field and the values they attach to the associated tasks. Both of these are also highly influenced by sex-role socialization, cultural norms and personal experience in general. More recently she has looked at the impact of parents' and teachers' beliefs on girls' achievement in math and science.

Eccles' model explains the differences in these areas, building on the work of psychological theorists such as Lewin and Atkinson, who have studied both the factors motivating people and the factors to which people attribute their success or failure at a particular task. Eccles' own model states that expectations are shaped by three factors: how confident men or women feel about their abilities relevant to a particular occupation, how difficult they think various occupations are and how formidable they see the barriers to their success. But the value people assign to any occupation depends on their personal short- and long-term goals (typically very different for men and women) and how well the job fits with the image of who they think they are and who they want to be. People also take into account what they think they'll have to give up to engage in this occupation or training.

Unlike prior models of achievement, which viewed any failure to achieve as an indication of some kind of deficit in a person, Eccles' model emphasizes choice. At the same time it acknowledges the problems of applying the traditional male-value based definition of achievement to women. Women, she suggests, may be choosing different occupations than men because they're positively motivated to do other things, not because they're avoiding male-associated activities due to lack of self-confidence or fear of success.

In the interview that follows, Eccles applies her research to explain specifically the very different participation rates in mathematics and science among men and women. She also shares insights into how these forces shaped her own early career. Finally, she suggests how individuals and educational institutions can help both women and men make career choices more consistent with both their talents and interests in math and science.

A Case of Stumbling into Science

Smith: *How did you become interested in women's career choices and more specifically in the influence of mathematics upon the career choices of women?*

Eccles: I really became interested in women's career choices about the time I entered UCLA as a graduate student, after having been in the Peace Corps for two years and having my first child. I really didn't know what I wanted to do. I was fairly traditional at that point, so I sort of stumbled into grad school. And I hadn't thought much about discrimination against women at all.

But around that time, 1968, the Women's Movement really took hold and consciousness-raising groups began in the L.A. area. After the first year I met four other women students. We were all taking the same classes and gravitated towards each other because we were among the few women in the department. There was virtually only one female faculty member in psychology out of sixty or seventy and she was in neither developmental nor social work, my interest areas. So we women students started sharing experiences about what had made us different. We knew we weren't quite like either the male students or our female friends who found staying home with babies absolutely satisfying. Yet in high school I'd never thought I was any different from other women.

So we five formed a very strong collegial group, which, I think, had a tremendous impact on my life. Three of us, in fact, shared research interests in attribution theory and ended up forming the female half of a research team. We were also activists. After starting our own informal conscious-raising sessions we decided to call a conference on the psychology of women and tried to change undergraduate and graduate training at UCLA. We helped start a women's studies program on campus along with a course on the psychology of women, which we convinced the psych department to teach. As a consequence we made contact with Karen Page, a faculty member at University of California, Davis, who was conducting a large survey of women. We convinced her to include questions to assess the impact on female undergraduates of their taking the new women's studies program and psychology of women course. That launched us into the whole research area of what influences women's attitudes and career choices. While we were still students we completed a study on the kinds of family experiences that lead women to make nontraditional choices.

Later, the way my studies linked up with mathematics was totally serendipitous. After Berkeley I'd gone to Smith College for a time to teach and then to Michigan in 1977. At Michigan I was told the National Institute of Education was calling for papers. They had a large amount of funding to study why women weren't continuing in math and sciences. Now I'd always been interested in achievement in general so I thought, "That's a perfect way to start my research in the field." I really wasn't interested in mathematics per se but here was this wonderful opportunity for a grant to look at the general question of achievement in a specific area. It became clear quickly that focusing on the social influences on math career choices was promising. There wasn't a lot of evidence for major biological differences in math ability even though some people wanted to believe it. Instead a substantial amount of the discrepancy in the numbers of men and women going into math/science careers appeared to be due to attitudinal and social factors.

Smith: *If you look at your own life before graduate school can you see some of these influences at work?*

Eccles: I've thought a lot about that. At the time I really had no idea why I was going to graduate school. It wasn't a career choice but a good way to spend four years when I couldn't think of anything better to do. School was always something easy and fun for me. I'd had the baby at Christmas and within two months I knew I wasn't going to be able to stay home. I was going out of my mind. But I figured by going to school I could take care of kids and at least have something to keep me alive and aware of what was going on in the world. I mean, sitting home with a baby, watching TV and cleaning the apartment while my husband studied full time for a masters in social work wasn't satisfying at all.

What's interesting is that I still wasn't accepted when I first arrived at UCLA and I'd only applied to that one place. I, of course, did the typical female thing of saying to my husband, "I told you so. You've been accepted but I'm not good enough for graduate school." But he said, "There's a mistake. There's no way you couldn't have been accepted." Then he forced me to go down there and, as it turned out, it was a mistake. By accident, the department never had a complete file on me and so couldn't accept me.

But when I went in to complain to the head of the department I had my first conscious encounter with sexism. I rolled in with my baby because I'd been in Africa for two years and women there took their babies everywhere. This behavior I'm sure convinced him he'd made absolutely the right decision by not accepting this flaky woman who'd bring a stroller to a faculty member's office. He rattled off pat reasons, "Well, you know, it's hard to get in here. You have to come from a good institute." I told him that I'd gone to Berkeley. "Well, you have to have very good grades." I was Phi Beta Kappa. "We focus a lot on science." I was a biochemistry major until my senior year. "You have to have very good GREs." And so on. He'd never even seen my folder. The secretaries had screened it out. But the last thing he said was, "Probably what kept you out was that we tend to be biased towards men. We really have problems getting men into developmental psychology."

Leduc: *That blatant about it?*

Eccles: That blatant, right across the table, saying, "Probably you weren't admitted because we had to choose between you and a man. And we pick men because there are so few in developmental." Well, they didn't have a single woman professor in development on the faculty! The next day I received a letter noting that they didn't have my transcript. I replied, "It should be there. I sent it a year ago." And once that issue was resolved, I was admitted.

I remember then going to see my advisor who asked me what I was going to do with my degree. I said, "Maybe teach at a small college." At which point he looked across the table and said, "Never say that again while you're here. We're not training teachers at UCLA. We're training researchers." So in a short time I learned two salient lessons about what was expected of female graduate students.

Smith: *Who had the predominant care of the baby when you were both at school, you or your husband?*

Eccles: Somehow it always turned out that I was more available. As I look back I have to wonder why. Yet at that time my husband and I were both convinced my load was much more flexible, although he's a man who to this day will say he's committed to taking care of his kids. He espouses all the right liberal attitudes and certainly was the one who encouraged me to go back to school. Then after he finished his MSW and began his doctorate he did take on almost a full-time job so his load truly was less flexible.

Smith: *What were your parents' backgrounds?*

Eccles: My dad was in the military and my mother a homemaker. She never worked outside the home but she was very smart and creative. She was also an alcoholic, just slightly tipsy most of the time. It took the edge off and helped her deal with life. If I look back, it was clear she felt she made tremendous sacrifices being a military wife. She never did fit the image. Instead she sewed, knit, painted, and wove. You should see some of the things she created.

My dad grew up in Oklahoma on a farm. His parents were pioneers with a very egalitarian household in which there was no division of labor between males and females. When it was time to plant or harvest, everybody went out and planted or harvested. My grandmother was a very tough lady who ran the household and I'm sure was the reason the family survived. Actually it's a recurrent theme with women that it was their grandmothers, not mothers, who'd done the unusual things in life. So my father was not the reason my mother never worked. He would've been happy for her if she'd wanted to work.

Dad treated my sister and I like two sons. I was the oldest so I played ball with him and chopped wood and generally helped out. We were expected to do well and that was a big influence on me. Moving around so much also shaped me because I had to learn to adapt to new environments. From the time I was four to the end of my junior high years we lived successively in Germany, Japan and Okinawa, then back to California. I found that challenge stimulating and enjoyed learning new things. Also I've always been fairly independent. And with exposure to many different cultures I didn't grow up with pat ideas of what men and women could do. Still, at the time I married, I had a fairly traditional image of what as a woman I was going to do, or at least try to do, until I found out I was going to die of boredom if I followed that route the rest of my life.

Leduc: *Was there any expectation from your family, spoken or unspoken, that you'd go to university or graduate school?*

Eccles: Certainly not to graduate school. My dad was not big into education. Neither my mom or my dad were college graduates and they grew up in environments where that wasn't necessarily the high status thing to do. My father clearly wanted me to go to school if I could, but he wasn't going to pay a lot. Luckily I lived in California and Berkeley was inexpensive and also a very good school. But I think if I'd lived somewhere else, I'd have gone to some state college. My parents couldn't afford to contribute to my graduate school funds and took a long time to understand my career motivation. They probably would've preferred an attorney or physician or some other profession that led to a tangible job. They still don't know what university professors actually do.

Smith: *You said your dad didn't have any objections to your mother working. I wonder why she didn't?*

Eccles: First of all we moved around a lot. Another factor was the limited range of work available to her, basically clerk or grocery store worker. She hadn't been to college so she couldn't teach. She had some typing training, but married right out of high school because of World War II and had me shortly after. To do anything would have meant more education. But when you don't know how long you're going to be in any one place it's hard to get started. I've done some research on choices gifted women made in Terman's sample, women in my mother's age group. If you think about the options open to them at the time, maybe staying home was their best choice. It at least gave them the opportunity to be creative.

Smith: *Were you in girl-friendly classrooms all the time?*

Eccles: I don't remember any that gave me a hassle. I was in a small high school and that was a real advantage. I had the same math teacher for three years, a male, but he was a very good teacher and he liked us all. Out of my graduating class of one hundred and eighty there were probably thirty of us, males and female, that were tracked from the time we entered to take the AP [advanced placement] math, chemistry and physics classes. There was never any question that the women weren't going to make it through all those courses and I think that was a real influence on me. My science teachers never gave any messages that women weren't as competent. And by having always the same teachers you came to know them well. But I wouldn't say that's a girl-friendly classroom. It's person-friendly.

Leduc: *Did you ever experience math anxiety?*

Eccles: Not at all. I love math. In fact, if anything, I have English anxiety. I still don't think I write well. One reason I became a psych major was to take objective tests and not have to write essays or papers. I would've gone in the direction of the sciences if for no other reason than to avoid what I thought were fairly arbitrary grading standards in the humanities and many of the social sciences.

I suppose being exposed to multiple languages should have made me more comfortable with languages but I think math just came easy for me. I don't believe in this right brain, left brain stuff but I can still think much more comfortably in the mode of mathematics and the sciences than in the mode of humanities.

Smith: *In talking to other successful women in science one common theme, in their high school experience particularly, is having close women friends who were also academically and mathematically oriented. It seemed to convey a message that it's okay to do math and be a woman. Did you experience anything similar?*

Eccles: We were such a small group that gender didn't make that much difference. I can remember about eight or nine of us, half girls, half boys, who actually completed all the advanced science courses together and became fairly good friends. There was no thought that the women might opt out to take a second language or AP social studies. We all had only one elective each year. And I think that kind of system is more likely to keep women involved because it doesn't let them select themselves out prematurely.

Smith: *Do you remember any incidents you found particularly encouraging or discouraging?*

Eccles: They didn't really happen until I got to graduate school. Berkeley was a very large place and it was easy to go unnoticed. Nobody singled me out to get involved in research although I did very well in my classes. So it wasn't that I was discouraged but certainly I didn't have any mentoring. That's why I blundered into grad school. All I knew was that it was four more years of school and something I could do at the same time I was taking care of babies.

Leduc: *How did the idea to go to graduate school germinate?*

Eccles: Well, they talked to us in Peace Corps training about it. That was the only real career counselling I ever received except for one adviser at Berkeley. I never talked to him much because he had hundreds of advisees but he looked at my transcript one day and said, "Have you considered going to graduate school?" I said, "Why would I?" I don't know what I thought I needed to get into graduate school but I certainly didn't think I had it. He said, "With your record you really ought to think about it. We don't usually take our own students but they might take you here."

Then when my husband and I went to the Peace Corps in Ghana our trainers took us under their wings. At the end of the first year they said, "You ought to think about what you're going to do a year from now. It's time to start applying to graduate school." And I did, because I was supposed to. So I was really shaped by random events. Probably I'd have eventually tried graduate school even if I hadn't gone into the Peace Corps, but I might also have ended up in business.

Smith: *Did being in the Peace Corps give you independence training, a chance to really test yourself?*

Eccles: I'd already done that as a military kid. The Peace Corps was not a whole different experience in fact. We were schoolteachers in good housing so it was not a survivalist experience. But it gave me a different view. African women still work full time with the kids on their backs everywhere they go. That changed my view to "Gee, having kids doesn't necessarily mean giving up the rest of my life." So I had two, a boy and a girl.

Smith: *Is there any particular part of your life that you would single out as atypical for women in your age group.*

Eccles: Lots of parts. First I moved all over. And I think the fact that my dad had no notions about women's limitations helped. He didn't necessarily encourage me to do anything atypical but he never indicated that women were different. In fact he expected us to do everything around the house that he did. He'd say, "All right, it's time you learned to chop wood," or "This summer you're going to mow the lawn. Here's the power mower." I even got baseball bats for Christmas. Since he didn't know what to do with girls for fun we'd go out in the back yard and do gymnastics with him or go swimming and dive off the rocks twenty feet up in the air. If you said, "I'm scared, Dad," he'd reply, "Oh, don't be chicken."

Smith: *How did your mom react? Did she participate?*

Eccles: Oh yes. She didn't do as much as we did but she didn't have fears either. She rode horses as a kid and was a pretty good athlete. She certainly thought it was okay for girls to do sports. We all did a lot of swimming. They didn't have organized sports overseas but the base operated a pool all of the time. My mother, in fact, became a life guard.

Smith: *What about your sister? What's she done with her life?*

Eccles: She's six years younger and a tax accountant but she doesn't especially like to work at it. What she does is go on these great adventures. She taught herself to sail and build a boat by reading a book. Then she and a friend set off from Oregon to sail down through the Pacific without ever having a class in sailing in their lives. She's also sailed the Atlantic three times in a two-person boat. What she often will do for money is come into port during tax season and do taxes for the rich Americans. She can support herself very well doing that only three months a year. She's never had children and has no desire to have any, but I think she wishes she could find some occupation that's also an avocation.

Leduc: *Your mother is still alive. What's her feeling about two daughters, so strong willed and successful. I consider your sister a success too because I like that in-and-out life style.*

Eccles: Yes, many of the things my sister's done are far more impressive than going down the traditional track. I wouldn't dare set off across the Atlantic in a two person boat. But I think my mom has mixed feelings about us. We've talked about it a few times and she knows she should be happy her daughters are doing well but she's never really come to grips with her feelings about her own life. She does have regrets. She doesn't pin it down to a job but I think she wishes she'd spent less time putting other people's agendas ahead of her own. I don't think she ever really knew what her own desires were but would've liked to have had the opportunity to discover them.

Smith: *You're written that it's difficult to judge the real contribution of women who've put all their energy into families, whether their effort might have produced children more gifted than they'd be otherwise. Can you see that influence in your own family?*

Eccles: I think so. My mother did nothing to deter our ambitions. She was always there for us and we were a very close family. But I think also to some extent people who pick my lifestyle are a bit neurotic. At least I feel that way. It's as if I've spent a lot of time trying to prove something to somebody. I'm not sure who that is, what I'm trying to prove or why. But Mother's ambivalence about our succeeding probably set the groundwork for this sort of self-doubt. It was just really clear she was unhappy and didn't know what to do about it.

Smith: *What about your own daughter. Has it made a difference in her choices that you've combined motherhood and a career?*

Eccles: She's just finished high school. But like many daughters of women with consuming careers, she rejects my kind of life. I think she doesn't want that pace and there's probably an element of wishing there'd been homebaked cookies for her after school. Many times I was away for meetings. Two times I missed her birthday and I've never heard the end of it. I think part of her independent behavior is a concern that "Mom's life is just too tough a model to follow." So she's set her aspirations far lower than her abilities and I've told her so. She just says, "I don't want to do what you do." Now that's fine with me. I think in many cases people would be nuts to do what I do. But I don't want her to avoid it because she's afraid of failing. Yet my career is a hard act to follow. In contrast, no matter what I did I was going to go further than my mom. I wasn't going to let her down if I tried and didn't succeed.

Leduc: *Does your daughter contemplate staying home with a family?*

Eccles: Well, she does want to have kids. You know, my son is in the marines and my daughter wants to be an elementary school teacher. Having spent a lifetime studying gender roles, I think they did it just to get me [laughs]. It will be interesting to see what happens to her, because I think she's very independent and smart. She may have exactly the same experience I did with traditional roles and decide later she wants more autonomy.

Women in Math and Science: The Critical Filters

Smith: *We've discussed how you eventually "stumbled' into a research career. Since then, what trends has your research uncovered in women's participation in science and math?*

Eccles: Let me first go back about twenty years. In the mid-1970s the U.S. National Institute of Education did a nice job of gathering the relevant research and statistics on why girls were not going on in education. One study they noted by Lucy Sells in the mid-sixties had looked at how much mathematics men and women had when entering the University of California system and how that affected their qualifications for science courses. What she found was that women had taken approximately half as much high school math as the men and consequently were shut out of over half of the university majors. She coined the term "critical filter" to describe the impact of that deficit on women's careers.

What's ironic is that this situation was an aberration. Historically the critical gender difference in high school has been not the amount of mathematics but physics and chemistry. However, from about 1965 to 1972 high schools began to be "relevant" and let college-bound kids have lots of options. That's when the girls stopped taking math. But earlier, most college-bound kids took four years of math, or at least three. And the data since have shown that, on the average, females and males again don't differ in the number of math courses taken until the last half of senior year and then only by a half year. So college-bound females average three and a half years of high school math, college-bound males four. Girls are dropping out of that last advanced class once they've been accepted into university. They take another literature course or an elective social science course but they're not fun electives. Females don't seem any more likely to take easy courses than males, although they both take more of those than we'd like.

But the much bigger differences have remained in physics and chemistry. Women are more likely to take high school biology, men more likely to take physics, especially AP physics. And that's been true as far back as there are good national records. The trend is amazingly stable. At university it's also the case that women are less represented in the physical sciences and applied mathematical fields, engineering being the best example. A mere three percent of engineering degrees have traditionally gone to women and that figure remained fairly stable until the mid-seventies when the big push began to get women into the sciences.

But in math itself that's not true. I have a chart going all the way back to 1920 that shows the proportion of B.A.s going to each sex in math, and about 30 to 35 percent of those degrees have always gone to women. Until recently that was also the proportion of women going to university so that's as large a percentage as one would have expected.

Leduc: *What about female participation in biology or behavioral science?*

Eccles: That's been stable. At university the biological sciences show no under representation of females. And in the behavioral sciences at the bachelor's level, if anything, there are more females. But what's interesting is that at the masters level the numbers of women begin to drop off, with still fewer at the Ph.D. level, even in fields predominantly female at the undergraduate level. For example in education, women earn about 80 percent of the bachelors degrees yet less than 50 percent of the Ph.D.s. So at the graduate and post graduate level we have tremendous problems attracting women. It's expensive, there aren't many fellowships and the training is long.

Smith: *Are the number of undergraduate women increasing in the physical sciences?*

Eccles: The numbers for chemistry and physics haven't changed much. We've seen an upturn in the proportion of women in those fields from 10 to 15 percent or something like that, but not much more than predicted by the increase in the overall proportion of females in the college population. Women are now more than 50 percent of U.S. undergraduates. But the engineering case proves educators can get women interested if they work at recruiting them. For example, engineering went from 3 percent women to a peak of 18 percent in 1985 and then dropped back down again. It's now hovering around 15 percent and nobody knows exactly why. Some speculate that schools are admitting more females into engineering, their attrition rate in undergraduate engineering may be higher than men's. I've not seen all the statistics but I suspect that's indeed the case.

Leduc: *Why do you think that's happened?*

Eccles: Why? The way engineering is taught at university is horrendous. In most cases it's anything but person-friendly. In many cases it's absolutely the worst possible example of an environment designed to drive people out. You still hear stories about how on the first day of school the engineering dean will say, "Look to the right of you, look to the left, only one of you three will be here to graduate." And they're proud of that. There's also little support in these classes if you're having trouble understanding the material. There's this idea that the student either understands on her own or she's dumb. They really want to get rid of people any way they can and one way is to make courses so difficult that students get discouraged.

Women are disproportionately likely to give in to that kind of pressure. We know from high school data that females say, "Why bother?" And at the college level even with higher grades women are more likely to say, "I don't have what it takes to go on." They may earn a B plus grade point average yet feel that's not good enough to be an engineer, whereas a male with only a C will say, "That's fine. I don't want to be a superstar engineer. I can get by as average."

Smith: *But aren't women also subjected to a double standard? Don't people in general criticize a woman more than a man for getting a mere B plus?*

Eccles: Right. I think women do pick up that message. They also hear little opposing evidence, such as "Wait a minute, you can be an engineer with a C." So they're allowed to select out. There's no mentoring and there are too few of them to form support groups. Clearly they're sexually harassed by male students. In our studies we also heard example after example of engineering professors making derogatory comments in class, such as "I don't know why you women are here anyway. You're just going to go off and have babies."

Smith: *It sounds like some administrators have decided they want more women in engineering but the word hasn't filtered down to the firing line. As far as people there are concerned it's business as usual. Let's shrink classes by pushing out the most vulnerable.*

Eccles: Absolutely. Not all are like that but it happens with enough regularity that it's understandable why women get in, then quit. However, many seem to leave for the biological sciences so they don't drop out of science all together.

Leduc: *If high school math isn't the critical filter for women in science-related majors, what is?*

Eccles: The critical filter becomes calculus freshman year. Except for the women who know immediately they're going to major in math or engineering, a disproportionate number of females don't take it, not realizing how that will shut them out of many courses later and make it very difficult to switch to a science major. They'd have to make up calculus.

Smith: *But isn't the trend today to take five or more years to graduate, providing time to make up courses and shift majors?*

Eccles: It's still very hard in the sciences to make up courses. I know Michigan's administration was pushing the sciences to stop requiring so much because, to get a four-year degree, students had to come in with several AP courses completed in order to jump into advanced classes first year. For example, the biology degree requirements were two or three times the requirements for psychology. You had to start filling them early and even then you'd likely need five years if you couldn't carry a full load every semesters. You also had to get into every course exactly in sequence. Engineering is even worse.

Smith: *What's the role of cost here?*

Eccles: Well, parents are less likely to fund five years for a daughter. They're far more likely to sacrifice financially for a son. If they get in a financial crunch daughters are more likely to drop out of college than sons. It may be that girls are more sensitive to their family's financial plight and say, "I really don't deserve it," whereas boys say, "I'm entitled."

The Job Market for Women
with Science/Math Degrees

Smith: *We've taken the story for girls in math/science now through graduate school. How many are going to actually use that science background once they graduate. And is that changing?*

Eccles: My reading of the latest statistics is that women are getting hired, but it's difficult to know what's really happening from the unemployment rates. People have not studied movement in and out of the labor market, at least in a way where one could follow particular people. But if you look at those who call themselves unemployed, that is, still consider themselves in the labor market but aren't yet employed, there's a higher proportion of women in the sciences across the board in every area.

Smith: *The graduate level too?*

Eccles: Women with Ph.D.s have higher rates of unemployment than men, and a higher proportion of women are underemployed, working at jobs requiring a lot less training than they've acquired. And I think that exists independent of the science field. But some other statistics suggest, in fact, women scientists may be doing better than women nonscientists. So a qualified woman is more likely than not to get a job meeting her qualifications in the sciences at this time. That could be because scientists are desperately needed and, of course, institutions are under pressure to meet affirmative action.

Leduc: *So are the numbers of women educated and employed in a field equal yet? Or are we still dealing with tokenism?*

Eccles: We're nowhere near having the number of women in the workplace match the number currently getting degrees. There's been an increase at the Ph.D. level in the proportions of women, sure, but it will take a very long time before the labor market reflects that. One problem is all the people who've been hired in the last twenty, thirty years and who are still a long way from retirement. And in some fields the statistics are still appalling on the number of female doctorates graduating. Something like three female Ph.D.s in Physics graduated in the United States this year and that kind of scarcity is what university faculties often face when they try to hire women in the sciences. It will take a long time to get enough women through the educational pipelines to fill just the token slots.

Leduc: *Are women paid less than men in the sciences?*

Eccles: Actually they come closer to equal pay in the sciences than in the other areas. I'd recommend that parents say to their daughters, if they have any science skills, "Look, your best economic decision is a science major because you've a better chance there of getting hired and paid what you're worth." That advice, of course, doesn't take into account the proportion of degree holders who actually go on to jobs and it may well be the case that female science degree holders are more likely to drop out of the labor pool.

Smith: *So the ones that do end up staying are perhaps highly motivated or gifted, a selected sample.*

Eccles: We don't know. We really need a study to track down every woman who earned a science degree and find out what they're doing five to ten years later. Believe it or not we don't know what proportion of women degree holders go back into the workforce, and after how much time. These statistics are not being gathered. In general we know women still move in and out of the labor market more than men and want to work less hours. Those are the biggest gender differences in career patterns.

Smith: *Then it seems our culture assumes if a woman doesn't stay in the field, full steam ahead through her twenties, she's lost to science. But the realities of women's lives may be that, yes, for a while they do pull out, but in their thirties or forties they're ready to go back and work straight through for the next thirty years.*

Eccles: If they're given that option, that's right. If undergraduate women knew they could interrupt a science career like that and still find a job later, I think they'd be delighted. And a lot more women would be attracted to the field. But what they actually hear is "If you want to get into science, you're going to have to do it the man's way and it's going to be tough. It's going to consume all of your life and a hundred percent of your energy if you want to do it right." Of course women want to do it right, just as men do. But women also think, "If that's what it's going to take, maybe it's not for me."

However, I think many of these occupations are becoming more responsive to women's needs, frankly, because of economic pressures. Highly trained scientists are so much in demand. U.S. statistics show over 50 percent of the people taking advanced degrees in the sciences now are not from North America. That means we're having to import most of our scientific work force. And universities increasingly understand that. They're becoming much more flexible about people returning for education after a variety of nontraditional career paths. And of course schools are going to find out those alternative paths work just fine.

I think industry has also registered that message and the U.S. Department of Labor too is saying, "Here's this labor pool already educated and very skilled, but they took time out. Now give women a chance and we'll help pay for retraining to bring them back up to speed."

Smith: *Then women don't necessarily have to be lost to science at an early age, given enough job and education flexibility.*

Eccles: And given more acceptance of the idea that working 30 hours a week is just fine as opposed to 60. Having two people work 30 hours a week may be, in fact, far more productive than one working 60 hours. But that requires shifting what it means to be dedicated to a profession. The sciences, at least the research sciences, tend to want people to be highly dedicated, meaning it's their primary commitment. We're also fighting the belief that if you haven't made your creative contribution by age 30 you won't ever do it. So there's no reason to hire a new assistant professor at 35 in math. Her brain must be dead.

That belief is hard to disprove because statistics don't control for the amount of time since professors received their degrees, only their chronological age. It may well be that people are most creative right after their training but that tends to coincide today with a person's twenties. Now it is the case in mathematics, for example, that most contributions are made before 25 or 30 but that could be a consequence of most mathematicians finishing their Ph.D.s before 25. But because that belief has guided graduate admission and hiring policies there aren't enough newly minted, older Ph.D.s for anyone to even challenge it.

Influences on Women's Interest in Math/Science Careers

Smith: *You've written that growing evidence suggests there's probably no difference in math ability between men and women.*

Eccles: Actually, that's not really clear. I'm not willing to rule out the possibility of biological differences, but I think that will account for a very small portion of the variance. Maybe we'll never achieve 50 percent women in the physical sciences but we certainly could go a lot higher. The differences now are clearly much, much larger than biology alone can account for. And in the biological sciences there's no reason not to achieve 50-50.

Smith: *Is some of the evidence coming from the greater participation of foreign women in these fields?*

Eccles: Some, yes. People look also at math test scores, for example, on the Scholastic Aptitude Test used in the U.S. for admission to universities. There, gender accounts for about 3 percent of the variance in scores, yet 85 percent of engineers are male. So why aren't all the women with math scores high enough to get them accepted into engineering actually going into these programs?

Smith: *But you've written we shouldn't look at these differences as a deficit in women. Maybe there are good reasons why women choose different careers than men?*

Eccles: I think that's true. We've focused more on why aren't women more like men rather than why did they pick their chosen careers. So why should we worry about women in math and science? Why not let people pick whatever career they want and never intervene? I think that's not wise because people make career choices very early and on limited information. Neither men nor women are doing a good job of assessing their strengths or the costs and benefits of various decisions. I say both sexes because the question can go either way. Why aren't more men becoming nursery school teachers or nurses? I'm concerned about all people making informed choices, not being discouraged from entering particular areas for reasons having nothing to do with talent or whether they'd ultimately like the job if they knew more about it.

Value differences also affect the occupations people select. But they may again be ruling out occupations quite compatible with their values if they were more familiar with the occupation. For example there are many opportunities within engineering to improve quality of life, something that interests many women. So a young women who had good spatial skills and enjoyed mathematics and tinkering in the physical scientist mode probably would find it a very exciting job to use these skills to design a community to be more responsive to residents' needs. But nobody tells her that's one of the things engineers can do. Nobody ever tells kids the **value** of being an engineer or doctor other than making lots of money. We don't point out the humanistic or spiritual or ascetic values of different occupations and for females that's especially relevant.

We also know there's a set of characteristics about certain science programs that make it absolutely understandable why women are more likely to stay enrolled. One is that women are more likely to be interested in the field's practical applications rather than the abstract theoretical exercise. Engineering, for example, tends to be structured around disciplines. A particular course will focus on a subset of engineering rather than the problems engineers have to solve. Yet in real jobs, problems don't fall out nicely into subdisciplines. They're interdisciplinary. Courses that integrate across disciplines seem to appeal to women. Competitiveness is a factor too. Many courses are still taught in a highly competitive way which raises women's anxiety level and makes them less willing to continue. But some faculty think gearing up the competition gets the best out of people. Well that's a very male view of motivation and not always the case.

A Berkeley mathematics professor did a study along this line. He wanted to know why recent Asian immigrants were doing so well in his course as compared to blacks and whites. What he found out was that Asian students worked as a group and divided up problems, using peer coaching and co-operative learning. Both the black and white students typically didn't do that. In fact they said it was cheating. They'd been told along the way that such a learning mode was immoral. Yet we know that teaching math and science using a co-operative rather than competitive framework gets far more women interested. They do better and stay enrolled. Furthermore, actual professionals don't necessarily work competitively, especially in industry. They typically solve problems in teams. Yet training programs are geared to a very different learning style and may screen out exactly the people who could make the largest contribution to the occupations.

Leduc: *The way that science has traditionally been taught could be more an endurance test, a ritual, than anything else. "This is the way we've always done it This is the way we're going to do it."*

Eccles: Exactly right. It's a way of screening out people based on an assumption of what true dedication means. But no criteria whatsoever back that definition. In fact it's increasingly obvious in many professions that it's outmoded.

Almost anything you do to keep women interested in science keeps men and minorities interested too.

Changing Math and Science
Teaching to Benefit All

Leduc: *Then what do you suggest policy makers do?*

Eccles: Let me preface this discussion by saying that almost anything you do to keep women interested in science keeps men and minorities interested too. So we need to treat everyone differently, not just women. The sciences have always turned off large numbers of people. Fortunately a small set of males has always been willing to put up with bad educational practices. Now that pool is no longer big enough to meet our needs and we're stagnating by shutting out other people who could provide new directions to the fields.

We could do lots of things at the university level. Change the way math and sciences are taught, for example, and that's happening. I'd recommend governments put money behind these programs to help universities rethink curricula. And universities have to open educational slots at all levels for people seeking education through nontraditional routes, for example, by teaching more courses at a time convenient for people with jobs and not seeing part-time study as lacking commitment. One sad trend in the last ten years is the drying up of support for women in science programs. The American Association for the Advancement of Sciences recently reported more funding for minorities in the sciences yet special women's programs have essentially disappeared. So industries will have to also put money into recruiting and training women and minorities out of sheer economic necessity. The labor pool is shrinking and they have to ensure adequate numbers of people to fill their jobs.

We also have to introduce different teacher training methods for secondary schools so that math and science teachers know co-operative and interdisciplinary methods. I like to use the metaphor of "weeders versus cultivators." Science teachers tend to see themselves as weeders but we can give them the skills to be cultivators if we make those kinds of practices part of the required teacher training curriculum.

Other recommendations? Well, I think, given my focus on choice, that many women opt out of science because they don't know what these jobs are like. I'm talking about policies that break down the barriers between training and jobs, that allow early apprenticeship opportunities to establish a close link between course work and experiences in the real world. We could give promising high school and junior high kids opportunities to work in university, industry and government labs in the summer so they don't rule science out before they experience the fun of it.

The Critical Influence of Parents
on Girls' Career Interests

We also need to work on parents. Their role is critical. Many are discouraging daughters from math and sciences, or at least not encouraging them. Our data suggest they underestimate their daughter's talents and think if she's getting good grades in math and sciences it's because she's working hard. They tend to think she's better in the humanities or social sciences even if she's getting good grades in both areas and in general are less likely to give her career counselling or talk to her about her future.

For example, we asked 3 000 parents what they wanted their children to do in the future. Well, they were much more likely to say they wanted a daughter to be happy, have a good life, all those kinds of things, whereas a son should be "something." They don't do this for malevolent reasons, it's just how they view their parental role. But girls need to know about the world as much as boys do and we need to make that point to parents. I think one of the biggest differences in the messages boys and girls hear as they grow up involves the importance of being able to support yourself and your family. Today that's an equally important value for both girls and boys, and I think girls get the best shot in math and sciences at making a comparable wage. If you get that message across, young women look at occupations very differently. Otherwise economic realities play havoc with their lives, making them vulnerable to abusive husbands and poverty.

Leduc: *Especially when you consider the numbers of single parents.*

Eccles: That's been a big change. Parents finally understand there's a 50-50 chance their daughters are going to be divorced and not receive child support, and that's changing the guidance they give their daughters. At the policy level, the government could help fund educational materials that parents receive on a regular basis, for example, telling them all the things girls can and can't do without high school physics. Now I don't want to imply that it's not okay for girls to pick a nonscience career but they need to be supplied with the information to make an informed choice.

Leduc: *Are you saying career education would be a shared responsibility between parents and teachers? And are you calling for more education of the teachers themselves about providing bias-free information?*

Eccles: Absolutely yes to both questions. Teacher education is the first step because I think the way you get to parents is through the teachers. Teachers should go out of their way to talk to parents of daughters with potential about giving their child information on opportunities in science and math careers. Teachers have to reach the parents, their natural allies, so parents can help get to the kids.

We can no longer expect women to be satisfied with less money and status just because they're dedicated to children.

Side Effects of Change

Leduc: *But isn't there still a danger here that we're undervaluing women in traditional career choices?*

Eccles: I have some real concern here because there is a real cost to drawing women out of the traditional careers. The fact is that, historically, those women were the secondary or elementary teachers of math and sciences. There were as many women math B.A.s as men but those B.A.s did very different things. The women went out and taught school. The men went on to graduate degrees then into industry or somewhere else, typically for much more money. Now we've had a real shift. Women more and more are following the male model because it's more lucrative and they're being actively recruited. Consequently, the quality and number of people training to teach math and science, at least in the States, has dropped substantially at both the primary and secondary school levels. You see it in their test scores, which are substantially lower than even ten years ago when the best women in science went into teaching. The solution is to change the amount of money and prestige attached to those professions. We can no longer expect women to be satisfied with less money and status just because they're dedicated to children.

I also think we shouldn't assume that the male model of achievement is the only model, and that people who aren't following it are dissatisfied with their lives. Terman's gifted women by the male definition of success were nowhere near as successful as the men, but they lived longer and certainly reported more satisfied lives. Given all the changes in society, the women now have some fairly specific regrets but so do the men, such as not having taken more time to be with their family. And so each, as they reach the end of their lives, are acutely aware of the cost of sex-role stereotypes.

Almost every study now is reporting changes in young people's attitudes towards work. We just finished a study of high school seniors where we asked them what kind of jobs they wanted and how much they wanted to work. The amazing thing was that nobody wanted to work full time. The sex difference had disappeared, not because the women now wanted to work more but because young men wanted to work less.

Smith: *So they don't see any glory in working themselves to death. Does this mean that the men are going to be more available for child care and the kind of support that wives have traditionally given male professionals?*

Eccles: It would be nice but that's a resistant change. I've done a national study that found a wife's working status has virtually no impact on the way her husband or children spend time. It affects tremendously the way she spends **her** time but it doesn't look like family members are modifying their household support for a working mom. Perhaps men's jobs have been slow to change to give them the flexibility necessary to provide that support, but men may start demanding it.

Research Needs

Smith: *Looking at what we know about career choices for women in science and math, where are our research gaps? Where do we need more information to develop wise policies?*

Eccles: Those are two different questions. I think we can make wise policy decisions right now without more research. On the other hand there are many areas that could use more study. We certainly don't know enough about involving parents, which is critical. We clearly need more funding for innovative intervention projects. We really don't know what works best because we've not tried the full range of strategies. I think the question of biological differences is also completely open, although we really don't need an answer to establish new policy because we're so far from ever pushing up against that barrier. But it would be nice to know if there are individual differences in learning styles linked to gender.

I got a letter the other day from an irate parent who'd heard a news report on one of my studies which looked at how parents' stereotypes affect their views of their kids. What I said was that parents who believe boys are naturally better at math than girls tend to view their own daughters in stereotypic ways. The letter writer was just furious and asked didn't I know "it was all biological and that men and women just came that way." It was proven long ago and shouldn't I get "caught up?" He cited three studies he'd heard about on the radio. It was a case of just enough knowledge to be dangerous, because the experts in this area agree we don't know any of these things.

What heartens me is that whenever I give my public talks I don't find the backlash you read about in the papers. A few people will say, "Why do you want girls to go in science? What's wrong with the way things are?" But by and large I find audiences want the best for their kids and are appalled when I point out the effect of telling daughters that they're getting good grades because they work hard rather than because they're smart. Parents and teachers want to do what's right for girls but don't know what that is today. They feel overwhelmed and need to be told concrete, simple ways to do things differently.

Math Ability and Gender

Smith: *What do you think about the Benbow-Stanley study of math ability and gender?*

Eccles: Benbow and Stanley have never proven any cause for their findings. Their studies simply report test differences exist and then speculate about what might be the cause. I follow their work because they make sure I do. I get letters from them containing their latest articles, but they've never documented any possible cause for the differences or ruled out any explanations.

Smith: *Is the difference shrinking?*

Eccles: It depends on which tests you look at. In some you'll see a decline. In others you won't. The last five years of data suggest it's shrinking but the last twenty show essentially a curve going up and down. We could be on either an up or a down slide today. The study that needs to be done is the effect of anxiety on test scores. We know girls report higher levels of test anxiety. We don't know if they actually have higher levels because it's macho for boys to report no test anxiety and no one has ever accurately measured their actual levels during a test. What we do know is that standardized tests are specifically designed to elevate anxiety. We also know there's a curvilinear relationship between anxiety and test performance. Up to a point anxiety improves it but too much anxiety begins to be debilitating. If girls start out more anxious, an anxiety-provoking situation may throw them over the top so that their performance is impaired. In contrast, the majority of boys may be put in just the right situation to produce maximum performance.

One way to test that would be to take away time limits. Tell testees they can have as long as they want to complete the test. Now it turns out that people won't take a whole lot more time because they can only sit for so long until they're burned out. One small-scale study in North Carolina looked at this, using both spatial skill and math tests, and found that without time limits the sex difference disappeared. So if I were ETS [Educational Testing Service] I'd take away the time limits in one whole state and see what happens. The sex difference may well reflect nothing more than test anxiety or test-taking style. But some say the ability to work under pressure is exactly what the tests should be measuring.

Leduc: *Why do you think more boys are considered mathematically gifted?*

Eccles: First of all, the difference isn't as great as you'd expect if it were all biologically determined, and boys are more likely to be nominated by their teachers as gifted whatever their math test scores. But it is true that when the children labeled as gifted by teachers were given the advanced math test there was a much higher proportion of males among the very top scorers.

Leduc: *Could the difference still be due to test anxiety?*

Eccles: It could be, or we could be talking about a very unique population at that point. That's why I'm not willing to rule out biological differences. In the top one percent there are some ten times more males than females. We've also known for a long time that the variability in males' test scores is greater, which means just as there are ten times more males scoring at the very top there are ten times more males at the very bottom as well. We know also that males are more biologically vulnerable from conception on. So perhaps something happens *in utero* to stretch out the male ability distribution at the extremes, which has nothing to do with the majority of us who are neither geniuses nor mentally retarded. Maybe those males at the extremes have been bombarded with hormones and as a result have any number of things wrong with them—are myopic, asthmatic—but also happen to be math geniuses.

Sex and Science in the Classroom

Leduc: *You've also studied differences in the ways the genders are treated in the classroom. What have you found?*

Eccles: What's interesting is that when we go into classes to observe a random sample of teachers we don't find much of a relationship between what teachers do in class to what students report about their own math ability or interest in math. We also ask the kids if a teacher treats boys and girls differently and then try to relate their responses to their attitudes towards science or math, but again we don't find a big difference in their attitudes. Yet the anecdotal stories we collect suggest teachers do make a lot of difference. If I present this study to a group of high school kids or a group of college women, immediately out will come horror stories. So I've been trying to reconcile these stories with the fact that when I watch a class none of these effects jump out.

Leduc: *Are the teachers sensitized to your being there so they're on their best behavior?*

Eccles: No, I don't think so. We sit in classrooms for a long time, for weeks. That's why I don't think it's just that teachers are on good behavior. We're around too long for them to sustain it. A particularly bad or good teacher can have a unique impact but our data would suggest we can't yet predict who that teacher is going to be. It's the chemistry between a particular kid and a particular teacher that's important. And we get stories about those processes all of the time. A few teachers will put off everybody and some will turn on all the kids, but they're rare. An individual student over her school years goes through many teachers whereas when I go in and study a particular seventh grade teacher there may only be two students in the whole class who've been strongly affected by that person. But that's not a big enough effect to show up in my data. Yet if I talk to those seventh graders all of them can come up with some other teacher who's had a unique impact on them.

So the anecdotes say teachers can have a tremendous impact but it is hard to pin down the causes. We can name behaviors that generally produce positive or negative effects on female students but those aren't the things students talk about. Their stories reveal something fairly special for each student. For example, a teacher might pick one student out in a year and say, "Come be my research assistant." Or a teacher might reply to a student, "That's the stupidest thing I've ever heard." That teacher may have been in a bad mood that day and has never said anything like that to anybody before. But this student is just devastated and may be turned off math forever.

So we didn't find a lot of differential treatment of boys and girls. But we did find a sub-set of classrooms where the brightest girls, on the basis of a teacher's nomination, were being treated very differently by that teacher than were the brightest boys and these seemingly sexist teachers were about equally likely to be males or females. It was almost as if they were consciously avoiding interacting with those girls. The brightest boys were getting lots of attention, praise and opportunity to participate whereas the brightest girls were given little chance to participate and the least praise. And it was not all the girls who were treated this way, only the brightest.

I received two kinds of explanations from these teachers for their behavior. The women gave me a maternalistic reason. They said, "I have to worry about the brightest boys dropping out of school because boys are at risk for getting into trouble in adolescence. So I have to pay special attention to them to make sure that they stay in the sciences whereas we all know girls are good students, get good grades and don't drop out of high school." Of course they said this before all the publicity about women not going on in the sciences.

In contrast, the male teachers said, "I can act buddy, buddy with the bright boys but if I touch or get friendly with the girls I'm going to get called before the school board for sexual harassment." And from a psychodynamic perspective there is a kernel of truth in that belief because those males are likely to be more sexually attracted to the brightest girls. They obviously weren't worried about problems with the girls they thought less smart.

Smith: *I wonder if that occurs even more at higher levels?*

Eccles: I think the older the female the more likely those dynamics are operating, and I don't know how policy can intervene there. Especially, now that everyone's hysterical about this, with males thinking, "Wait a minute. If I have any doubts in my mind that I might engage in this behavior the best way to protect myself is to have nothing to do with women."

Smith: *And it's women who ultimately will pay.*

Eccles: So we need more studies that look at those dynamics in the classroom. The other possibility is that teachers are reacting to different interaction styles. Bright boys may be insisting upon attention but bright girls aren't. So that sub-set of boys insists on dominating the classroom and the girls won't compete. The bright girls may think, "I don't need special help. I can get by just fine." They sit there quietly and don't draw attention to themselves.

Smith: *Does that mean we need more sex-segregated classes?*

Eccles: I don't know if that's the solution. Many teachers can get all students to participate, can keep a class room orderly and not let sexual dynamics get involved, though they're in the minority. So I'd rather push for better treatment for everybody rather than single sex opportunities. I prefer integration of the sexes. But you have to worry about critical mass, not have a token situation with only one female. If that happens it would be better for her in an all-female class.

My data, however, shows parents have a bigger impact than teachers. Kids are with the same parents their whole lives. They're with different teachers every year so it takes a unique, salient experience with a teacher to have an effect.

Smith: *Have you encountered the belief among parents that if a girl is talented she shouldn't have to work hard. So she feels bad if she does have to study.*

Eccles: I think that attitude exists. Mathematics is hard for anyone but this culture believes math ability in particular is biological. It's useful to counteract that attitude anyway possible. I have a wonderful anecdote from China to illustrate my point. I spent two months there teaching. One evening a woman in engineering told me that in China men still can get into university with lower test scores. The reason is that teachers think test scores are more diagnostic for females. If a male gets a low score it could just be because he was sowing his wild oats and once he's finished he'll do fine. Whereas all females work hard so if they score low it must really be due to lack of ability.

This young woman then said, "You know, I decided I was going to do a little test of that belief. I had all my fellow students keep track of how much time they spent on homework and I tabulated the results. Sure enough it was true. On the average men spend less time on their courses but men also were making the worst grades. If I looked at the people making the best grades, men and women worked the same amount. To get the top grade it took exactly the same amount of effort from both males and females."

Smith: *Does that apply here too?*

Eccles: No one has done the study, but I suspect it does. People have this idea men don't work as hard then infer they're still successful because they're smarter. Well, as in China, it's probably the case that men don't work as hard but that's why they don't earn the grades. But somehow people always forget the second piece of the relationship, men's lower grades.

Key Changes

Leduc: *What needs to be done to facilitate women's participation in math and science?*

Eccles: The key is not to take a simple-minded approach. We've tried many intervention schemes and they've taught us that simple solutions don't work. We have to attack the problem from a variety of perspectives and over a long period of time.

Smith: *So suddenly announcing the availability of ten thousand scholarships for women in engineering is not a solution?*

Eccles: Not when they get there and are treated badly. They'll just leave. Another key point is that it's never too late for intervention. We can involve women in math and science at many points in life, five-year-olds to forty-year-olds.

Leduc: *Any advice for individual women?*

Eccles: I'd say it may be difficult but it's never too late to change your mind about a science career. And tell girls it's OK to brag, to say to themselves they're talented.

References and Recommended Readings

Atkinson, J.W. & Raynor, J.O. (Eds.) (1974). *Motivation and achievement.* Washington DC: Winston.

Benbow, C.P. & Stanley, J.C. (1980). Sex differences in mathematical ability: Fact or artifact? *Science, 210,* 1262-1264.

Eccles, L.S., Adler, T.F., & Meece, J.L. (1984). Sex differences in achievement: A test of alternate theories. *Journal of Personality and Social Psychology, 46,* 26-43.

Eccles, J.S., Jacobs, J.E., & Harold, R.D. (1990). Gender-role stereotypes, expectancy effects, and parents' role in the socialization of gender differences in self perceptions and skill acquisition. *Journal of Social Issues, 46,* 182-201.

Eccles, J.S. & Jacobs. J.E. (1987). Gender roles and women's achievement-related decisons. *Psychology of Women Quarterly, 11,* 135-172.

Eccles (Parson), J. et al (1983). Expectancies, values and academic behaviors. In J. Spence (Ed.), *Achievement and Achievement Motivation* (pp.75-146). San Francisco: W.H. Freeman and Co.

Eccles (Parson), J. (1984). Sex differences in mathematics participation. In M.L. Maehr and M.W. Steinkamp (Eds.), *Women in Science, Vol. 2, Advances in Motivation and Achievement* (pp.93-137). Greenwich, CT: JAI Press, Inc.

Eccles (Parsons), J., Midgley, C., & Adler, T.F. (1984). Grade-related changes in the school environment: Effects on achievement motivation. In J.H. Nicholls (Ed.), *The Development of Achievement Motivation* (pp.285-331). Greenwich CT: JAI Press, Inc.

Eccles, J. (1985). Why doesn't Jane run? Sex differences in educational and occupational patterns. In F.D. Horowitz & M. O'Brien (Eds.), *The gifted and talented: A developmental perspective* (pp.251-295). Washington, D.C.: APA Press.

Eccles, J. (1987). Gender-roles and achievement. In J. Reinisch, L.A. Rosenblum, & S.A. Sanders, (Eds.) *Masculinity and Femininity, Vol. 1* (pp.240-280). New York: Oxford University Press.

Eccles, J.S. (1987). Adolescence: Gateway to gender-role transcendence. In D.B. Carter (Ed.), *Current conceptions of sex roles and sex typing* (pp.225-241). New York: Praeger Press.

Eccles, J.S., & Midgley, C.M. (1989). Stage/environment fit: Developmentally appropriate classrooms for early adolescents. In R.E. Ames and C. Ames (eds.), *Research on motivation in education: Goals and Cognitions, Vol. 3,* (pp.139-186). NY: Academic Press.

Eccles, J.S. (1989). Bringing young women to math and science. In M. Crawford and M. Gentry (Eds.), *Gender and Thought: Psychological perspectives* (pp.36-57). New York: Springer-Verlag.

Lewin, K. (1951). *Field theory in social science.* New York: Harper & Row.

Sells, L.(1973). High school mathematics as the critical filter in the job market. In: Developing opportunities for minorities in graduate education. *Proceedings of the Conference on Minority Graduate Education, University of California, Berkeley.*

Sells, L.W. (1982). Leverage for equal opportunity through mastery of mathematics. In S.M. Humphreys (Ed.), *Women and minorities in science* (pp.7-26). Boulder CO: Westview Press.

Significant Events in the Life of Jacquelynne Eccles

Attending University of California at Berkeley during Free Speech Movement.

Remaining at the University of California, Berkeley over my parents protest when they went to Germany and wanted me to go with them. This fundamentally changed my life and my relationship with my parents.

Marrying my (ex)husband. He is responsible for my going to graduate school.

Serving in the Peace Corps in Ghana as a secondary school teacher.

Having and raising my two children. This also fundamentally shaped my life trajectory.

Forming a close group of colleagues as graduate students at UCLA.

Teaching at Smith College.

Moving to the University of Michigan and becoming exposed to large scale survey research. This changed the direction of my research orientation.

Getting a grant from the Federal Government to study girls and math.

Moving to the University of Colorado. This put me in touch with Richard Jessor and with the MacArthur Research Network on Successful Adolescence in High Risk Environments. This has again fundamentally changed my research agenda for the next several years.

7

Surviving Nontraditional Careers: Health, Safety and Educational Issues

An Interview with Lesley Lee, M.T.M. (Masters in the Teaching of Mathematics), Consultant on women and mathematics, Montreal; and Karen Messing, Ph.D., Professor of Biology, University of Quebec, Montreal.

René de Carufel

Meeting in Karen Messing's kitchen in Montreal over her bountiful Sunday brunch, the authors learned from the two researchers just how difficult it is for women to survive nontraditional jobs, particularly those in the sciences, trades and technology. Women must first run the gauntlet of training designed with males in mind, often involving math skills that female socialization still discourages them from gaining. Then to stay on the job, they must cope with not only harassment but also health and safety issues. That's because employers in general have failed to adapt jobs to women's particular strengths and needs. However, by co-operating with each other and convincing employers of the very real fact that workplace changes will benefit women as well as men, women are carving out their own successes in these fields.

Lesley Lee learned all about these special stresses on women in nontraditional fields during her education, a B.Sc. (Honors) in math and physics, then a Masters in Teaching Math. She taught math for a year at Acadia University in Nova Scotia and twelve years in a French language CEGEP, Quebec's unique system of post secondary/pre-university schools. Observing the trials of her female students she grew concerned with the way they were required to act and think like men in math and science classes. This experience among others prompted her to take on a strong leadership role in resolving the women's issues fermenting in the Quebec Confederation of National Trade Unions (CSN—Confederation des Syndicats Nationaux). She went on to win election as president of the women's committee for the union central.

She left teaching in 1983 to work as a consultant on gender and math education, and as a union counsellor on women's issues. She also teaches courses to promote the math and financial capabilities of the general public and conducts an ongoing research program to understand how men and women learn algebra.

Karen Messing started out to be a social worker despite her superior mathematics skills but, inspired by the words of Betty Friedan, decided to prove she wasn't afraid of science and ended up with a Ph.D. in Genetics. She was drawn gradually away from classical cellular genetics by her participation in union-requested research and courses on women's occupational health and safety issues. Fortunately she can do this as part of her university workload through her university's agreement with CSN and other unions that allows the unions to request help from professors to conduct research and courses for the unions. Through her involvement with the union she met Lesley and they've since co-operated to identify ways to improve working conditions for women in the trades and technology. Messing also co-chairs a feminist research group to help achieve these goals.

In the following interview the two scientists discuss their own nontraditional backgrounds and what they've learned from their studies: the challenges women face in nontraditional jobs and how women are discouraged from getting the math and science background needed to qualify for many of these positions. They also suggest some ways to begin removing these barriers.

A Tale of Two Scientists

Smith: *Lesley, let's start with your background. First of all, when did you decide you were interested in a nontraditional career?*

Lee: Well, I don't know. My main interest in high school was gymnastics and dancing. Math and physics were just courses that came easily. I never would have gone to university because of my family and cultural background. My mother was a secretary who thought before marriage a girl should be a secretary, or a nurse if she were really ambitious. My father was an Anglican priest and thought women just got married. But he thought that airline stewardess was a pretty neat job too. He certainly saw no reason for wasting money on university for a girl. What helped me was we moved to Kingston, Ontario in my high school junior year and I was put in the Honors class. We were marched over to Queen's University across the street and enrolled and made to fill out forms for bursaries. It was just expected everybody in my class was going to university.

Smith: *So you didn't have to make choices.*

Lee: No. I remember my three buddies and I made an appointment with the registrar who said how nice it was we were coming to Queen's and then asked for our majors. My best girlfriend had said math and economics so I couldn't say that. I don't know why but I said "math and physics." And then I immediately got all the attention. This was wonderful but I had no idea I would find myself in first year physics with about 400 guys and two girls.

Leduc: *Was your friend in class with you too?*

Lee: No, she was in economics. At least we could share math. But I was completely cut off from other girls. I got into this male culture and was cut off socially too because it was a very heavy Honors program. We had labs all day Saturday and spent Sunday writing up the labs. Also I had only a $400 bursary so I had to work on top of that heavy load. I got permission to live off residence, which ordinarily was compulsory for first-year girls, because the Dean of Women was my former English teacher and understood my financial situation. So I missed out on contact with other girls again. I didn't have that beautiful social experience at university you hear about. I was just with the guys in my class, so the indoctrination process was that much stronger. I adopted male values and looked down on anybody going into teaching or all those female things. But it was the result of being cut off. It took me 20 years to even revisit the university. It was a dark period of my life.

Leduc: *Why didn't you quit?*

Lee: It never occurred to me. What would I have done? I was alone in this town, my family had moved away and I was cut off.

Leduc: *So you had support to get into a nontraditional environment, but the support wasn't there once you were in.*

Lee: Well, there was some support in the fact that I didn't fail courses. I got good marks. But I had no image of a career path. In my second to last year, I was hired by Atomic Energy for a summer job, but at that point I decided to marry a guy in English literature. I actually took a year off after my third year because he'd finished. Anyway I didn't take the Atomic Energy job, and now I think what a lucky break. I never would've left to see anything different. Those were the days where companies used to sign us up in first year. As a girl I was ignored but I had a male name and that eventually got me into a few interviews. So my experience trying to get student jobs was very different from that of the guys. They were in companies from year one. When I tried to get a job in my field they'd say, "Can you type?" I couldn't, and didn't want to learn because I knew I'd spend my life typing. So I waitressed and made a lot more money.

Smith: *Getting married and dating, did that reconfirm your femininity? Or compensate a little bit for some of your indoctrination?*

Lee: No, I had boyfriends all along but I don't think that confirmed anything. A lot thought I wasn't a real female because of my field. They found it threatening. I never dated guys in my classes of course. They were sort of socially backward although we had a lot of "buddy" fun. Yet by dating guys outside my field, I encountered all this stuff about "I suppose your father wanted a boy."

Leduc: *Were you treated as a boy when you were young?*

Lee: Well I was considered a tomboy, probably because I had an ultra-feminine sister and I had to find a different role. I had two sisters, an older and a younger. My brother was the youngest. I liked marbles a lot and was very competitive. But certainly I didn't look like a boy or move or talk like a boy. But I had an investment in being tough. It still comes up every now and then. I say, "Look out 'cause I'm really tough." It's a way of protecting myself I guess. I was very sensitive and so had to put on a facade.

Smith: *What were your parents' expectations of you?*

Lee: There were no expectations and they really didn't understand why I wanted to go to university. I have one anecdote that tells it all. A girlfriend a year younger was living in Ottawa. My father met her on the street and she told him she was graduating that year. My father thought that was funny because she was supposed to be a year behind me and I wasn't graduating. So my father thought maybe I'd flunked. She explained that "Lesley's in an Honors program and it's four years." Well he phoned and was irate. "You mean you could have finished in three years and you took four? What's going on?" His idea at that stage was I was going to get married anyway. So why put in all this time?

I think later they were proud when they finally cottoned to the fact I had a university diploma and could probably get an interesting job. But my mother has been so disappointed that I haven't translated that into a "big bucks" career. Every time I got pregnant she was so depressed. She invested in me all the career dreams she never fulfilled and said, "Why, if you've had this chance to get an independent life and financial security, have you opted to be dragged down by five kids and work in popular groups and unions?"

Leduc: *You earned satisfaction instead.*

Lee: Yes, but they don't understand the satisfaction of the union work. In my family, unions and the Mafia were about on par.

Smith: *Have you thought, Lesley, of doing a Ph.D. in math?*

Lee: Not in math and science anymore, although the older I get the more I'm interested. I'm one of these suckers for books on physics and the latest developments. I love it but it's just personal satisfaction right now. What would I do with a Ph.D.? I don't want to be a research mathematician or physicist.

My concerns now are students and trying to find out through interviewing them what they believe and feel about math. And also intervention in these areas. Like Karen I'm very interested in what we call popularization. For instance when we had fiscal reform here I gave sessions to help people understand what was behind reform. I was also the co-ordinator of the Quebec Coalition against the Goods and Services Tax, the GST. By breaking down all the myths people have about math and science we're putting finance in the hands of the people so they can make decisions and stop placing "experts" on a pedestal.

Smith: *Let's turn now to you, Karen. How did you choose a nontraditional career?*

Messing: I wanted to be a social worker and got a bachelor's degree in social relations. Then I had a baby just after graduation. As I was nursing him I read the *Feminine Mystique* by Betty Friedan and saw a line that said women don't like science or are scared of it. That aroused my ire and so I took some science courses. I ended up getting a Ph.D. in genetics. At the time genetics was a very romantic new area and I was quite fascinated.

Smith: *What other factors besides Betty Friedan influenced you to switch?*

Messing: Well, I'd always been a superstar in math. I took super advanced math because of my grades but nobody ever thought this would be relevant to my future.

Leduc: *You didn't need it, you're a woman.*

Messing: Right. When I took the SATs my scores on the English aptitude and math aptitude were only six points apart, both very, very high. My guidance counsellor told me that mathematical reasoning was really a form of linguistics and my score was artificially high because I was good in English. So it never crossed my mind that I'd do any kind of science. The other thing that happened was that I skipped my final year in high school through a series of events. I'd had a chance to take only one science course, physics, in which I was the top student again. Now they sent a number of people off to summer camp in physics that year but nobody ever thought I should go and I didn't think of asking either. And so when I skipped, I may have said to people that "this means I won't be able to take any other sciences" but nobody felt this was important.

Lee: But this is still true today if a girl has high math marks, even in university. I was at the top of my class. Even in physics I was among the top three in a class of about 400. But my performance was dismissed as hard work. Girls just don't have it to be top mathematicians and they get good marks only because the boys haven't started working yet. When the boys get serious they're going to take off like jet planes, so I spent my whole academic career looking behind me, waiting for the boys to take off. I finished a B.Sc. honors in math and physics and I was still waiting. I was never told "you're good, you should continue." My high marks were almost an embarrassment and that's still going on today.

Now I wasn't about to tell my teachers the reason I was in math was because I was damn lazy and I liked courses such as math where I didn't have homework because I figured it out so quickly. And I didn't have to memorize things like in history which I dumped as soon as I could. But, you know, a girl who does exceedingly well either gets categorized as a boy and socially not feminine or likable by other girls or she gets categorized as not really bright—just hard-working. And of course some day this will show and she's going to top out, game over. You can imagine the panic a girl feels the first time she hits a rotten professor in a new subject and can't make head or tail of it.

There is a downside for boys too. I have sons who are always telling me they're also hard done by sexism. Associating success with math and science and technology, and with masculinity of course, means if they seem to be working hard but not doing well, their masculinity is up for question. Whereas girls who don't do well in math get high points on femininity. So girls like to talk about how badly they're doing.

Messing: Yes I spent a lot of time bragging about how badly I did.

Lee: It must have been hard!

Messing: It was difficult, because you had to figure out how to explain you were doing badly when superficially people wanted you to do well.

Leduc: *Did your parents encourage you to go in any particular direction or was there any ambiguity in their support?*

Messing: No. My background is different from Lesley's in that way. Probably because I don't have brothers. My parents put a lot of emphasis on academic success. They were very proud of me although they were a little upset when I had two kids and got married. But they are always waiting for me to find the perfect man to take care of me for the rest of my life and every time they realize I haven't found him, they get very upset. So their comfort level is more tied up with my sexuality than with my professional career. But they nevertheless supported me through graduate school.

Smith: *You had already had your kids when you went to school?*

Messing: By the time I finished my Ph.D. I had two. It took me a while to do my Ph.D., because my Bachelor's was not in science. And I worked for a while. The whole procedure took about 12 years of which maybe half of that time my parents were supporting me. I was 32 when I finished. And in terms of professional support there's been no faltering, although my father is a little disappointed I'm not a professor at Harvard.

Women's Health and Safety in Nontraditional Jobs

Smith: *Karen, how did you become specifically interested in the health and safety barriers women face in nontraditional jobs?*

Messing: I was initially involved in Applied Genetics and classic lab work with human cells to determine the effect of environmental toxic agents. Eventually I became more and more involved in a relationship our university has with the Quebec labor unions in which the unions can ask the University to provide expertise in certain areas. So the unions requested information on what happens to people exposed to radiation and toxic chemicals in different workplace situations. Because I was a woman, the questions I got were mainly about conditions dangerous for pregnant women. I did a whole bunch of educational sessions for the unions about the potential causes of genetic damage in pregnancy.

But the more I tried to answer those questions the more I realized that the narrow disciplinary perspectives and concepts I'd learned weren't appropriate to answer the real questions asked by women workers. I was like the new woman in the machine shop who was given tools too large for her hands. So about five years ago I decided to determine the real concerns for women's occupational health and the appropriate methods to deal with them. And I got some retraining on sabbatical to look at women's work.

Smith: *What tools or methodologies did you learn?*

Messing: We haven't developed them all yet. One example that I can give you is with pregnant women. The usual approach to limiting damage in pregnancy is to look at a thousand women who are exposed to, for example, toluene in the workplace. Of those you might get a hundred pregnancies and then you see out of those pregnancies how many are miscarriages or babies born with malformation and so forth. Then you repeat the study with benzene, again with carbon disulphide and still again with another chemical. The problem is that in the real workplaces you never have just one agent or one condition. So this testing of agents one by one is a totally inappropriate way to go about things. And also there are a hundred thousand chemicals used so that by the time you test all of them there are going to be a lot of malformed children out there if any of the chemicals are dangerous.

Leduc: *So the old model was more for simple injury, a discrete event, and not designed for a long-term interactive process.*

Messing: Right. It's also a matter of whose point of view you're taking. If you're talking about pregnancy, the employer's view is, "I'm not going to clean up my workplace until somebody shows me each of these chemicals is dangerous. By the way, I'm also making up rules so that the only correct study is also impossible to do." That's one approach. The other is that of the pregnant worker herself who doesn't want to be there if it's dangerous and who wants you to show her how to make it safe. Right now the rules are not set up for the pregnant woman. They're to protect the employers.

Lee: In fact, we've talked a lot about developing a mathematical model to deal with a hundred thousand chemicals interacting at the same time and yet provide a simple coefficient that says, "This is a dangerous workplace." But the mathematics for dealing with complex work situations isn't well developed or of interest to many people. Who's going to put money into it?

Other Obstacles to Nontraditional Jobs

Messing: Another interest of our research group, a feminist occupational health and safety research team, is the obstacles to the integration of women into nontraditional jobs. We look at mostly ergonomic obstacles, but you can't treat ergonomics [the study of work activity] factors by themselves. You have to look at social obstacles too, so we're developing an integrated approach to the problem.

An example of an obstacle we found was in a study of a 1500-person machine shop. One woman had more backache than her colleagues. The reason was her partner was 190.5 cm (six feet, three inches) and she was 168 cm (five feet, six inches) and the work surface wasn't adjusted to take into account both of them so she was constantly having to work in a very uncomfortable position. Also her tools and gloves were not the right size for her. She spent a lot of time turning wrenches, and when she would do this her gloves would slip. She had less physical strength than her partner and that disadvantage was compounded by the inappropriate equipment and tools. So the two factors together gave her many more physical problems than her male colleagues and we were involved in making recommendations to improve her situation.

Smith: *This woman had already chosen shopwork as a career?*

Messing: She actually had a Bachelor's in biology. There weren't many jobs for women with that degree unfortunately. So that's what she decided to do. She was a member of a Montreal women's group which was at that time struggling to get her employer to hire women. The shop was a large government employer and the group succeeded in getting about ten women in but seven promptly left. The working conditions had a lot to do with the attrition. In general, I have very pessimistic things to say about affirmative action programs in industry.

Smith: *Did she stay with it?*

Messing: She'd been laid off last time I heard.

Smith: *Certainly what you've just brought up is interesting. The physical situation to which someone first gets exposed may back them right off from a job.*

Lee: Yes, and legislation's not enough to fix it.

Messing: No. We're doing a series of interviews with workers in a large municipality where both a union and a women's group worked to get women into blue collar jobs. But these interviews are very, very sad because of the harsh treatment these women receive from both their foremen and colleagues. They don't dare ask for any equipment adaptations. We hear stories of women having to drive a truck to roll down fresh pavement but the truck's seat is set so far back an average-sized woman can hardly reach the pedals.

When I asked a young woman, "Have you said anything about this?" she replied, "We have enough to do just to keep the job. We can't make changes." She talked about one of the more dangerous jobs, using a clipper to clip hedges or prune trees. The handles are too big and far apart, and she can't hold it right. She said in this desperate way, "Well, I can't do anything about it." Because at the same time that she's dealing with this inappropriate equipment she's dealing with guys for whom the only woman they ever talk to is either their wife or some go-go dancer in a cabaret. So if she's not either of those, who is she? In fact, studies of blue collar jobs have shown that 92 percent of men work in areas which are, or almost are, men only. They're not used to dealing with women as co-workers. So there's the attitude problem combined with equipment and work station adjustment problems. Which means that the workplace a woman finds herself in is designed for the male body, the male mind, the male cultural approach and the male schedule.

One of the problems with a male schedule, in the particular city we're studying, is the idea that manpower should be totally flexible. That means when you get up in the morning you don't know what part of the city you're going to be working in or your assignment or even if you'll be working overtime. Arranging day care is just a total nightmare. And the result for women is tremendous difficulty and an enormous attrition rate.

Also, because the women have been hired more recently and are more junior in status, none have regular jobs. They're on call. They don't know on a given day whether they're working or not. So you can legislate equal access but you'd have to legislate a whole bunch of other things at the same time. And this applies to many aspects of the problem of integrating women into nontraditional jobs.

Even my nontraditional job as a biology professor has been designed with a male career pattern in mind. For example, whereas my male colleagues in high school all took Electronics 101, I took sewing, or more accurately, flunked sewing. So I don't know very much about machines. This is a real pain in the neck for me whenever I work in the lab. Also the style of behavior in departmental meetings is not mine. Once we had about five women in the department, we legislated that one of the chairperson's roles in a meeting was to ensure that the women could speak. Because otherwise we'd say three words and get interrupted.

When women express the real problems they have in their jobs, it's interpreted as hysteria.

So the same issues come up in both blue collar jobs and my academic job. The work is defined according to the male model and a woman has a tremendous amount of trouble either fitting herself to it or getting it to change so that she can be comfortable.

Now I work in occupational health and the concept of what is occupational health and what is a risk to it were also designed with male career patterns in mind. When you think of an occupational health problem, you think of an accident, somebody falling off a building.That's not the kind of thing that happens commonly to women workers. It's going nuts from work as a telephone operator being monitored by a computer. But when women express the real problems they have in their jobs, it's interpreted as hysteria.

Lee: I'd like to pick up on that because it ties in with the research I did. I worked for several years on women's issues as a union counsellor and one of the fun sessions I had to do was a whole weekend with construction workers in which they were obliged to talk about women's issues and the integration of women into construction. I was scared stiff to give this session and I wondered how we were going to keep them a whole weekend in Montreal. Of course at lunch time they all went to the tavern and this other woman and I, who were giving the course, were left on our own. I thought they'd never come back. But they did come back and they did stay. What we discovered by the end of the two days was that they'd been as scared of us as we'd been of them. We were the unknown and they thought "what are these raging feminists going to say to us?" They were quite surprised that we turned out to be fairly nice.

Smith: *No horns.*

Lee: They actually ended up being one of the most appreciative, polite groups I've ever addressed in the union. It started off just beautifully.

We also did a counselling session for the first women bus drivers in the city. There were all sorts of obstacles and fights to win these jobs. There used to be constraints like five years of experience driving heavy trucks, that sort of thing.

Messing: And there were seat design problems.

Lee: There's that side of it too. It was the same old problem of no adaptation. First of all they gave them men's uniforms. You know Quebec women are among the most proud in the world about their appearance. And here were these gals who'd wear make-up and earrings when they drove the bus and then they're put into men's uniforms too big for them. Looking just ridiculous. And faced with direct harassment for being there. So for them to complain about the fine points of "I can't walk in these shoes and wear this uniform because they're too big" really turns out to be a luxury.

Messing: But they're not a luxury. They're the issues that make women drop out eventually, yet can't work on changing them because they have to do so much running to stay in the same place. And some of the guys' objections are quite legitimate in a sense. For example, they integrated women into hospital kitchens, but the problem is these great big heavy objects. Nobody should be lifting them but the guys have been doing it for years. Sometimes they really don't like it, but it's part of their job. Maybe they've even been trying to get the loads lightened. But right now somebody's got to lift them and when the woman who's just come in and gets the same salary they do says, "I can't lift this, will you help me?" some guys will say, "Yes of course." Other guys will say, "You're getting the same money as I am, lift it yourself." In a way you can understand the anger because in order for there to be real integration of women, a lot of things should've been changed, but weren't before the women even started.

Leduc: *And those changes would have made the job more humane for both genders.*

Lee: That's what we have to convince union people of, make them see that change is in their own self-interest. Because in most factory jobs, for instance, where the new person traditionally gets the heavy duty job, that requirement makes the job also unavailable to a lot of men. And the older they get, the less available it is or it wrecks their backs and so on. It takes a while for that message to get through.

Messing: It's not like the guys would object to having a load lightened or to having that particular entry level job made easier. It's just that for them it's not so essential that it warrants a major struggle. But for the women it's critical. And it's a real fight because the management has not been overwhelmed with happiness by having to hire these women in the first place. They're doing it because of public pressure or the laws. If, on top of that, we ask them to change the jobs themselves, I mean, come on, what is this? And we're having a bad recession in Quebec now too.

The other thing is that boys get reinforced for being lazy, you know. It's sort of masculine and this why we have such terrible problems with our male students. And if you send men into a workplace and ask them to do something like count and weigh the number of packages handled by a cashier you can't rely on them to do it right because this is drudgery, which is more appropriate for women.

Lee: Right. Men are saving themselves for the creative stuff!

Messing: In a poultry slaughterhouse we studied, both the employer and the workers described the greatest obstacle to getting women into men's jobs: "If you ask the women to do the men's job of cutting up and hanging the big, heavy turkeys, probably they'll be able to do it." And the women said, "Yeah, actually we could do it right now, but then we'd have to rotate all the jobs and the guys couldn't do ours right, separating out the viscera, and we'd have to do it over again because it's a picky little job." And so the major obstacle to rotating jobs was that neither the employer nor the women wanted the guys to do the women's job because they'd screw up.

Leduc: *And that's all part of the socialized beliefs that there are appropriate types of work for males and females.*

Lee: Yes. Karen and I have talked lately about how deep-rooted that is. We've been reading Valerie Walkerdine's work and Cynthia Cockburn's, "Machinery of Dominance" about the experience of women in technology. It involves this whole genderization process that is so much a part of our fears and fantasies and our image of what we want to be. For example, every object existing has a gender in some sense. We've even genderized thinking. So looking at women's problems as only an equal opportunities issue, as we did in the past, doesn't work. We thought we'd just have to put up a few posters and get a law passed. We realize now when you probe people's actual images of what life is all about, these fictions about femininity/masculinity are fact in their minds.

I think Jane Gaskall in British Columbia did a wonderful revolutionary study revealing people's images of the reality of their lives. In it she talked to some adolescent girls about why they didn't want to go into nontraditional areas. They looked at their dads, who didn't share anything in the home. They looked at the young men around them who weren't going to share anything in the home. They knew they wanted to marry and have kids, so they wanted to get out of high school fast, get a job, make a bit of money and have some fun before they hit family life. And when you look at it from their point of view, with their hopes and dreams and their clear look at the reality around them, it doesn't make much sense to tell those working-class girls, "Actually, you should go into more long-term nontraditional jobs and risk being considered non-female and have to deal with all the myths and worries about combining a family and career. And of course men are going to change, and you're going to have this wonderful existence of shared tasks." When they hear all this, it's not surprising they think you're science fiction.

Messing: We've just been doing similar interviews in a cookie factory about why the women don't take the men's jobs and they're also absolutely right. If I were in their position I wouldn't either. Number one, with the women's jobs they get to all sit together and chat and that's the only thing that makes the day on an assembly line livable for them. They don't want to have to carry heavy, big sacks around. They know they'll hurt their backs, because they see the guys all hurting theirs. They also see some of the machines as dangerous and don't have appropriate training in fixing machines. Anyway they don't think their husbands would like them spending all day running around with a bunch of guys. And they're quite right. So, why the heck should they want to change?

Smith: *Are the women who do take on a nontraditional job initially interested in the specific jobs they're training for?*

Messing: Oh yes, very much so. To get into a nontraditional job, a woman has to go through so many obstacles that of course she's very interested in that job. You've got a highly selected population there. If they aren't passionately devoted to their jobs, extremely courageous, extremely insensitive to being hassled and pinched and having photographs of nude women all over their workplace, we don't see them anymore. They're back in the cookie factory on the assembly line.

I had a student in my women's occupational health course last night say she was going to give her talk for my course on how women can't enter nontraditional jobs. She said, "I tried. I decided I wanted to be a carpenter. I'd been a nurse. So I went into carpentry class and first the teacher says, 'OK, you guys can understand this because it's just like taking the transmission apart in your car.' And I thought, 'Wait a minute, I never took the transmission apart in my car.' But the guy goes on and on that way. So you have to go through all your courses like that, and then you go into the workshop and get a backache. Your arm hurts and you cut yourself, and all the guys have had all this experience with machines and they know how they work and you don't. And then nobody wants to hire you, and I said, 'To heck with that, I'm going back to being a nurse.'"

Smith: *But do you find women justify dropping out of these jobs with the excuse "I'm no longer interested in this?"*

Messing: No. Certainly, this young woman was still interested, but she was just very sad and defeated. Women tend to say, "I'm still interested in doing it but I'm not good enough." In fact one of the things that makes me very angry is all this talk about women being equal now and having full access to nontraditional jobs, and the only problem with getting them in is they're not interested enough. But in fact what happens is that women, because of all these messages, go in saying, "OK, I can do it, if I'm any good at all." Then they can't do it and they think there must be something wrong with them. We go through it even as university professors because of the ferocious opposition and evil treatment we receive. We women constantly feel, "I'm not good enough, I shouldn't be here. They were right when they said this wasn't the place for me."

Smith: *They take it personally, not realizing a lot of people encounter these obstacles.*

Messing: Yes. Also they don't have the tools to deal with the issues because there aren't many tools for coping. What do we tell them to do? The only reason I'm where I am today is because I have a sort of twin. I co-direct my research group with another person. She was the first woman professor in our biology department and I was the second. When I came in, she says that she was able to relax. It took us about a year to realize that we'd better stop being rivals for being the sexiest woman biology professor and then we mounted this research group together. We phone each other about once a day and tell each other, "It's OK, you're not stupid." We have a lot of rivalry as well and have to deal with it. But if we hadn't had each other there's no question in either of our minds that we wouldn't have been able to do anything at all.

Leduc: *You're bringing up the importance of co-operation.*

Lee: We've concluded this in every area. The importance of a network, a support group. When I went to a Women in Trades and Technology, WITT, Congress a few years ago, there were more than 100 women there all talking to each other. I never saw a group of people who liked their work so much. And yet what they were living through in their unions and work places was just a horror story. The obstacles—all the problems of training in mixed gender technical schools where you're a minority. It went on and on and yet, they didn't bring pictures of their kids, they brought pictures of themselves at work. They were really an enthusiastic group and very proud and dignified.

Leduc: *What made them different was that they'd found the support?*

Lee: A support network. There are groups all over now. They're trying to set up a newspaper, a bank of names of contacts and a trade school for women in Canada. None of them come out of any feminist tradition that I can see, and probably wouldn't even call themselves feminists, but they've realized that survival involves sticking together. It seems the absolute key. Women can really increase their strength by getting together and forming groups to pressure for change.

Encouraging Women to Stay
in Nontraditional Jobs

Leduc: *What would help encourage more women to enter nontraditional jobs?*

Messing: Well I don't want to encourage women to enter unless there are mechanisms to let them stay. That's what I would emphasize right now—putting programs into effect to enable them to stay on the job. What allows women to stay right now is being stubborn and extremely resistant. I don't think a woman should need these superhuman qualities to succeed so the emphasis shouldn't be on the individual and her strategies.

In the educational system I'd emphasize teaching boys to share domestic tasks. Young women don't think it's going to be a problem because until the birth of the first child tasks are shared. It's statistically true. We've done studies of it, other people too. But all the additional work brought by the first child is done by the woman. This starts a cycle. The woman does more of the work, therefore she can put less emphasis on her career, therefore she earns less, therefore it doesn't make any sense when one of them has to take time off to be with the kid for it to be the guy. Therefore the woman does it and her career is slowed down even more. Therefore the guy takes on more and more importance, and finally it doesn't make much sense for the woman to put any energy into career development.

Another thing is to legally oblige employers to examine all aspects of jobs, organizational and ergonomic, which may pose problems for women. Employers need to understand that reproductive damage is not confined to women. The States are excluding women from jobs with lead exposure and it's so ridiculous because lead is about the best established male reproductive poison. There's no reason women should specifically be excluded and every reason to reduce exposure for **all** people of reproductive age. So there's a need to educate people that male bodies also can be hurt by the work place. But as far as encouraging women to enter nontraditional jobs, I wouldn't put any more pressure there right now. The focus should be on reducing obstacles.

The Male Model in Education and Training

Lee: The idea of the male model in the work place is in the schools too, in technology particularly, even in mathematics to some extent. I did a huge review of the literature for the Quebec Ministry of Education on why girls don't go into nontraditional courses. The major factor was course content. It's set up for boys. If you take a calculus course, what are the classic problems you study? Missiles and bombs falling, maximizing profit, minimizing losses. Instead of environmental problems, such as population growth or nutrition and growth rates.

Leduc: *So you learn to use math to beat down the competition.*

Lee: Yes, in fact one of my colleagues during the Iraqi war had his class figuring out the trajectory of those Scud missiles.This male model has been built into the very content of the courses and even dictates acceptable behavior there. That's what I brought out in the article I wrote about my experience in physics. I had to learn to behave like a male to be acceptable. I dressed in blazer jackets so my breasts didn't show. And I opted for invisibility. In one situation my professor piled chairs on top of desks and climbed up to repair equipment on the ceiling. I let out a gasp of concern. He gave me this glacial look and I was so embarrassed.

Leduc: *You weren't supposed to express concern or caring. Math teaches the male role model, be competitive instead of co-operative, be stoic or invisible.*

Lee: Yes. And talk like a male. We're both reading this book by Deborah Tannen about how males talk and to my dismay I'm on the male side. I thought how did I get this way? Objectifying everything and leaving myself out entirely. I don't talk about what I'm feeling, at least it took me a long time. And when I wrote that article about my experience in physics I just about died saying even "me" or "I."

Smith: *That's certainly the training you get in science.*

Lee: Yes. When a woman goes into training for a traditionally male job, she really wants to succeed. But ten years later, when you can get some perspective, you realize the damage you've done to yourself as a woman in order to make it. Then you have to go through this whole effort of trying to put the "I" back into your work. Of course that's not considered scientific. So I have a problem continually when I'm writing a research report. Every now and then some feeling slips in and it's immediately crossed out by whoever is reading it.

I'm reviewing a book right now called "Gender and Mathematics" from an international conference on women and math education, involving women reporting various research they've done or programs they've tried. There isn't a single "I" or "me" in it. It could've been all men writing it. And these are the people supposedly the most concerned about women's math education.

Messing: Sometimes it's only appropriate to be angry or have emotion. I experienced this problem when I was studying in France on sabbatical. At one point I was analyzing the work activity of train cleaners, particularly toilet cleaners. Because in France, as in Quebec hospitals, the only people who clean toilets are women. The men have jobs called "heavy work" which involve driving little tractors around. The women do jobs called "light work" which involve sticking their heads inside of a toilet bowl and scrubbing.

When I started this study we'd measure the number of times the woman changes her posture, and how long it takes her to clean a toilet—63.4 seconds to clean one train bathroom in which time she changes her posture 28 times. And they wonder why the women all have backaches. So I wrote a report in the "proper" style and couldn't stand it. I had to write down also how I reacted to the fact that the women all had backaches. Two out of seven were sent by their doctors for cures for being too fat. This enraged me because of course it had nothing to do with their weight. It was because of their terrible jobs. But since doctors never ask you what you do for a living—especially if you're a woman—they couldn't understand these backaches.

So I started this article about how the women should be changing their jobs. I found it very difficult. My anthropologist friend had to sort of hold my hand. She kept saying, "You're not telling why you're so upset. You're supposed to be writing your feminist feelings, your solidarity with these women." But it had been trained out of me.

Leduc: *But we learn that emotion is not appropriate way back in grade school, or whenever biology begins, when we have to dissect frogs. Don't feel for the animal.*

Messing: Yes, it's not relevant. And it doesn't matter how many animals we destroy because there's always this endless supply. So to feel for the animal, to feel for the whole process is not appropriate for anyone in science. That could be one of the first instances where women say, "This doesn't fit me because it's not according to what I see as relevant for the world."

But if you're going to be a woman scientist or technologist you must learn the whole process of desensitizing yourself. Which is going to be very useful to you later on when you encounter the normal vicious criticism of your papers or projects. When you live in academia, for example, one of the most difficult experiences is getting back these anonymous comments on your grant proposal or paper where nobody ever bothers to try to be nice or tactful.

You have to desensitize yourself to your students also, because the whole scientific endeavor is done by cheap labor of young scientists staying in the lab 24 hours a day. In order to supervise somebody under those circumstances you really have to be heartless. I've had students come to me to do graduate degrees because they say, "Well, I wanted to go with Dr. Big Important Name but he told me that it didn't matter if I had a kid"—in fact this young woman had two kids and was pregnant—"he still wanted to see me there on Saturdays and Sundays." He wasn't there on Saturdays and Sundays, but she had to be. Well she couldn't do it. But if you persist, you have to constantly squash all these little voices that say to you, "This is not right, this is not the way I want to live." If you succeed, you can become a scientist. But it means you turn into another person.

Leduc: *It's almost a form of brainwashing.*

Messing: It's like being squished into a mold. A Procrustean bed is the best example. If your foot doesn't quite fit in, just chop it off! What Lesley was describing before, I think, is trying to grow some of those parts back. And it's difficult. But neither of us are responding to those pressures anymore. We've gotten into areas which are not quite classical in our field but which permit us to profit from our female perspectives. That way we can stay alive and still contribute something.

Now if I were going to be a microbiologist producing Nobel quality work I would still have to submit to that. But at one point I decided I couldn't stand one more meeting of the Environmental Mutagenesis Society because the only women who survive are either young students—and I don't want to speculate on what the relationships between them and the men at these meetings are because I lived through it myself—or one or two much older women who look or act like nuns. There are no successful women scientists at my level to talk to because they've been winnowed out.

Influences on Women's Interest in Nontraditional, Math-related Fields

Smith: *What educational conditions have you found that influence women's interest in nontraditional or math-related fields?*

Lee: One barrier is the teacher using male models for learning, speaking, reasoning. There is also direct discouragement in the form of actual harassment by peers or even teachers when they think girls shouldn't be in these classes.

I did a little survey once for fun, because I heard the guys say, "Everything's changed now, there are more women in math than there used to be." So in the course of a departmental meeting I said, "Would you all write down your present courses and the percentage of each class that's female." Then I got the official list and counted. They'd grossly overestimated the number of females in their class. It was as though like having a few females present means they're taking over. But my female colleagues didn't have this problem—they seemed to realize what percentages of their classes were female.

There's been a lot of research on the benefits of female math and science teachers and it seems that female teachers are slightly better for girls. Some evidence suggests female teachers don't play the game of mystifying math and science quite as much, are more concerned about getting the information across and don't try to impress or put a distance between themselves and the students. But it's still not 100 percent sure that female teachers are best. From my own training I know they've also become men in a sense.

One thing research does suggest is that educating girls together in nontraditional fields is an advantage. I think it has a lot to do with bonding. If you're only surrounded by girls you're not "weird" because you're all doing this and so you build up strengths that would be lost in an all male class. I found it interesting that women with experience in mixed trade schools came very early to the conclusion that we need trade schools for women only. And I found out when I was doing union training that if you get women together they can develop and share strategies—when the guys do this or that what are we going to do? If you put one male in that class, the whole discourse changes. Women are not going to confide and the man is going to do half the talking.

Looking through the literature it's clear the orientation and administration of schools are also part of the problem. I found evidence for how the school spirit, its values and images all become very important in the messages girls receive. A rich school, heavily into discipline and uniforms, which many parents want these days, tends to have traditional graduates. The girls come out in girls' jobs and the boys come out in boys' jobs. Whereas an alternative school tends to produce girls who'll go into nontraditional fields. Support for finding one's own way, is important.

In addition, I pulled out of the literature the idea that students are influenced by factors like the classroom itself. In a conference workshop I had a group of women collectively draw a picture of a typical math class. We had everything on a grid—the chairs, bare walls, the atmosphere, the design, the air conditioning, the lighting and so on. Then we designed how it would look if women considered how they would feel in it—bringing in texture, plants; changing the lighting, windows and color and providing seating for groups and comfortable chairs where people could talk. It was a total redesign to make women feel at home. It said, "We want the classroom to be a place where we share and grow together."

Leduc: *Are text books being rewritten to reflect the real life problems that women encounter?*

Lee: No, not really. But I think the fundamental barrier in the workplace and the classroom is this whole absurd gendering process where we talk differently to male and female babies from day one. We all participate in it. Why are certain objects female or male? Why has the computer become a male object although it's equipped with a typing board? How is it all of a sudden that girls stay away and boys zap onto it? Really, although we do have different hip joints than men and a lower centre of gravity—there are physical differences—there's no reason for all this gendering.

Leduc: *The difference is not that significant.*

Lee: No! And we're more alike than different. So gendering is a social creation. The bottom line is the power given to the masculine. That's what's valued, what's normal, and the problem we're facing with women in nontraditional occupations is women are not "normal." We've created everything in the image of men, and women don't measure up.

Smith: *We're square pegs going into round holes. But are you optimistic at all about the ability of adults to change their attitudes towards math and technology-related activities?*

Lee: I am optimistic, but in the long term. I don't believe I can do a three-hour session with some women and change them. But I believe I can put questions in their minds that are going to gnaw at them for the next twenty years, and might eventually take hold, or I can put them in situations where they start thinking for themselves. One of the things I teach is an introspective exercise where they say to themselves, "I am a solver of mathematics. Now how do I go about it? What happens when I block?" So they're doing the problems but also standing back and observing the process. And that's been a real breakthrough for a lot of people.

Valerie Walkerdine did some research on pre-school girls and their attitudes towards math. She's a psychologist and former teacher from England who's into the business of the most revolutionary thing we can do right now—telling other stories. We hear repeatedly the same tales, "Girls don't do well in math and if they do it's because they work hard. We've got statistics to prove it." We've millions of stories like that and she's saying we've got to introduce stories where gendering didn't work. Tell what we really feel about math and science and our anger and all of the experiences that go against these repeated myths.

Needed Research Directions

Smith: *Are there particular areas regarding women in nontraditional jobs that need more research?*

Messing: In terms of job engineering there's an awful lot we don't know. Everybody thinks women's bodies are sort of little men's bodies, but they aren't. They're proportioned differently, work differently but we don't know how differently. Studies haven't been conducted, for example, on the specifics of male/female physical strength differences and what jobs and activities are comfortable for men and women.

One local company had a big affirmative action program with applications from 300 women for the first 12 positions for women in a nontraditional job. They put all these women through a 100 different tests they never gave the guys. And they finally chose 12 and put them through physical and technical training programs to help them do the jobs just like the guys, even though the women were much more highly selected. The approach was that women should learn how to work like the men even though the equipment wasn't designed for women. There was no idea that the women should be allowed to adapt their jobs to match their own personal needs or strengths.

But this lack of adaptation is very dangerous in a physical job. For example, when climbing hydro poles, you can fall off the damn things if the angle of attack of the heel of your boot to one of those nails you have to stand on isn't just right. But a woman's hip is not the same as a man's and therefore the heel of their boot doesn't create the right angle if their boots are just little men's boots and not re-engineered. This kind of thing has not been researched at all.

Smith: *If one fell they could say, "See? It proves women are clumsy."*

Messing: Well that's what they did. They showed women had more accidents than men. Until they changed the boots. So there's a whole big research area that we're involved in.

Lee: I've just been looking at some research on gender and math. What astounds me is it's so small-scaled and underfinanced, all these individual studies of "my class of 26 students." Or you have a large-scale study on some other topic, carried out usually by men, and they tack on a women's question and it ends up either showing nothing or showing what they want to show. One international study on math reported girls inferior to boys in what they call higher level thinking, which was defined as higher level in the first place because the boys do better on those questions.

Leduc: *So of course it **must** be a higher level of thinking.*

Lee: Yes. They come up with these results but they've asked a question that has little to do with reality. For example, one study concluded "British Columbia has only three percent female math teachers but almost no sex differences in math ability. Therefore we can reject the hypothesis that girls don't do well because they don't have female role models." But we don't know how this study got the statistics. We don't know if only three percent of the students who wrote that study's math test in that year happened to have a female math teacher in their last year of high school. There's a lot of this kind of sloppy, slippery large-scale study. Or else you have somebody on their own time and initiative, without any particular training or funding, trying to make sense of what's happening to girls or trying some little project to change things. And they end up saying, "But of course none of this is conclusive because it's a small sample with no comparison group."

Smith: *So maybe we won't even publish it.*

Lee: Or we'll just share it with a few friends. So there's got to be money available to actually go out and ask people why they don't go into math and science, but these studies are not a priority.

Leduc: *Do you think it will become a priority because of the labor market? In the next ten years, we hear, there'll be a shortage of the typical white male worker.*

Lee: Perhaps, but if that's the basis, they'll try to turn those new workers into white males. That's what the courses are about. If that happens, which is the way private enterprise would go, we've got problems. We've already had open door policies and affirmative action programs and as Cockburn says, "There's no line-up at the open door of opportunity."

[Karen Messing has had to leave the interview at this point]

Advice for Training Counsellors

Lee: So who is responsible for change? Certainly counsellors are important. But school counsellors are trained using male models based on male studies. They know nothing about the full range of female work possibilities. They've had no training in women's work issues, so the experience of women students who've gone to counsellors has usually been poor. In fact, we had one girl in our CEGEP years ago who wanted to work in an outdoor job. She liked physical activity and went to the counsellor about this. He had no idea of any outdoor jobs for women and on top of that he thought she should see the psychologist.

Leduc: *What do counsellors reading this interview need to do?*

Lee: Well, half of the content in training counsellors must be on women. They can't just have two hours. They've got to know all the job possibilities and obstacles for women. The tests they are using are sexually biased, and they're not aware of it. There's got to be a whole attitude revision.

Towards the end of high school my stepdaughter went to a counsellor who actually said, "For a good-looking girl like you, what you do is not very important. You're going to get married in a few years." I never forgave him. I thought "that jerk is getting paid fifty thousand a year, he should be hung." So the problem is the initial training of counsellors and the need to update them because many were trained years ago. They've still got their hang-ups and old attitudes towards women. But if you just tell them, "There are no more problems, girls can go into everything," you're also not doing any good.

Final Words of Wisdom

Smith: *Any advice you have for our readers about how much math or science they should take if they're interested in nontraditional jobs?*

Lee: Well, I gave this advice to my kids: "Take as much math as you can stand. Take college level courses if you can possibly stomach it, because the day will come, though maybe not right away, when you may decide you want a particular job and very often the barrier is your mathematical training. If you have to go back to Grade 9 to catch up, you're not going to do it. And the barriers more and more to retraining women are lack of math and science."

Smith: *So keep your options open.*

Lee: Yes, if you put an X over everything involving math, there isn't much left these days. So I say to reentry women, "Look, there are really neat night courses in the high schools. You can work at your own pace. Keep taking them." And then some of them get to like it. That's what I've seen with so many girls who in high school thought, "There's no way in my life I'm ever going to need math or science." But the statistics show that ten years after graduation they'll likely find themselves single parents who have to get out and earn the daily bread. And if they're in some field like hairdressing or waitressing where there's no advancement, then math becomes important to get out.

Smith: *So math is the key to a good economic future.*

Lee: It's used as a filter for a lot of subjects. People look at the math marks to decide if you're intelligent or submissive enough, or will work hard enough. So it's important in that sense. And you need enough math to do social criticism and not opt out when you're on the board of a shelter for battered women and somebody sets out the budget. If nine out of ten women around the table go all fuzzy at seeing numbers we have problems. If you're going to be a responsible citizen today you need math.

References and Recommended Readings

Cockburn, C. (1986). *Machinery of dominance: Women, men and technical know-how.* London: Pluto Press.

Friedan, B. (1963). *The feminine mystique.* New York: Dell.

Gaskell, J. (1983). *Career differentiation in the high school: The perspective of working class females.* Communique at AERA, Montreal.

Lee, L. (1987). Des epouvantails qui effraient les femmes: Les mythes en science. *L'ecole des femmes,* Goulet & Kurtzman (Eds.), UQAM (pp. 87-100).

Lee, L. (1986). The scientific exclusion of women from science. *Resources for feminist research / Documentation sur la recherche feministe, 15*(3), 21-22.

Lee, L. (1986). Demystification des mathematiques aupres des femmes adultes. *Femmes et mathematique,* L. Lafortune (Ed.), Les editions du remue - menage (pp.137-151).

Messing, K., Dumais, L., Romito, P. (1992). Prostitutes and chimney sweeps both have problems: Toward full integration of the two sexes in the study of occupational health. *Social Science and Medicine, 36* (in press).

Messing, K., Haëntjens, C., Doniol-Shaw, G. (in press). Sugar and spice: Health effects of the sexual division of labour among train cleaners. *International Journal of Health Services.*

Tannen, D. (1990). *You just don't understand: Women and men in conversation.* New York: Morrow

Walkerdine, V. (1990). *Schoolgirl fictions.* London/New York: Verso.

Vézina, N., Tierney, D. et Messing, K. (1992). When is light work heavy? Components of the physical workload of sewing machine operators which may lead to problems. *Applied Ergonomics, 23,* 268-276.

Significant Events in the Life of Lesley Lee

1963	Birth of my first child and only daughter
1966	Birth of my first son
1967	Moved to Quebec with a new and vibrant culture and language
1968	Birth of my second son
1973	Birth of my third son
1977	Became involved with the women's movement that was building in my union both at the local, regional and finally at the provincial level where I was a member of the national women's committee of the Confederation of National Trade Unions and its president for four years.
1978	Returned to studies to do a master's degree and subsequent involvement in research which is still ongoing
1979	Birth of my fourth son
1980	United Nations women's conference in Copenhagen
1983	Quit my teaching job to freelance which freed me up to do a lot of exciting contracts in research, training & development in the area of women/science/technology. At that time I was elected to the board of a local shelter for battered women and children where I remained involved for a number of years and learned a lot about the victims of violence and the difficulties of keeping such initiatives financially afloat.
1989	Moved to Montreal and the start of an exciting new life as a single parent city dweller
1992	Returned to school for Ph.D. in math education

Significant Events in the Life of Karen Messing

1943	Born
1963	B.A. cum laude Social Relations, Harvard University
1963-70	Two sons born
1970	M.Sc. Genetics, McGill University
1973	First publication: *Molecular Genetics, 122:323-330.*
1975	Ph.D. Genetics, McGill University
1976	Professeure, Départment de sciences biologiques, Université du Québec à Montréal
1990	Directrice, Centre pour l'étude des interactions entre la santé et l'environment, Université du Québec à Montréal
1990	Muriel Duckworth Prize, for research most contributing to the advancement of women, Canadian Research Institute for the Advancement of Women, given to the team headed by K. Messing and Donna Mergler
1990-91	Training in ergonomics, Conservatoire National des arts et Métiers, France
1991	"Woman of the Year" (Environment) Salon de la femme du Québec 1991
1991	Key publications —*Occupational Health and Safety Concerns of Canadian Women: A Review/Santé et Securité des travailleures: document de base.* Labour Canada. 110 pp —Putting our heads together: Academic and feminist perspectives on women's occupational health. *National Women's Studies Association Journal 3*: 357-63 —co-author: Analysis of work activity of a job in a machine shop held by ten men and one woman. *International Journal of Industrial Ergonomics, 7*: 163-174
1992	Closing speaker, International Round Table on Gender and Occupational Health, Health and Welfare Canada

Section Four

Where do We Go in the Future?

After all the labour force has changed, the demands have changed, industry's changed, more doors are open to women now than there used to be. And that means that a woman can consider relatively easily a number of options that would have been very difficult before when I embarked on our career development research.

—Donald Super, Ph.D., personal communication, American Assoc. for Counseling and Development AGM, Reno, Nevada, April 24, 1991.

Despite the optimism of Donald Super's comments above, the women we interviewed for this book have been only guardedly optimistic about how level the playing field is for women in the workforce. They've summarized the systematic, socialized and often frustratingly subtle kinds of obstacles women face everyday as they strive for equality in the workforce. And over and over, they've brought up the need for change—in educational access, in parent/teacher/employer attitudes towards young women's career aspirations and in workplace practices.

But there is hope and there is progress. The last three interviews discuss several types of institutionalized change that could help women overcome these obstacles and genuinely expand their career options.

In Chapter 8, Linda Gottfredson of the University of Delaware presents a brief overview of the strengths and limitations of the Diversity Programs set up by many organizations in the United States. Acting beyond the scope of affirmative action, these programs are concerned with hiring and promoting more women and minorities and also with making organizational environments more welcoming to these individuals.

Then Sharon Kahn of the University of British Columbia presents the intricacies of a Canadian approach to recruiting and keeping more women and minorities in nontraditional careers. These programs require employers to follow the guidelines set out by the Employment Equity Act and the Federal Contractors Program. Employers must review and revise their own recruiting, hiring and promotion practices to eliminate discrimination against women and minorities; in other words, re-evaluate, as Kahn summarizes, "the day-to-day routine we follow unthinkingly that may disadvantage others." These programs also involve establishing hiring goals for traditionally disadvantaged groups.

But while employers struggle with the above long-term strategies to make better use of the real capabilities of *all* workers, the busy career counsellor needs ways to help women clients here and now. In the last interview Sharon Crozier of the University of Calgary addresses this pressing issue—how to improve career counselling for women. She covers such specific topics as choosing a feminist counsellor, using interest inventories more wisely and avoiding bias in counselling. She also suggests more structural changes, such as improving counsellor training and extending career education in the schools.

8

*Finding (Economic) Strength through
Diversity: A Workplace Adaptation to
Welcome Women*

*An interview with Linda S. Gottfredson, Ph.D., Professor of Educational
Studies, University of Delaware, Newark.*

Increasing competition in the global market may be one of the best hopes women have to see the workplace become more receptive to their career aspirations. That's because one way of increasing worker productivity, which employers must do more and more to survive, is to help all employees, women included, develop their skills to the fullest extent possible. To that end many organizations are setting up "diversity programs" to make their environment more "welcoming" to women and special groups. But, like anything else still developing, these programs contain potential pitfalls for those trying to reap their benefits.

For this interview Linda Gottfredson agreed to sketch her views of the strengths and weaknesses of diversity programs (see Recommended Readings for her more in-depth discussions of the issue) as well as some related implications for women's career choices and counselling. The discussion took place one quiet November afternoon over the dining room table of her suburban home, disturbed only by the occasional muffled honks of migrating Canada Geese and the raucous calls of blue jays foraging in the lush backyard. She also spoke about her life-long concerns for social justice in the workplace and her own youthful struggles to follow her career interests and aspirations. Two Raggedy-Ann dolls guarding the entryway to her home hinted at the multiple roles which she, like many women professionals, must juggle; Gottfredson is a now single mother of twin daughters as well as an internationally respected social scientist.

As a social scientist, Gottfredson is probably best known among vocational psychologists, and anyone else interested in women's career aspirations, for her 1981 monograph, *Circumscription and Compromise: A Developmental Theory of Occupational Aspirations*. Her paper observed that all social groups share the same images of occupations, based on job sextype, prestige level and field of work. It described the progressive and usually permanent narrowing of the occupational preferences of both boys and girls from preschool through the college years according to developing self-concepts of gender, social class and intelligence. Her theory then laid out the strategies later used by young people to reach a compromise between these preferences and job availability in the real world. People first sacrifice their preferred field of work while hanging onto hopes for prestige as long as possible. But what threatens people most, she concluded, is the idea of taking on a job of the "wrong" sextype.

Gottfredson's wide-ranging interests regarding the job market's structure and the principles of social justice have also led her to study many other areas of interest to people grappling with the factors circumscribing women's career interests and aspirations, such as fairness in employment testing, the beneficial use of vocational interest inventories and job composition by race, sex, prestige levels and type of work.

However, because of limited space, the following discussion touches only on (1) how Gottfredson's own youthful aspirations were potentially circumscribed (2) how diversity programs could expand the options for women and minorities, as long as political agendas are held at bay, and (3) how women can adapt to these changes to increase their competitiveness for the career of their choice.

Science and Social Equality: One Woman's Quest

Smith: *How did you become interested in career choice, the whole field, not just women's careers?*

Gottfredson: The general issue tying all my work together is a fundamental interest in social inequality. What's its nature, how does it come about and how does society handle it? It's an interest that goes back to college. But my interest in science goes back even further. I always loved math and science. When I could imagine myself having a job it was as a scientific technician of some sort.

Smith: *Any particular science that caught your fancy or just science in general?*

Gottfredson: Primarily biology. I also took chemistry. We didn't have much else in my high school in the way of science. But I was always a kid who was interested in nature, perhaps because we lived in the country and I loved wandering around and collecting insects and stuff like that. And I worked a whole summer in an NSF Science program for high school juniors. I loved that too, working in a laboratory where they studied things like botulism. Then I worked two years in various capacities in labs to support myself while I was going to college so the love of science was always there. I was interested in how nature works first then later interested in how society and people work.

The interest in social inequality really developed in my college years. It was the sixties civil rights era and I was concerned about racial inequality. I volunteered to tutor in a ghetto school and worked for the Oakland Human Relations Commission as a work-study student. I enjoyed that a lot, investigating among other things, the disproportionate representation of the races in journalism. At that time human relations commissions were new, so I also developed a brochure for them to advertise their services. After college I went into the Peace Corps. So I've had a long standing interest in why people end up different and to what extent these differences are fair or not.

Smith: *Did you grow up with other brothers or sisters?*

Gottfredson: Yes, three. I'm the oldest and I have a sister two years younger, a brother four years younger, who is multiply handicapped, and then a brother eleven years younger.

Smith: *Did having a handicapped brother influenced you in any way, for example, made you doubt if justice and fairness existed for all?*

Gottfredson: I don't think so. All I know is that when I was at Berkeley for two years, 1967 to 1969, during the anti-war demonstrations, I disapproved of a lot that was going on. I thought so much public demonstration often was a form of self-aggrandizement for the individuals involved and didn't alter much. I had a sense that what the human relations commission was doing, or sought to do, was the real hard, important work for society, for example, influencing how people found housing or jobs. Arguing with the police on Telegraph Avenue was not the way to help. People I talked to in the demonstrations sometimes had no patience for changing conditions. Their actions seemed like a lot of posturing.

Smith: *How did your experience in the Peace Corps affect your sense of social justice? You must have seen a lot of poverty and inequity.*

Gottfredson: Malaysia, my assignment, was hardly as poor as other countries in the region, like Indonesia, where I also traveled. What I became aware of, acutely, were the complexities of ethnic relations because Malaysia is a tri-ethnic society, Malay, Chinese and Indian. That's where a lot of my concern first developed about how easily well-intentioned strategies can impede social justice.

I wasn't sure I was going to be able to go there at first because of racial tensions and riots. About that time the government, which is Malay, made Malay the official language, instituted quotas for Malays in various jobs, and ended the use of English in professional schools, which disadvantaged both the Chinese and Indians in the name of some sort of racial quota system. I had a sense of the problems that could cause. But as Peace Corps volunteers we weren't allowed to speak about political issues.

So I've always been one who cared about fairness and justice and doing the right thing. Being competent and being fair to people was a very important part of my self-concept.

Smith: *Did your earlier socialization also contribute to these values?*

Gottfredson: They took on a special importance to me possibly by substituting for other things in terms of social regard, peers. I grew up in the countryside with one neighbor and I am naturally shy, so I think all of that conspired to make me feel alone, a wallflower. It was difficult to make friends and to feel easy with people. But I gained a lot of self respect from doing well in school and being a good person.

Smith: *Was there anybody in your life who had a big influence on your values?*

Gottfredson: There are various professional people who I owe a lot to because they've influenced me in one way or another. John Holland is one. I also like being interdisciplinary so I've gotten a lot out of people who've introduced me to other fields. Robert Gordon, my second husband, taught me about the role of intelligence and was also very supportive of my career and shared responsibility for taking care of our family. I deeply appreciated that. More recently, Jan Blits has exposed me to political philosophy.

As for scientific role models they've been people who've combined competence with high intellectual integrity. For example, one person I've always held in high regard is Arthur Jensen, one of the best researchers I know for getting at the heart of a question, and then pursuing it despite arguments that, well, one shouldn't do those sorts of things. There are many others I could also name. So I've always admired people from my earliest years who did what they thought was right although it cost them. As a child those types of people were my heroes in the movies.

Smith: *I'd like now to return to your own process of career choice. For example, how did you decide to go on to graduate school? When did the big change in your career aspirations happen?*

Gottfredson: In high school it's often hard to gauge realistically what you can and can't do. It was only after the Peace Corps, when someone asked me, "Why not try graduate school?" that I thought of going on. Then after working at The Johns Hopkins University as a research assistant for a year, doing some of the same intellectual work as the professors, I realised, yes, I can do this too. Before that I'd never considered myself as material for anything higher than lab technician. I applied for graduate school and went straight through, switching from psychology to sociology for my graduate work. But I ended up in psychology anyway, with the work that I did.

Smith: *You did make fairly traditional academic choices, psychology and sociology. Do you think that was a result of socialized limitations as your theory suggests?*

Gottfredson: Well, I think it's consistent with my *real* interests. I love what I do and think various people have found my work useful. I can't imagine a better job than one where you're paid to pursue your intellectual interests.

But what restricted me before graduate school, I guess, was a view of myself as a mother. I married at 19. I'd never really questioned the traditional view of what a mother does and doesn't do. I remember the reasons I wrote in my undergraduate application for wanting more schooling. And it's embarrassing. They all had to do with being a better wife and mother if I could work.

Really, two things affected my aspirations. One, I didn't know my capabilities. I knew that I'd done very well in high school and college but I thought professionals must exist in a different intellectual realm. Two, I considered whether the time and training demands were consistent with being a mother. I can remember as an undergraduate thinking, "What work can I do that will be consistent with having a family?" All I could come up with was doing something out of my home, which wasn't very satisfactory. I really didn't consider beyond that. I always imagined I would be the traditional fifties wife and mother.

Smith: *It sounds like you were circumscribed by your traditional gender role very early. Whatever you were going to do had to be consistent with that primary role of wife and mother.*

Gottfredson: I didn't question it and no one else around me did either. I don't remember anyone saying explicitly that I should follow that role, but there also wasn't any discussion of doing anything outside of it, which might have made a difference. And second, I felt that compared to males in my family and my first husband's family, people just took me less seriously. It really didn't matter much what I planned for a career. Actually, when I think about it, I really did have a lot of reinforcement for staying home with the kids and not working if you don't have to. And at that time, lacking experience, I just accepted it.

You see, one thing that's always made a difference with me, and I suppose it does with a lot of people, is actually having the chance to be in situations where you learn for yourself what you can and can't do. You start questioning all the things you've taken for granted. So I advise people to seek out experiences that are a little out of the ordinary. The Peace Corps was that for me. It taught me a lot about myself and my own society by being away from it. I gained a strong sense of how much socialization and environment affects a person.

Origins of a Theory: Circumscription and Compromise

Smith: *Gradually you overcame the social forces that threatened to compromise and circumscribe your own career. Then how did your specific interests develop?*

Gottfredson: Let me explain my overall interests first. They combine concepts in sociology and psychology and one of sociology's key concerns is social stratification, why are there inequalities and what's fair and unfair. As a graduate student

I was steeped in this area, probably because that was the kind of topic I was already drawn to. I became associated with John Holland, who was in the Sociology Department at that time, and interested in his theory of interests and job choice. I saw how it could apply to certain sociological questions. Sociologists were missing some of the key distinctions in jobs at that time but generally weren't interested in psychological constructs.

At the time my interest in vocational psychology was the sociological issue of who gets ahead, and the systematic characteristics of jobs. For example, how many jobs are there of different Holland types? Then I looked further—how many jobs are there of both different levels and types and what kind of skills and education do they actually require? All these studies provided some insight into the jobs themselves and the distribution of people across them, such as, where are women or blacks most highly represented or underrepresented?

Smith: *At this point you weren't specifically interested in women, just special groups in general?*

Gottfredson: Right. Various kinds of inequalities or differences and their outcomes—social class differences, sex differences, racial differences. I also began studying handicapped people, dyslexics, where they end up. I was really interested in the whole job system and why different groups seemed to want to go in somewhat different directions. Sociologists in particular seem to assume that everybody wants the same kinds of high level jobs. It's just a matter of what's blocking their way, who gets bumped out of the competition. But sociologists know that equally bright people from different social classes don't have the same social aspirations. That suggests it's not just workplace barriers that turn their eyes away from those jobs. Yet that inconsistency wasn't being addressed by sociology. In contrast, psychology paid a lot of attention to why people have different career aspirations, though mostly for different interest fields, not different levels.

So even before I developed my theory I'd done a lot of work trying to combine the sociological and psychological perspectives on career attainment. Sociologists are interested in women to some extent but more in social class in general, whereas vocational psychology was to a large extent a study of women versus men. So I combined those two as the circumscription and compromise theory.

Smith: *What was exciting about it for you personally?*

Gottfredson: Well, it was the culmination of a lot of research and thinking. I see some of those ideas in my earlier papers, some pieces of the puzzle that were starting to take shape. I can remember sitting in my basement with piles of papers and it was so exciting because things started to come together. What I loved finding were anomalies that suddenly I could explain. Why do people want different jobs when they all say they admire the same things? Then after working on it, things would just start falling in place.

Smith: *But to synthesize all those ideas and come up with something new, you have to have it all in your head, you have to be focused.*

Gottfredson: It's not just having it all in your head but being able to pursue it in such a concentrated way without big distractions. Not having to put it aside for a couple of weeks for something else.

Adapting the Workplace to the Needs of Women and Minorities

Smith: *I'd like to turn now to some of your more recent research on changes in the corporate work environment that could realistically broaden women's career options. You've written that our society must work harder to help all workers, women included, develop themselves to their fullest not only in the interest of social justice and equal opportunity but also to maintain global competitiveness. One way is the widespread adoption of diversity programs, part of the "managing diversity" movement described in your chapter in "Working through diversity: Human resources initiatives." Could you explain first of all what we mean by diversity programs?*

Gottfredson: Well, it depends on which one you pick. There are a lot of different kinds. It's become a very popular term in the last four years or so. Some are much better than others, some perhaps even harmful. But I think there are two concerns underlying the notion of such diversity programs in either industry or public employment. One is really an extension of affirmative action and includes not only the old employee entry and hiring issues but also promotion. Organizations have discovered in the last decade that they may be able to hire increasingly larger proportions of women and minorities but this has not been matched by their rates of promotion. So now we hear discussions of the glass ceiling and how to develop ways for women and minorities to break through.

The other aspect, which goes beyond affirmative action, is a concern with changing the climate of an organization, so that it actively welcomes and values women and minorities. These programs focus on efforts to lower the turnover rates among women and minorities by fostering both career development and satisfaction with the organization.

Smith: *Can we define climate?*

Gottfredson: There are many kinds of organizational climates. One definition is to call it the type and tenor of interpersonal relations in an organization and the rigidity of the behavior required of employees. I think the kind of climate we've been interested in with regard to diversity programs is one that at least tolerates, and better yet, accepts and values people from different social, racial or gender backgrounds. We're concerned about the acceptance of different political, intellectual and business views. So it's making the work environment more pleasant, accepting, supportive. But you have to be aware that other groups may perceive that special treatment is being given to some people but not them. The targeting of women or minorities for assistance has frequently led white males to feel neglected. Some white men may say, "Well, I've never found the environment supportive of me either." Then you are sowing the seeds of discontent. The change has to have wider beneficial effects, not be selective.

Career and family are two absorbing things and in this society we have not worked out how to do both in a way that works well for everybody.

Sometimes you get conflicting ideas about how to integrate diverse kinds of people into the workplace. Some involve making certain kinds of jobs more available or feasible for certain groups, let's say, women. Looking back on my own work life, as a woman and mother, I think some of the considerations that disproportionately affect women include organizational support for child or elder care, and flextime or job sharing. These ideas really involve restructuring both the jobs and their benefits. For example, there have been "Mommy tracks" suggested in industry, which allow part-time or flextime work for mothers, without jeopardizing their seniority rights or future promotions. Likewise, in some universities, people with child care responsibilities, male or female, can take time out, so to speak, from the clock ticking towards tenure decisions. Those kinds of changes greatly ease the burdens which women face in pursuing certain careers, especially those with longer or less flexible hours. I think those steps should help women in pursuing those jobs, if they have the interest.

For now it's very difficult to combine career and family. I can testify to that, with nine-year old twins, raising them more or less alone. But it was hard before I was alone too. Career and family are two very absorbing things and in this society we have not worked out how to do both in a way that works well for everybody. Employers need to adjust to the family needs of their workers, both male and female. A lot of men would like to spend more time with their children but it's not been the manly thing to do.

Smith: *They might have felt they'd be penalized too. It's competitive out there.*

Gottfredson: I've heard men criticized for spending too much time with their family because that's not how you get ahead. So more family orientation will benefit a number of men as well but it's essential for women or any single parent.

Smith: *So both time and benefits need to be made more flexible?*

Gottfredson: Yes. With benefit programs the idea is to allow people to choose what their benefits package include, not have a one type-fits-all package. Child or elder care can be one choice. What people often argue, and I think it's true, is that a lot of these changes benefit the entire work force or many segments beyond the group stimulating the concern in the first place. Also, organizations are taking steps which don't change the job itself necessarily, but do change selection or promotion procedures, such as having alternative routes to management positions that don't require the usual four-year degree minorities disproportionately fail to have.

The other major focus of some diversity programs is to change the attitudes and behaviors of employees towards each other. For example, groups of employees meet to confront and discuss their stereotypes and biases.

Now this is where a lot of controversy over diversity programs comes in. Some people fear discussing stereotypes could drum them into people's heads even as we try to root them out. Or merely shift the form of stereotype. In the past we've viewed women in one fixed way that's now considered bad, yet today we're ordering people to look at women still as a group, but in a different way that's possibly equally bad. I don't know that I like women being characterized as all alike in some way, whether it's being more intuitive or less logical or whatever. Individual women differ a lot. I've seen reports, for example, of Indian women, saying, "That description of Indians doesn't fit me nor my tribe and I don't like it."

So while the intent often is good, in showing that stereotypes don't hold for many people in a group, you don't replace them with other stereotypes. Employers have to be aware of average differences in interests, aptitudes or values among groups but they also need more appreciation of the range within any group. I wouldn't want them to think that all women interact differently than men. Or classify all women or all Indians and so on as different from men on some other trait. What I do want is for the men to see that more than one kind of behavior is acceptable.

In some of these programs, what happens, I fear, is that politically correct views become established. There are certain things you're supposed to say or believe about men or women or special groups and any variation isn't tolerated. When a program verges on enforcing such an orthodox belief it can create a lot of underground resentment.The programs I like are the ones emphasizing the importance of the individual, recognizing that each person has his or her own individual needs, constraints and contributions to make. These programs also focus on the variety among individuals, which may be broader now that we have a more diverse workforce. But we shouldn't balkanize society or organizations into rigid groups and assign different privileges to them.

Smith: *To paraphrase what you've just said, the guiding principle of these programs becomes "develop individuals, not groups." No individual should be assumed automatically to be representative of his or her group. It also sounds like there has to be a lot of careful planning to develop an effective program.*

Gottfredson: Yes, it's an ongoing process. The best programs I've studied are always ongoing anyway, where you're constantly trying something out, discovering its side effects and then changing it accordingly. There's a lot of experimentation, a lot of failure that has to be tolerated as people grope for better ways of doing things. Right now there's lots of good experimentation in the United States, within and across organizations, but what is useful for one company will not necessarily be useful for another. Some companies have a lot of geographically dispersed branches that have to adapt to very localized circumstances and different workforces—for example, a mostly female or Mexican-American work force or old or young and so on. They obviously have to take a more flexible view about the types of diversity programs in place in their various units than, say, a very unified, centralized corporation. So whether a company can get by with one policy or needs several localized policies will depend on the circumstances.

A general issue for employers is to make greater use of the workforce since the number of incoming workers is shrinking and consists more of minorities, women and more hard-to-train people. No longer do organizations have the luxury of picking employees who fit the organization but must change the organization to fit the employee. People discussing diversity initiatives often point to the fact that employers simply have to make better use of all their employees now. That includes men too. I think one could rightly say there's a lot of room for improving the career and skills development options of all workers. Therefore what may be driven in part by desire or need to integrate women and minorities is leading to a general change in how one views the work force, towards less turnover perhaps.

So the most constructive diversity programs in my view are ones that involve good management anyway, and somehow meet the needs of everybody. They pay attention to the particular skills, weaknesses and constraints of individual workers, which differ for women and men on the average, but also differ among men themselves. Men are differentially skilled and have different family circumstances and needs in career development.

Smith: *Are these kinds of programs actually increasing the numbers of women entering and staying in the nontraditional jobs in industry?*

Gottfredson: I assume they are, but it's hard to get hold of any evidence, probably because it's so politically and emotionally charged. The programs are also new and the few evaluations done often have been incomplete or unsystematic. And a lot of companies feeling vulnerable to public criticism may not want their evaluations known, especially if they fail. So there's a lot of hype. Often the evidence put forward to show the programs are working has nothing to do with their original goals. Or a strict body count is used—"we've gone from 10 to 20 percent female employees"—which simple quotas could also achieve. It's not clear what's producing the change in numbers or what's the resulting quality of the work climate. It's hard to call a program successful if the women are happy but the men are not.

Smith: *Let's turn to how the results of these diversity programs fit in with your theory. You've said that narrowing of career possibilities occurs in the early years of life. Do you think the climate changes occurring in organizations are actually encouraging young women to re-expand their career options?*

Gottfredson: What's viewed as acceptable for women has changed a lot in the last couple of decades so that a lot more young women are considering professions, getting higher degrees. But I don't know if that has anything to do with the diversity initiatives per se. Starting with the Women's Movement there was concern and effort to have women open up their options but, and this is only a hypothesis, they've primarily aspired higher in the same fields as before, rather than moved into different, less traditional interest fields. There's still the relationship between gender and interest. For example, we have ten times as many women going into graduate physics as we used to but still only about twelve percent are women. On the other hand, women continue to be overrepresented in education.

This may be due to men and women on the average being fairly different in their interests. Why that's so is not clear. Some of it may very well be biological and any biological difference is probably magnified by society. That certainly seems to be the case so far. For example, we have lots more women in medicine, but women have always been interested in biology, helping others.

Smith: *But now they become doctors instead of nurses. And instead of being an elementary school teacher, a girl might aim to be a high school principal or college professor. But that's still an interest in teaching.*

Gottfredson: Yes. Now in Holland's Conventional field, such as office or secretarial work, you may see women leaving for something more congenial to their interests. There isn't much higher level Conventional work to aspire to and their interests may not have been there anyway. Many women go into secretarial work because it's temporary and doesn't require a lot of credentials or retraining to go into the job market. But as their options open they'll move into something more feminine, perhaps social or artistic fields. Women generally don't go from office worker to construction worker, even though they're fairly closely related, in fact next door in Holland's theory. But one is still very stereotypically feminine, one stereotypically male. The number of women is probably not increasing much in mid- and lower-level traditionally male jobs.

Another possibility is that women will move up into work which is really androgynous. Physician is not masculine, lawyer is not really masculine. At one time physician may have been more masculine in the sense that it tapped into investigative talents but you can imagine a field or job changing somewhat as the mix of people or genders in it changes. In fact I've written a paper on how that can happen. For example, I've heard people say psychology's becoming more feminized. More women are entering psychology and they tend to be interested in clinical psychology. I don't know if that's contributed to the fact that the U.S. has two psychological associations, one research and one clinically oriented. But I bet you'll find women mostly in the latter.

Research Needs in Diversity Programs

Smith: *You've stated that evaluation of diversity programs is difficult. Therefore what research do we still need to do in this area to find out the best ways to make the workplace congenial to women and special groups?*

Gottfredson: For one thing, it's not clear to me why women, minorities and other special groups do or don't get ahead or what the problems are behind differences in promotion rates and so on. One of my concerns is that there's been so much emphasis on the advantages of the white male, the unfair obstacles, that people may not realize how hard it is to get ahead for reasons other than race or sex. Some may say, "Well I'm in. The wheels should be greased." But it's not like that. We also can't expect women to end up with the same distribution of jobs as men even if we eliminate discrimination. For a variety of reasons women do have different interests and we'll find fewer with interest in engineering, at least at this point in time.

So parity of numbers in a given job is not an appropriate criterion for assessing whether there have been unfair barriers. Different people come in with different interests, values and abilities and that produces differences in employment outcome. I'm not sure we've always appreciated that. For example, I'd expect that fewer woman with families would feel they realistically have the option or desire to be promoted into jobs demanding a lot of time away from home. In the past a lot of women have simply ruled out jobs or careers for reasons having nothing to do with ability. Now as jobs change, maybe their choices will also differ.

Smith: *Do we need more research to find out what's happening in those areas?*

Gottfredson: Well, we need to be more open minded to these issues anyway. I'm not sure more research will help. There's so much sensitivity in this area, so many political agendas.

Smith: *Then it's not just our knowledge gap that limits the kinds of programs set up to help women and minorities fit into the workplace. There are other more dominating considerations?*

Gottfredson: Yes, and they affect the extent to which you'll learn of the effects of these programs. I recently read an article in *Science* magazine on the relationship between social science evidence and social policy. It pointed out that failure to link the two could come about for several reasons. One is lack of knowledge, but then among others are political constraints, which means that even if you learn certain things from more research you have to ignore them.

Smith: *Does that mean a woman going into a nontraditional field may have problems finding out what she's getting into because of the lack of candid information?*

Gottfredson: Well, it's tough for anybody, but especially for people going into settings where there aren't many like them to talk to or learn from, such as women with families who've had to handle the job. If you're a pioneer, you face an unknown territory and sometimes you have to grapple with the problems as they come.

Getting Information on Diversity Programs

Smith: *If a woman has been thinking about entering a particular career, then landing a job in a particular company, is it useful to find out first if the company has a diversity program, its rates of promotion of women, etcetera?*

Gottfredson: I think a person looking for a job in any organization would want to know something about its climate and the degree to which it recognizes individual differences. That's obviously a concern for a person going into a cross-sex atmosphere, male or female, though it's more often women facing that situation. At the same time I wouldn't want to go in and seem like I had a chip on my shoulder or was ready to find bias everywhere. So instead of asking what do you do for women in particular, ask what kinds of monitoring or career development assistance do you have for employees. Are there mentoring or personal development programs? Don't be surprised to find many have none.

And certainly I'd be careful in evaluating what I was told. Are you going to be ghettoized in some way by the very measures supposedly helping you fit in? You also want to distinguish what's hype and window dressing, what isn't. There's such diversity in programs that I'd try to exercise independent judgment about what they're doing and not take the line as given.

Counselling Considerations

Smith: *I'd like to ask you to take a more general view now. Given the changes we've just discussed in the workplace, what advice could you give young women about choosing a career?*

Gottfredson: One major dimension to consider when looking at your options is the mental difficulty of the job—skill demands. It seems to me that any sort of useful and realistic counselling has to take that into account. My concern has been that vocational psychology had not paid much attention to ability as opposed to interest differences. So in my own work I set out to characterize jobs according to their ability requirements. That's how I developed the Occupation Aptitude Pattern Map, to give people a view of the entire workworld using a manageable number of job categories, little more than a dozen, rated by interest type and skill level. The job levels were related mostly to the amount of intelligence demanded. The job types were related to specific abilities, interests or activities required on the job. I've also developed but never published—I got side tracked by other issues—a counselling strategy starting with this map.

Smith: *Can this strategy help women widen their traditionally narrow range of career choices?*

Gottfredson: Well, there's been concern that women, and other groups, only explore a narrow area. So how do counsellors open choice up without making it unmanageable? Using my map as a counselling tool, I argued that people should look first at broad job categories and descriptions on this map and find what intellectual level they wanted to work at, not worry immediately about the particulars of any job. Next the person should look at adjacent general job areas, explore them and then zero in on something. As a counsellor you challenge them with, "Why this choice, what about that career?" in a general way so they can see the relationships among all the groups. Only then do you give in-depth information about anything and start them exploring how to be competitive in those areas.

Smith: *This approach requires clients to be very aware of their ability levels and interests?*

Gottfredson: Not necessarily. I had it arrayed according to five educational levels and people can pretty much assess if a level is too difficult or easy for them. They'll say, "Professional is too difficult for me. I'm more the nurse type." Maybe they're using test scores, grades, SATs, who knows what. But you say back to them, "Okay, now I want you to look at one level above the one you've chosen and one level below," to encourage them to consider all their options.

Overall, I think you want to encourage women to examine their options and be realistic about their skills. The issue is not to decide immediately where you fit, given your interests and abilities, but where you want to go and how to make yourself more competitive to get there, especially if you're not competitive in some way now.

Smith: *So the key is assessing the skills required to get you where you want to go and not giving up because you don't have them now.*

Gottfredson: Right. My work tries to reconcile the goals of promoting exploration and promoting realism. People have to be realistic in the sense that they need information about themselves and the jobs, to know how competitive they are and which jobs are better bets, but they can also start thinking about becoming more competitive. Then they can set their sights higher, with probably a fall back position. So think of several possibilities you're interested in, then plan how to improve your competitive position. If a kid is in the lower half of a test score's distribution, a counsellor could say, "You might get into this program with those scores but you should develop other skills to increase your chances."

Smith: *Getting a crack at the career you want is a matter of odds?*

Gottfredson: Your odds of getting in and succeeding may be low or high but you can change those odds. On the other hand, you can't overlook them. If you're not competitive you can't go in and say, "Well, here I am. I sure hope things turn out." They might and they might not. But most people have lots of untapped potential and if you put yours to work you can be more competitive. Now you may have to always work harder in some areas than other people in the same job, but if you want to make that trade off you can. Of course, some things you can't trade off below a certain level. You simply may not be bright enough, but often special talents can offset that deficit.

Smith: *You could find a niche within a field by developing special talents.*

Gottfredson: Yes. A lot of people stumble through career development. They wander from job to job, taking what's easy and available and end up doing that for life. But I think if you take a more self-development point of view, you can often increase your odds of doing what you want. Employers are always looking for employees who can become greater assets to the organization, though that depends somewhat on how tightly bureaucratic or open they are.

Smith: *You mentioned earlier the role of experience in your own life. How important is it in general for making career choices?*

Gottfredson: If people are not giving you feedback about what you can or should do, all the possibilities, then you need to gather personal experience to learn that on your own. I've talked to other women who finished professional or advanced degrees a little later than normal because they worked for a while first. What they've said is the work experience gave them a chance to slowly grow into realizing what they could do on the one hand and what really satisfied them on the other. Sometimes you decide to try something and surprise yourself by enjoying it although that activity may not have been typical for your mother's generation. Those of us who ended up in our careers that way are lucky. I've been concerned for a time about some young women being pushed too hard to do new things. There are a lot of women out there who are the first wave into many occupations in large numbers and maybe other people don't realize the costs to those women of pushing.

Women have to be careful when making any choice, traditional or nontraditional, and not let themselves be pushed by the expectations of others.

Like in law. I remember reading some years back about a number of talented women who entered that profession and found it wasn't for them. There were big conflicts between family, work and their interests. They'd followed the new prescribed route for women as unthinkingly as other women had followed the old. Women have to be careful when making any choice, traditional or nontraditional, and not let themselves be pushed by the expectations of others. I can imagine a fair number of women out there whose mothers felt cheated because they didn't have a job and now their daughters feel cheated because they didn't have a family of their own or the time for the kind of family they wanted.

Smith: *Final question. Do you think that being a mother, with first-hand experience in balancing family and career, has influenced your theories about women's career choices?*

Gottfredson: I can't say it's affected my theoretical orientation but it has made it more personal. I know I think about my daughters when I think about the work world—what kind of world I want them to live in and what kind of women I want them to be.

References and Recommended Readings

Gottfredson, L. (1978). An analytical description of employment according to race, sex, prestige, and Holland-type of work. *Journal of Vocational Behavior, 13,* 210-221.

Gottfredson, L.S. (1981). Circumscription and compromise: A developmental theory of occupational aspirations. *Journal of Counseling Psychology, 28,* 545-579.

Gottfredson, L.S. (1985). Role of self-concept in vocational theory. *Journal of Counseling Psychology, 32,* 159-162.

Gottfredson, L.S. (1985). Dilemmas in developing diversity programs. In S. E. Jackson (Ed.). *Working through diversity: Human resources initiatives.* New York: Guildford.

Significant Events in the Life of Linda Gottfredson

1969	Receives BA, Psychology, University of California, Berkeley
1969-72	Peace Corps volunteer, Malaysia.
1976	Takes position as Research Scientist, The Johns Hopkins University
1977	Ph.D., Sociology, The Johns Hopkins University
1981	Publishes monograph, "Circumscription and Compromise."
1982	Two daughters born
l986	Takes faculty position, University of Delaware. Edits special journal issue, "The g [Intelligence] Factor in Employment."
1988	Co-edits special journal issue, "Fairness in Employment Testing."
1989	Receives tenure, University of Delaware, with strong support from department.
1989-90	Publishes articles with Jan Blits on race-norming in employment testing, spurring a national debate
l990	Promoted to full professor despite strong opposition from department.
l990	University bans Gottfredson's source of research funding on ideological grounds
1989-92	Gottfredson and Blits charge that the University of Delaware is repeatedly violating their academic freedom in teaching and research, failing to protect their rights, and retaliating against them for defending their rights.
l991	A national arbitrator orders the University to rescind its 16-month-old funding ban.
1992	Gottfredson and Blits reach an out-of-court settlement with the University of Delaware resolving all outstanding disputes. Gottfredson begins projects on the relationship of employment testing to national debates over civil rights and economic productivity.

9

A Canadian Perspective on Developing Equality in the Workplace: Employment Equity

Sharon E. Kahn, Ph.D., Director of Employment Equity and Associate Professor, Department of Counselling Psychology, University of British Columbia (UBC).

Governments and employers can no longer expect women to mold themselves to fit into the traditional, white male-dominated workplace. Instead, new economic and social realities require that organizations create fair and equitable job/educational opportunities for all. This was the central message Sharon Kahn communicated to one of the authors in an authoritative interview in her campus office sunny October day. Drawing upon her experience as director of the University of British Columbia's (UBC) Employment Equity program since 1989, she discussed Canada's Employment Equity Act and Federal Contractors Program, two legislated solutions to the problem of increasing the numbers of women and minorities in the workforce. Kahn's task over the last three years has been to oversee a total reevaluation of UBC's practices and policies in the areas of recruiting, hiring and promotion in order to eliminate systematic discrimination against women and minorities. To accept this challenge, she took a temporary leave from her professorial duties.

Kahn's leadership in Employment Equity is a natural application of the counselling skills and interests in women's careers she has developed ever since her grassroots participation in the Women's Movement in the late 1960s. After finishing graduate training, she continued to hone her feminist principles through more than fifteen years of teaching gender-fair counselling and supervising other counsellors of women with work-related concerns. She also established her own research base on women's vocational choices and the ways women cope with work-related stress.

"Counsellors remain frustrated that the workplace has not adjusted to women's careers and families," Kahn has written. Fortunately, the philosophy behind Employment Equity, she notes, fits well with the feminist counselling belief—that environmental constraints and gender-role socialization play a primary role in the problems women have with employment. "How effective legislated employment equity and federal contract compliance are, only time will tell," she says. "UBC has made significant progress, but much still remains to be done."

Career Development of a Feminist Psychologist

Leduc: *Could you start out by telling us something about your personal history? Such as what your parents did for a living?*

Kahn: My father was an accountant with his own firm in Kansas City. And my mother was a bookkeeper who worked with him in his office.

Leduc: *You came from a middle class background?*

Kahn: Yes, but how do you define middle class? If you use my father's occupation as an index, there is no question that we were middle class. My mother's parents were fairly recent arrivals in North America. In terms of occupation, her family was working or low middle class. Neither of my parents completed college. Looking back now, I see my background distinguished not so much by class as by ethnic and religious considerations. I was raised Jewish more than anything else, and at home, there was always pressure to achieve.

Leduc: *Did your parents expect you'd go as far as you did in your education?*

Kahn: I always knew I'd go to college, and soon after I began my first year at Washington University in St. Louis, I knew I wanted to go to graduate school and hoped to find a career in university research and teaching. Both my brother and I have Ph.D.s. My undergraduate degree was in English literature and my graduate degrees are in counselling psychology. My parents insisted that education was important—the key to the future. Interestingly enough, I also received a second message—that another benefit of graduate school was as a place to meet the right kind of marriage partner. Now I eventually married a man with an advanced degree, but I didn't meet him in graduate school. I met him here at UBC.

Leduc: *When did you make the career switch to psychology?*

Kahn: It really wasn't a switch because I think English literature is also about how people deal with their lives. In fact, I see the two fields as complementing one another. I saw counselling not only as work I'd enjoy but also as a way to improve and enhance my own social skills.

Leduc: *Did you go straight into graduate school from undergraduate work?*

Kahn: No, after getting my B.A., I was secretarial assistant to the editor of arts and letters at the *Atlantic Monthly*. It was an interim job. Since I'd finished my B.A. in only three and a half years, I had a half a year to wait before graduate school began. I think I'd hurried through because my mother died when I was 19, and after that I felt a real need to get on with my life. My mother's death had a powerful effect on me. I'm close to both my father and brother, but the loss of my mother forced me to be independent in ways that were both painful and beneficial. Anyway, that magazine job convinced me I wanted to work in the helping field rather than in publishing.

Leduc: *How did you become interested in women and careers?*

Kahn: Part of it was the social context in the late sixties—I began graduate school in Boston in 1968—so I was involved in the sixties' social activism. My introduction to feminism was made easy because I was in a city with a lot of universities, new ideas, and committed young people. I was involved in consciousness-raising from the beginning, and it became a part of who I am. That experience affected both my interests and personal life, so when I went to Arizona State for my doctorate, it was easy for me to carry on with feminism. I conducted a number of women's workshops in self-esteem and assertiveness training. Looking back, I see my personal life and my professional interests in women's careers and counselling as a single unit. I've also written about how I think feminism-inspired change has affected counselling and counsellors in general.

Leduc: *So you turned out to be a role model for the women you worked with.*

Kahn: Yes, it was easy to talk about the issues and identify with my clients. I was struggling with many of the same issues that I thought important to them. And as a single, well-educated woman seeking a good career and taking care of herself, I was in many ways a likely role model. So I think I was a very effective counsellor.

Leduc: *When did you come to the University of British Columbia?*

Kahn: I came in 1975. I'd been socialized in an academic world that was fairly mobile and growing, and I came here thinking "I'll stay for a few years and then move on." What happened was I liked it here very much. It became my home and the centre of my professional life. However, even if I hadn't liked it, academic mobility by the late seventies and early eighties had become much more limited.

Leduc: *Do you think you had more mobility initially because you were single?*

Kahn: Absolutely, but many of my single friends thought choosing UBC was particularly risky. They were also making independent choices, but not to move to another country or a city where they knew no one. My mother's death, in a sense, meant one fewer parent to worry about, and my father had remarried. So though coming to Vancouver did seem a risky choice, UBC's Counselling Psychology department wanted someone to develop its Counselling Women Program. That job was exactly what I wanted.

Leduc: *Now was that career choice or career chance?*

Kahn: I think it was a combination of both. I'll say one more thing about my career interests. A few years later when I was still pretenure I was told by the then Dean of Education that I should be careful not to narrow my focus too much. "Women" was perhaps too restricted a topic. Instead I should be aware that a broad base of counselling psychology and educational interests would be more appropriate. However, as it turns out, I have managed to make a career out of this "restricted" topic. But I hope many academic administrators today would see my focus area in a more positive light because the whole research area of gender and women has gained enormous credibility compared to the late seventies when I heard that advice.

Leduc: *And you're still maintaining a focus on women's careers even in Employment Equity, so you haven't grown away from it.*

Kahn: Not at all. I'm probably doing this job better now than I could have done it ten years ago. I think this is true for all of us. Whatever we're doing now, we should recognize that the years that went before were preparation because we bring to our work so much of who we are. It's not so much "Did I read the right book or have I taken the right courses for this job." I'm also contributing my past thoughts, ideas and experiences. I see that continuity very much in my own career. Now, certainly, my experience and training run the gamut of women's career counselling. But my expertise and interest right now are focused on Employment Equity and its practical application—how organizations and employers can deal with the social, organizational, and political demands for equity. Also, my current research is on women coping with employment-related stress.

Leduc: *Let me ask a personal question. Have you ever experienced inequities in the workplace?*

Kahn: I have to say "yes" because I know the system. I think the Dean's suggestion that "women" was too restricted a topic for authentic scholarly inquiry is indicative of the sort of systemic bias that chronically affects all women working in traditionally male-dominated careers. I'm not so much concerned by instances of overt discrimination, which are clear cut and can be addressed in the courts, as I am by instances of covert discrimination—the kind that both perpetrators and victims may be unconscious of.

Leduc: *It seems you've been able to break through the glass ceiling with your present job.*

Kahn: I think that's not true. I'm still in a middle management position. And my job usually is done by women. Indeed, people comment on the unusual fact that men administer the employment equity program at the universities of Alberta and Western Ontario.

An Overview of Employment Equity

Leduc: *Could you give an overview of what a Canadian employment equity program involves?*

Kahn: Yes, and I can use my present employer, UBC, to show how the program works.

In 1983, Judge Rosalie Abella headed up a Royal Commission on Employment which worked for a year gathering information and doing a number of studies.The recommendations that resulted included the establishment of the Employment Equity Act, which was brought down in 1986 and covers federally regulated employers such as the banks and transportation. The Employment Equity Act was Canada's way of saying that voluntary employment equity isn't good enough to protect human rights.

At the same time as the Employment Equity Act was brought down, the government established the Federal Contractors Program. It states that any employer of more than a hundred employees who wishes to bid on government contracts over $200,000 must commit itself to this program and, through it, the provisions of employment equity. The Federal Contractors Program covers approximately forty colleges and universities and seven hundred other employers not federally regulated but having federal government contracts. UBC joined in 1988 and in January 1989 appointed me to develop its Employment Equity program.

Leduc: *Does a university Employment Equity program differ much from those in non-university settings?*

Kahn: It differs in several ways. Universities are complex organizations. Unlike businesses—where the CEO gives an order and everybody falls into line—they're decentralized. Their model is more republican than monarchical. Another characteristic peculiar to a university is that its faculty is influential disproportionate to its size. Because the role of the university in society is to preserve and advance knowledge, those individuals most directly involved in teaching and research have most influence. Although UBC's faculty is less than half the size of its non-academic staff, its influence over university programs is large. A university employment equity program must make sense to an academic community, especially with regard to recruiting and hiring of faculty.

Another difference is that universities have a particular concern with equity because they are formal training grounds for women and minorities eager to take their places in the future job market. If universities aren't training them in large enough numbers, other employers won't have enough applicants to choose from. Women and minorities simply won't be in the qualified pools. One of the ways in which universities are unique is that they not only hire but also produce qualified applicants for future jobs.

Now given my background in counselling psychology, my interest in women's career development and my knowledge of the problems women have maintaining their careers, the Employment Equity Program has been a fabulous opportunity to put my skills to practical use. Another strength I brought to the job was that I already understood this institution. I knew who some of the important players were and something about how things got done.

Leduc: *So being politically aware, regardless of the institution, is helpful for establishing Equity.*

Kahn: Yes. Getting an Employment Equity program up and running requires several initiatives, and establishing new initiatives in the setting of an established bureaucracy of a decentralized university is a task that requires skill, diplomacy, and persistence, even obstinacy, sometimes. The first step is to have an institutional policy. Then there are two important tasks. The first is the survey or census of the workforce to determine the proportion of women and minorities currently employed. The second is an employment systems review of formal policies and informal practices.

In Canada, federally, there are four groups of people targeted by Employment Equity—women, aboriginal people, visible minorities and persons with disabilities. These four groups were designated because the Abella Commission studies showed they suffered higher unemployment rates and were often found working in low paying, low level, low status jobs. Keep in mind that the three minority groups are at least half women, which means women comprise a large component of Employment Equity, although Employment Equity does not deal only with women.

In the next decade, over seventy percent of the growth in the Canadian labor market will come from the four designated employment-equity groups. Indeed, right now, something like seventy percent of new entrants into the workforce are women and minorities. We have to ask ourselves, "What are we going to do to capitalize on these people when we know they are looking for work and we need them now and will need them in the future?" It's important to realize that Employment Equity was not devised simply to address discrimination. The program also addresses Canada's economic and social future because these four groups are gaining political power and will continue to increase their demands.

Leduc: *Will their evolving power result in a change in their socialization?*

Kahn: Yes and no. I know a lot of young women who think of themselves as having a reasonable share of job-market opportunities and I find their self-esteem heartening. Unfortunately, many of these same young women find themselves disadvantaged in the workplace, and I find that sad.

Leduc: *How in fact did you carry out the work force census?*

Kahn: Conducting and analyzing the census was very complicated. In universities dissent is common and openly expressed, and a number of factors cause people to think along lines like, "I don't like government intervening in university affairs" and "Central administration is getting too large." In addition, there are ideological reasons why people disapprove of the Employment Equity approach to multiculturalism. Then, too, academics are in the business of setting standards of excellence, so they tend to look askance at proposals that seem to threaten "merit."

Beyond the initial question "Should the university participate in an employment equity program by conducting a census of its employees?" stand many additional decisions, such as whether to include certain employees—for example, casual or student appointments—in the census; how to design and write promotional materials; how to follow-up with non-respondents, encouraging them to reconsider their original choice not to participate.

Finally, when the census is complete, decisions must be made about data analysis. For example, what are the appropriate qualified external pools with which to compare the organization's workforce? Accordingly, UBC compared university figures to two data sources from Statistics Canada—women who'd been granted doctoral degrees and women and minorities who'd been employed in 1986, the latest set of census data. Both of these data sets are incomplete for employment equity. Data on doctoral degrees granted in Canada omit essential information about international candidates and Canadians with doctoral degrees from outside Canada. Most importantly, both sets tell us who received doctoral degrees and who was employed, rather than who might have received degrees or been employed if sexism and racism had been eliminated.

Leduc: *Following the analysis, what was the next step?*

Kahn: Next the university set hiring goals based on qualified external labor pools. Statistics Canada data offer bare minimums, and UBC should be doing better than that. Some people would argue that if women make up 51 percent of the population, women should comprise 51 percent of all UBC positions. Others would argue that the university cannot hire 51 percent women faculty until there are 51 percent women in all the qualified applicant pools. To give you an example, women presently make up 3 percent of UBC's engineering faculty, and the qualified applicant pool of women with engineering Ph.D.s in Canada is 5 percent. So it's not possible in practice nor at present theoretically defensible to argue that 51 percent of our professors of engineering should be women. At UBC we currently have set a goal to hire women into 35 percent vacant tenure track faculty positions.

Following the census and the setting of hiring goals, UBC asked individual faculties to adjust the overall university goal of 35 percent women to reflect their faculty's appropriate qualified applicant pool, for example women with Ph.D.s in engineering. Clearly, a goal to hire women into 35 percent of vacant tenure-track engineering positions at this time is too high. For the 1991/92 academic year, UBC hired women into 38 percent of its vacant tenure-track positions, but that doesn't mean every department that hired achieved 38 percent. In fact, not one of the several engineers hired to teach on faculty was a woman.

The great danger isn't conscious bias, but prejudice that is systemic and therefore invisible.

Leduc: *What is the relationship between UBC's Employment Equity Policy and its hiring goals?*

Kahn: UBC's Policy on Employment Equity is merit driven. We want to hire the best qualified person, and so strive to enlarge the candidate pools from which we hire. We have no preferential hiring system, nor an affirmative action policy. Our current practice is to recruit actively and to encourage all qualified people, especially women and minorities, to apply, and then to scrutinize our selection procedures to ensure that they are fair and objective. The great danger isn't conscious bias, but prejudice that is systemic and therefore invisible. UBC's Employment Equity program does not promote alternate standards, but some people misunderstand the program by assuming that a hiring goal is the same as a hiring quota. In Canada, hiring quotas have only been set as court sanctions in cases where overt discrimination has been proven. Efforts to meet hiring goals are like mid-term marks in a course. They can be used to rate performance and to decide if and where improvement is needed.

Let me mention finally another role of the census. In addition to providing an ongoing data source to help set goals and monitor progress, the census also lets us communicate with new employees about employment equity objectives.

Leduc: *Isn't there a Canadian university now where every replacement is going to be a female.*

Kahn: Yes, the Royal Ontario College of Art established that particular replacement policy. Other universities state that in the case of equal candidates, they'll always choose women. There are also some universities that restrict certain jobs to women.

Leduc: *Does UBC's policy avoid the backlash from hiring women preferentially?*

Kahn: I don't know that UBC has or can avoid backlash from those who either misunderstand Employment Equity or who disagree with it on theoretical grounds or feel personally threatened by it. But I think UBC's policy avoids backlash from women because every female employee knows she's hired because she's the best qualified for a job.

UBC's review of its employment policies and procedures should produce a fair, objective system for everyone, not just women and minorities. Equity means examining unconscious and systemic bias, and then changing the way we recruit and select people. We uncover practices that may disadvantage groups of people and then try to modify those practices. I'm not interested in blaming men or individuals, but rather in changing systems and structures.

Leduc: *And still some people oppose Employment Equity.*

Kahn: Yes, their argument is sometimes about the rate of change we need to pursue in order to achieve a fair representation of women and minorities in the workforce. Some people believe today is already too late, and therefore insist on preferential hiring. Others believe that market forces will in the long run resolve the employment problems of women and minorities. However, if women make up less than twenty percent of Canadian university faculties today, our current rate of progress will take a hundred and fifty years for women to make up fifty percent of Canadian faculty. Accordingly, I believe in promoting change, and I believe UBC's policy is appropriate. Although the system is big, and like all big systems, moves slowly, I have seen it change.

Leduc: *What do the census results say about UBC?*

Kahn: Apart from its faculty, UBC looks like any other large employer. There are custodians, secretaries, managers, vice presidents, accountants, engineers. In terms of Employment Equity, UBC has looked very much like other large employers over past years. That is, women and visible minorities have made modest progress, but aboriginal people and persons with disabilities have made very little. It's difficult for Canadian employers to recruit aboriginal people, and it takes time to recognize the capabilities of and to provide reasonable accommodations for persons with disabilities. And like everywhere else in Canada, women and visible minorities have problems breaking through to upper-level management and academic positions, though at UBC we do have a number of women and visible minorities in non-academic, middle-management positions.

Leduc: *Are there still only two percent women in upper management?*

Kahn: The proportion of women in upper-level management positions is closer to 10 or even 15 percent. However, the number of women with appropriate education and experience who are underemployed proves that the glass ceiling still exists.

The Employment Systems Review

Leduc: *How does the Systems Review fit in?*

Kahn: The Employment Systems Review is the other major task in an employment equity program. We consider whether formal and informal practices may potentially disadvantage a particular group of people. Employment Equity is based on discrimination that is systemic, not necessarily intentional. Day-to-day routines we follow unthinkingly may disadvantage an entire group.

In our review we look at all current employment practices, procedures and policies. If the potential effect is to disadvantage women and minorities, we consider changes to our systems. For example, where are we recruiting? Do we advertise appointments, or do we simply hire through word-of-mouth? If the latter case, the same kinds of people will be in our recruitment pools over and over again. If we advertise, where do we advertise and how do we word our advertisements?

The number of women with appropriate education and experience who are underemployed proves that the glass ceiling still exists.

Similarly, there are special measures that women and minority groups may need if they're going to compete on a level playing field. Most people think of equality as treating all people the same, whatever their differences, but those people who work in Employment Equity think of equality as accommodating differences in order to ensure the same results. For example, we know that safety is particularly relevant for women. If faculty and staff must work on campus in the evenings or on weekends to get ahead, but women don't feel safe on a deserted campus, then as an employer the university is not providing what women need to achieve. Emergency telephones and good lighting improve opportunities for women (and men, too) to work during evenings or on weekends. In the same way, sidewalk ramps work well for everyone. Ramps intended for people with mobility problems are used also by parents with strollers.

Leduc: *What about childcare as a modification for women?*

Kahn: Absolutely. Child and other dependent care is important to both women and men. Many employed women are part of the sandwich generation. They have not only kids at home but family members requiring assistance. Without question, it's difficult to care for family members when all able-bodied adults in the household are employed. So yes, there are special measures we need to utilize the full potential of women, but these measures make the workplace and home better for men as well.

In addition to considering dependent-care benefits, UBC is reviewing maternity benefits. We have a number of unions and employee groups, each with different benefits relating to maternity leave. In our efforts to equalize maternity leave across all employee groups, we've realized there are also widely-shared concerns about dependent-care and parental leave. What about men needing to care for an ill spouse or elderly parent? As a result of the Employment Systems Review, the university has become aware of these issues and is seeking to address them.

Leduc: *And they're evolving.*

Kahn: Yes. The argument before was always based on cost. Now we hear arguments about the cost of employees who are unable to come to work because of sick children or whose attention at work is divided between work and family.

Unfortunately, labor-market myths too often blind us to reality. For example, not all women have children or stop work to raise them. In fact the latest statistics suggest that sixty percent of women with children under three are employed full time. Some of our myths about women and work have to change if women are to enjoy full opportunities in the workplace. Too much of the workplace seems to be built on the belief that there must always be a spouse at home to provide the domestic support all employees need in order to put in a full day's work.

A number of employers are looking at employee assistance and wellness programs, and child care, dependent-care, and parental leave provisions. The workplace is changing. I don't know if it's because employers are concerned about being fair to the growing numbers of employed women, but certainly initiatives that promote women at work and families are happening simultaneously.

Leduc: *Are the employers setting up these programs looking more at long-term benefits rather than the immediate ones?*

Kahn: I think that's true. Employers increasingly find that equity initiatives work to their advantage. They are beginning to realize that economic survival means providing an attractive environment for women and minorities because these employees have much to offer. Society can no longer rely on the traditional pool of young, white, able-bodied men. In Canada the birth rate is declining and there are tremendous changes in immigration patterns. The image of the "typical" Canadian is changing. Employers are realizing that employment practices must change, too.

But change is not easy. One way that employers have hired is by screening people so the employer ended up with the smallest subset of qualified candidates. Employment Equity now requires employers to screen people into candidate pools, which ensures the inclusion of qualified women and minorities.

Leduc: *Is some of the resistance to the program a problem of logistics?*

Kahn: Yes, some of the resistance results from the need to do things differently, but some of the challenge and excitement comes when employers confront the pragmatics of change. I was talking with a woman the other day about *bona fide* job requirements. She told me that when a particular municipality wanted to increase the number of women in its police force, the city advertised in a fitness magazine. Now, that was a creative tactic because they were targeting both women and men who would meet their physical requirements. Targeted advertising enlarged their pool of women who met the physical demands of the job much more than had previous newspaper advertisement.

Leduc: *What are some examples of specific gains that an Employment Equity program can achieve?*

Kahn: One example at UBC is improved monitoring of the hiring procedures for academics. For many years, faculty women have asked for some kind of report on the university's hiring procedures. Now we have a formal program—Employment Equity—to monitor and report on hiring procedures. The Vice-President, Academic, has produced this summary form for tenure-track positions, and departments must submit a recruiting summary along with their recommendation to hire. The summary reports on the composition of recruitment and selection committees, the measures taken to include qualified women in the candidate pool and the ratio of men and women short-listed and interviewed. In addition, the summary reports on specific advertisement wording and other active recruitment measures. These summaries assist in maintaining fair and objective hiring procedures for every faculty position. They are excellent consciousness-raising tools too.

Employment Equity is considered in most initiatives that affect faculty and staff. For example, a recently proposed project on training and development for UBC's employees addresses Employment Equity. Are women and minorities participating fully in opportunities that lead to promotion? Are managers receiving awareness training in gender, cultural, and disability issues? Are supervisors learning about recent labor market trends? Employment Equity is integrated into the proposal and this integration improves all aspects of training and development.

Employment Equity and Women's Career Choices

Leduc: *How does all of this affect women in terms of career choice?*

Kahn: As employers and governments encourage equitable working environments for women and men, they motivate women to pursue a wide range of careers. In my experience as a counselling psychologist, I know that motivated people become demoralized in the face of limited opportunities. There's a close relationship between motivation, hard work, success and opportunity.

I also think Employment Equity programs can provide opportunities for women in nontraditional areas. When there are female engineers on a university faculty, as there are at UBC, these role models socialize young women to consider engineering as a career. Increasingly, women are also changing the face of professions such as law and medicine, and these changes serve to encourage other young women to pursue nontraditional careers.

Leduc: Are you limiting "nontraditional" to blue collar or technology fields?

Kahn: The way I use "nontraditional" comes from my research. My colleague Bonnie Long and I identified as nontraditional those fields where women hold less than 35 percent of the jobs. Management is a good example, but management increasingly includes women, and therefore management is becoming less nontraditional. Currently, most of the blue collar and highly technical jobs are non-traditional for women. And because I believe that talent and capabilities are evenly distributed among groups of people, I think there are women who would do very well in nontraditional work.

Leduc: *I asked that question because often people think nontraditional means only the blue collar or technical fields—not realizing that at one point, management was considered very nontraditional and that the definition is still changing.*

Kahn: At the highest managerial levels, CEOs, chairpersons, and company presidents are predominantly male. University faculty also is a nontraditional area for women. Today about 17 percent of full-time academics in Canadian universities are women. Of course, there are more women faculty in nursing and education—these are traditionally women's fields—but even in those traditional women's disciplines, many faculty members are men. The same phenomenon is true in the public school system. Many of the principals are men and most of the teachers are women. Systemic discrimination segregates women and men into particular specializations, and too often segregates women into low-level jobs.

Leduc: *Support jobs?*

Kahn: Yes, or particular areas of specialization. For example, a female vice-president of a major corporation may be in charge of human resources as opposed to finance. In general, when there has been unequal opportunity for men and women, we see both job segregation and traditional and nontraditional patterns of career development.

Retaining Women in Nontraditional Fields

Leduc: *How do you think Employment Equity will help those women who choose to go into nontraditional fields? Not only to gain entry, but to stay in those jobs?*

Kahn: Employment Equity looks at hiring, training and promotion. At the University of British Columbia we've looked closely at recruitment and hiring, but not at promotion. Although women make up a large part of the UBC workforce, they're not present at all job levels, particularly at the highest. But women make up over fifty percent of university undergraduates. So somewhere along the way either women are not choosing nontraditional options or employers are not selecting women for nontraditional jobs. Ironically, women and minorities may be disadvantaged by academic training procedures. For example, an academic scientist's career involves postdoctoral study, and many young woman may lack the mobility to take advantage of those experiences, particularly if they have family responsibilities. Employers must consider how men's and women's careers differ, rather than ignoring differences in the structure of opportunities or just giving women special preference.

Leduc: *Then, it would not be a merit decision.*

Kahn: No. Employers need to understand that women's and men's careers follow different development patterns and consider the effect of these patterns on workplaces. As in hiring, employers deal with myths and stereotypes about merit and promotion. For example, in a department where playing handball together is important, a woman who is not interested in the sport may not seem like the right type, not because she can't do the job but because she doesn't participate in a non-job-related activity.

For a long time, the myth was that because women had babies, they weren't interested in the long-term commitment required by high-level jobs. Women are having fewer babies, they're not staying home and some do want to achieve at the highest levels. Maternity benefits, in fact, may be one of the best ways to ensure women have opportunities to compete. For example, consider the fact that women academics' pretenure period may overlap their prime years for child bearing. A woman who gives birth to a child is certain to lose time in which to produce the work required for tenure. UBC, here, has tried to address the problem faced by these women. Any woman who takes maternity leave during her pretenure period may have her tenure decision extended one year. I imagine some men who become parents during their pretenure period would also like to extend their tenure decision. I am not opposed to stopping the tenure clock for pretenure fathers.

Leduc: *Does UBC emphasize accommodating the individual?*

Kahn: Yes. Increasingly, we try to treat people as individuals as well as take into account group membership. The other day I argued on behalf of an individual case. One of UBC's support staff suffers from a degenerative disc disease. She has trouble sitting at a desk, and asked the university to provide her with a special chair. I argued that the chair's cost is little compared to the loss of her services and the expense of hiring and training someone else.

While employers must consider the needs of individuals, they also must be aware of the needs of groups, particularly groups suffering from discrimination and disadvantage. The psychologist, Dr. Faye Crosby, found that often individuals denied having experienced discrimination even though they knew they were members of disadvantaged groups. Therefore, relying only on individual cases might make it easy to dismiss discrimination, especially when it's unconscious, subtle and systemic. Thus large-scale survey data, such as the employment-equity census data, are extremely valuable in the development of social policy and equity programs. As an employer identifies patterns of discrimination within its work-force, policies and practices can be created and monitored to affect change.

Beyond Employment Equity

Leduc: *Employment Equity programs have been established as one means to produce change in the gender imbalance in occupational fields. What other solutions do you see help women and minorities gain entry into and maintain employment in careers matching their interests?*

Kahn: I believe that right now Employment Equity programs established by employers or government are one of the best ways to assist women and minorities. There have always been individual ways to deal with difference, such as improving one's skills or becoming more like others—in this case, white, able-bodied men. But I also think the world changes because structures change, not just because individuals want the world to be different. I am pleased to be part of a program where employers are doing some of the adjustments, rather than expecting individuals to make all the changes. Women cannot be expected to find better childcare arrangements by themselves or to take supervisory skills courses on Saturdays if they want to be supervisors. Employers must be part of the solution.

Leduc: *And thereby everyone benefits.*

Kahn: Absolutely. Everyone benefits from fair and objective employment prac-tices.

Leduc: *What do you see changing in this area by the turn of the century?*

Kahn: I see more women and minorities in nontraditional fields but quite honestly, I don't see breakneck change coming. My vision is that society will reevaluate employment, create new structures, and as a result, develop a healthier work environment for everyone that will enable men to take time out to care for dependents and women to pursue their highest goals.

Leduc: *If you had lots of money, where would you put it to improve the programs?*

Kahn: There's no doubt I would put money into educational equity. Both young women and men must understand that they're looking to a future where their partner will work outside the home and expect them to share family responsibilities. I think young men are poorly served by teachers who perpetuate myths about what adult life is all about.

Leduc: *What final wisdom can you offer women choosing careers?*

Kahn: Get all the education you possibly can. I have found as a counselling psychologist and as a director of Employment Equity that employers are looking for well-qualified women. If a woman has the educational training and background to do the job, she will be in position to overcome many workplace disadvantages. When those disadvantages are overcome, everyone benefits—both women and men, employers and employees.

References and Recommended Readings

Crosby, F., Pufall, A., Snyder, R., O'Connell, M., & Whalen, P. (1989). The denial of personal disadvantage among you, me, and all the other ostriches. In M. Crawford & M. Gentry (Eds.), *Gender and thought: Psychological perspectives* (pp. 79-99). New York: Verlag.

Kahn, S.E. (1983). Development and operation of the women's employment counselling unit. *Vocational Guidance Quarterly, 32*(2), 125-129.

Kahn, S.E. (1984). Astin's model of career development: The working lives of women and men. *The Counseling Psychologist, 12*(4),145-14.

Kahn, S.E. (1988). Feminism and career counselling with women. *Journal of Career Development, 14*(4), 242-248.

Kahn, S.E. (1989). Life skills for women. *Guidance and Counselling,* 4(4), 31-38.

Kahn, S.E., Long, B.C. & Peterson, C (1989). Marital and parental status and quality of life of female clerical workers. *Canadian Journal of Counselling, 23*(2), 174-183.

Kahn, S.E. & Lichty, J.M. (1987). The career plans of women. *International Journal for the Advancement of Counselling,10*(2), 123-130.

Kahn, S.E. & Long, B.C. (1988). Work-related stress, self-efficacy and well-being of female clerical workers. *Counselling Psychologist Quarterly, 1*(2 & 3), 145- 153.

Long, B.C., Kahn, S.E., & Schutz, R.W. (1992). A causal model of stress and coping: Women in management. *Journal of Counseling Psychology, 39*(2), 227-239.

Mawson, D.L. & Kahn, S.E. (in press). Group process in a women's career intervention. *Career Development Quarterly.*

Pearson, H.M. & Kahn, S.E. (1989). Women clerical workers: Sex-role socialization, work attitudes, and values. *The Career Development Quarterly, 37*(3) 249-256.

Significant Events in the Life of Sharon Kahn

1946	Born, Kansas City, Missouri
1968	B.A., English Literature, Washington University, St. Louis, Missouri
1969	M.Ed., Counseling and Guidance, Boston University, Boston, Massachusetts
1969	Counsellor, Boston University
1975	Ph.D.,Counseling Psychology, Arizona State University, Tempe, Arizona
1975	Assistant Professor, Counselling Psychology, University of British Columbia, Vancouver, British Columbia
1980	Associate Professor, Counselling Psychology, University of British Columbia
1989	Director of Employment Equity, University of British Columbia

10

Career Counselling for Women:
Current Issues and Future Directions

An interview with Sharon Crozier, Ph.D., Career Development Coordinator and Counsellor, University Counselling Services; Adjunct Professor of Educational Psychology, University of Calgary.

The best career counselling for women helps them towards greater awareness

of all their life options and to plan actively the lifestyles they want to lead. That's a summary of the eminently practical philosophy that Sharon Crozier offered one November afternoon in the warmth of her Calgary home. Fueled by cookies and herbal tea, she led the authors through a vigorous discussion of the multiple, complex issues women bring to career choice and counselling, whether they are (1) young women still grappling with how to choose and time a family and career, (2) mothers struggling with role overload or (3) thirty-something women seeking help to identify and validate their skills for re-entry into the workplace.

Crozier developed her insights into women's career planning as a result of wide-ranging professional and personal experience with career change, unemployment, life in a dual career family and the challenges of a nontraditional career. Over the last ten years she has privately counselled hundreds of women and men and developed, taught and coordinated career development/planning programs for Canadian universities and colleges. She co-authored a text used in the Career and Life Management course (CALM) that is mandatory for Grade 11 students in Alberta high schools. She has also taken an active role in the Canadian Psychological Association's Section on Women and Psychology and the Canadian Association of College and University Student Services. Her research has focused on applying Donald Super's Life-Career Rainbow to planning women's careers, using the theory that a career encompasses all of a person's roles across a lifetime, including spouse, parent, citizen, worker, leisurite, student and child.

The following interview presents an overview of Crozier's concerns with regard to women's career choices plus her suggestions for meeting more of their career counselling needs.

Crossing the Hexagon: One Woman's Resolution of Her "Opposing" Career Interests

Smith: *How and when did you get interested in women's career development?*

Crozier: Probably back in high school, when I was making career decisions myself. I initially chose math education, a nontraditional career for women. And I was very aware that my high school counsellor was taken back a bit by this choice. However, because I wanted to teach math, not be a formal mathematician, that made it more acceptable. So I've been aware of the problems women face making career choices and some of the impacts on their lives from the start.

Smith: *When you were in training to teach math did you get any questions, any comments about why you were interested in math?*

Crozier: Yes, but the reaction, in some ways, was good. There was quite an interest in my being a woman interested in math, but it was positive. And by the time we got to math methodology classes it was quite accepted that I was in that area because they needed math teachers. Yet what stands out in reflection was the fact nobody ever questioned why I was not planning something other than teaching math. I did very well with my math courses and was in general an excellent student. I have an honors degree. But nobody once said, "What about engineering, Sharon, what about accounting?"

Smith: *Why did you pick math? Was it an intrinsic interest?*

Crozier: Yes, I enjoy math and like analytical problem solving. I see it as part of my cognitive style. I also have a strong people interest although those two are often considered quite opposite.

Leduc: *What about the men in school with you who were tops in math too. Were they encouraged to go into science or math-related fields?*

Crozier: Yes, it's interesting. They were encouraged to go much further with their math background. A number of them have Ph.D.s. In contrast, it was fine for me as a woman to think of a teaching degree then stop there. There were a lot of those messages—"if you even get the degree as a women that will be enough for your life." Women are not given the message that it's good to be interested in math, and here are ways to also express your social side and integrate both into your life.

We've seen a real but unnecessary separation between someone who is in the math-sciences areas and someone who is in the social-interpersonal area.

Leduc: *From high school you went directly into a university education program?*

Crozier: Yes, I did a four-year degree and right after taught biology for five years in an alternative high school, where the students study on their own and you are more of an advisor than a class room lecturer. I also taught in open area schools and a vocational school, so it exposed me to a variety of types of education. I also spent some time unemployed in Victoria—I was 23, 24—and that had a major impact on my thinking about career issues for women. Upon leaving university with an education degree the only job I thought I could do was teach, but Victoria had a lot of teachers at the time and I could only get substitute jobs. I was at a real loss for any other occupation that I could do with this degree. My biggest recollection of that year is frustration and lack of knowledge and information. So I came back to Calgary and taught here three more years.

Smith: *Did you ever think of going to a career counsellor yourself?*

Crozier: Not at that point. I'd had no experience with career counselling in university. I never thought I'd do anything but teach. So, in my mind, why did I need career assistance?

Leduc: *At 23 probably the other young women you talked to were becoming established in relationships, getting their family in place and thinking, "What is this career stuff?" That could have influenced you too.*

Crozier: Yes, although I was not planning on having a family at that point so that made me unusual.

Leduc: *Did you have mentors in Victoria to help you figure out what to do?*

Crozier: No, some of my mentors came later. There was one guidance counsellor I got to know while teaching in Calgary who was very encouraging. "Yes," she said, "go on and do the masters. You're capable and it won't be so different from math." That was my concern—will I be capable of doing psychology with only a math background? Then within my graduate program I had two mentors, Dr. West and Dr. Herman, both male, both very positive about my capabilities and the kind of work I was doing. A lot of the messages I got regarding vocational psychology was that in a sense it was the poor cousin in counselling psychology to family, marital, interpersonal, and so on. But Dr. Herman had a strong background and positive belief in vocational career psychology and that was important to me.

Smith: *Can we ask how you happened to go to Victoria?*

Crozier: I went with my husband's career. We'd first moved to Lethbridge for mine, which didn't work out for him, so Victoria was a compromise for his career. It ended up frustrating me so we moved back to Calgary. I think that is another issue with dual career couples—how to manage whose career is going to take precedence and how to find suitable places for both and compromise.

Smith: *So you speak from experience when counselling the dual career couple.*

Crozier: Most women do. If they're married, it's almost a given the husband's working. So then you're in a dual career relationship. Whether or not a lot of women look at it that way is another question. The woman usually just goes along with the husband and doesn't even think of her job as a career.

Smith: *You were teaching math. What prompted you to go into counselling?*

Crozier: I went into educational psychology so there was still the education component. But my stronger interest was to work with individuals on life issues because of the experience I'd had teaching family life and sex education. I became very interested in the students' developmental process and saw a need to give more than just a quick counselling session in this area. In fact, I published some papers in the seventies on that topic. But I only taught one or two classes of it because I was hired as a math teacher and it was hard to break that mold. And to tell you the truth, I was a bit burnt out and couldn't face another fraction.

Smith: *When you started counsellor training, were you aware that women face any special circumstances in career choice?*

Crozier: No, I became more aware of the whole area of women's issues and their developmental prospective through the graduate years. Since then, in my own practice I've struggled with how do I deal with what these women say? How do I help them work with these issues when I don't find them in the literature?

At the graduate level I'd had training in career development but not regarding women's career issues as a separate topic. But as I started my own personal consciousness raising, becoming involved in women's studies courses and in counselling women and girls, plus the Women in Psychology Group in Calgary, my awareness of women's issues increased and produced a merger of my own two areas of interest. In my view, women's career issues are a fairly recent area for us to look at as separate from men's.

Issues in Career Counselling

Leduc: *What issues do women talk about in your counselling sessions?*

Crozier: A lot of the concerns involve struggles with melding career with home and family—"how do I satisfy my own desires and still meet the needs of my family that's so important to me?" They're really struggling with the limited models offered to them by the educational and work systems because those are structured for people who can have a singular role in their lives. Education has been set up for eighteen to twenty-two year olds being looked after at home and whose only major role is student. That is not the case for a lot of women I work with. Yet they are going into situations where they are expected to have that singular focus and not worry about a family.

The other issue I hear is, "How do I fit into the work world in a way that takes into account my need for relationship." I agree with Gilligan's view that women define themselves in relationships. They want to know what does this work mean in relation to other people, either directly if they're going to deal with people, or indirectly. Or what is the meaning of this career in society? I can't just do this for external rewards, such as profits, success, status, prestige. I need to make a contribution to society. I would say the majority of women still consider those factors strongly on their occupational criteria checklist.

Leduc: *Do you think that's a function of socialization?*

Crozier: Certainly socialization is a factor. Whether it's a matter of nature too, I don't know. That's a tough one. There are differences between men and women, and socialization plays a role in that. But I'm not to the point of thinking if we socialized people the right way, so to speak, we would end up with androgynous beings walking around. I think that for women relationships and nurturing are more significant and always will be. That's not to say that a large part of being a woman doesn't involve the issues of separate identity and external achievement, and vice versa for males. So there are differences that we need to start recognizing and validating. We are getting to the point of recognizing them, but still not good at validation. There are a lot of large systemic structures in our society that are difficult to change.

Smith: *Going back to your actual career counselling experience, have you seen any trends in your female clients?*

Crozier: I've been in university counselling five and a half years. And one trend we see is an increasing population of older female and part-time students. At some level women reach a time in their lives where they are ready to take career issues more seriously, possibly because they have established their relationships or they have been through a relationship and realize they need more than just that in their lives. Also, younger women at university are considering careers more seriously. Many of the younger women have a strong belief in having it all and it will be interesting to see how that works out for them. However, some of the mature students are really questioning that goal and struggling with how to balance their lives between career and relationships.

Smith: *Do you find younger women who think they can have it all come in with a lot of misinformation about what they'll face out there?*

Crozier: I would say more a lack of information, they are naive. There are things we could do to help them with that, but there are developmental issues involved too. They need some experience to effectively deal with these issues.

Leduc: *Has it changed so much from when you were an undergraduate? You were saying you didn't have a lot of information.*

Crozier: They have more information than I did but they need even more, plus more time and energy to process it. The knowledge needed to understand the world of work today is phenomenal. And it's not just women who have these needs. One of the interesting trends with men showed up in a recent career planning workshop I did with our university's alumni. Many men wanted to know how to have more balance between work and family. They had younger children and no longer wanted to put in all the hours at work. I hear comments like that from men every so often but certainly it's not as common as the media would have you think.

Smith: *So most men coming in are not trying to figure out this juggling act or worrying about having it all the way women are.*

Crozier: Not the younger men. Very few of them seem to have that mental frame. Now, we work with both men and women in the career planning workshops on lifestyle planning and home and family issues because it's important for both to have some awareness in that area. What's interesting is that the young men are surprised to be asked to think this way. They wonder where you're coming from.

Smith: *You mean to be asked "How are you going to integrate your family role with your work role?" This is news to them?*

Crozier: Yes, their definition of career planning is "help me think about the job I'm going to do." And I talk about all of your life roles across your lifetime and how career and work impact lifestyle. That perspective is unfamiliar to them quite often. Again, they need a certain amount of experience to start dealing with it directly. Now the young women have thought about it more but very often their concepts, in my mind, are naive—"well you will just have a man and all these kids and somehow it will all fit and you'll still be a corporate president or whatever." So we have made a decision in counselling services to keep our programs heterogeneous in faculties, gender and age so that people can learn from each other. Mixing ages is very helpful for me because I can have a real person talk about issues that I bring up more at a conceptual level, a person who has been through the process and who can say to the younger women, "Well, it does not quite work that way out there in the real world."

Smith: *Are there other differences between the various age groups of women that the counsellor has to deal with?*

Crozier: If I can generalize, the majority of older clients, say age thirty or so, who come in for career counselling would have a family already so they have all sorts of complex issues to cope with, such as managing the day-by-day child care situation or losing a marital relationship. They may be facing the rest of their lives alone but still have to deal with left over issues from the relationship and self-esteem problems. That's why to me it's important for a career counsellor to have a strong general counselling background, not just career counselling. People need integration of the self in career counselling.

In comparison, the younger woman may be in a relationship but "just thinking" about her career, not planning as seriously. Some of them need to recognize that statistics show women work probably three-quarters of their adult lives today. Prince Charming does not come along to save them.

Melding Reality and Dreams

Smith: *So how does all this life complexity you've described affect the older woman's career choices? Does it restrict her choices or motivate her to do more?*

Crozier: A little bit of both. It does have an impact on her career choice, no doubt about it. She looks at the world through a different lens. And a very important part of career counselling is to help her understand her world perspective, where she is coming from. For some women the demands on them are motivating. They've had other levels of work experience and are now ready to do amazing things. But other women look seriously at the structure of the work world and wonder how they can fit in. That's a major issue we have to look at—the way work is currently structured. There are some realities that women can't ignore, and I think as career counsellors we can't say, "The world of work is rosy and you can do whatever you want." Some women have the motivation to change the work structures they enter. Others don't because they're using their energy to achieve in a variety of roles.

The real issue is that sometimes society does not value balance. We value people that focus full steam ahead on careers.

Smith: *Can they make career choices to express their real interests?*

Crozier: Again it's a mixture. Some women will say to me, "I would love to do this if I had the money and energy and if I could go to school for another seven years." But given their values and all the roles they're trying to carry, they don't have those options. But we want to be careful not to label these choices as necessarily negative. In some ways they're positive because these women are choosing to have a balanced, varied lifestyle instead of defining themselves purely in career. The real issue is that sometimes society does not value balance. We value people that focus full steam ahead on careers. That is the male model, where you put all of yourself into your occupational role. So women do make their career choices in a different framework but it's not necessary to see that as a limitation.

Smith: Have you personally felt the tug between the traditional male model, focusing everything on a career, and the need and desire to diversify?

Crozier: That's an interesting question. I would say that I'm in the throes of that struggle right now. I put a lot of my energy into my career and defining myself that way and it is just recently—I am 38 soon—that I am rethinking it. I don't have an answer about what direction I will go in but I can relate to women saying this does not feel like enough. I think we're seeing women who followed the male model hitting a point where they step back and ask, "Is this where I want to be? Do I want to continue to put this much energy into work and career?"

Leduc: *It sounds to me that younger women are very idealistic: "I am going to have everything." But women coming for counselling at a later stage in life are more practical. They've had to juggle roles to maintain sanity and still enjoy life. Do you find they apply that same kind of practicality to choosing careers? For example, will a single parent look for an occupation with more stability in terms of employment and a higher salary versus a career that would be more heartfelt?*

Crozier: Yes and no. Again those are tough distinctions because she thinks, "I know some things about myself. I want to express them in what I do in this world."

But, that attitude may be tempered if she's a single parent by the reality that she needs money. She can't afford to be laid off once a year. So for me the challenge as a counsellor is to take the fantasy, their "touchstone" as Barbara Sher calls it, and fit that together with other life realities.

Smith: *Is the typical woman less self-knowledgeable along these lines than men?*

Crozier: No. Actually a lot of young men have idealistic, stereotypic expectations, although theirs would be often more about a career. For example, young men may think they will be professional athletes. But generally young women have thought more about who they are and where they want to go. They have their own hopes and dreams. Their idealism is refreshing and you want to validate it.

Smith: *I've read that women come into their own in their late thirties, forties. Men simply get locked in early and never unlock. But women don't get locked in and make actually better choices later on. Or is this a myth?*

Crozier: If we look at the career choice process as developmental, which I do, you find that for both sexes there are structures in our society that say at eighteen you graduate from high school and then you have to make choices on as much information as you possess at that point. But what's nice these days is that we are allowing for career change in both men and women. I use myself as an example in my workshops. I tell them, "I made a choice at eighteen to be a math teacher on the information I had about me and the world of work at that point. It was not a completely bad choice. But now both I and the work world have changed." So women are returning to career decision-making because their earlier choice often was not based on full information about relationships and what family life would be like and so on.

And men, as you said, can get locked into particular career paths which are often just as stereotyped as women's. Still, work-wise they have a few luxuries that women don't because they have more breadth of choice and better pay. After homemaking and raising children, women have a hard time validating those years out of the workforce and convincing the workforce they have marketable skills. In contrast, the male who has kept working, even if just in a laboring position, has a record that shows, see, he's been dependable, reliable, out there working every day. Some of my work with women is to help them see that homemaking offered them opportunity to develop skills—child rearing, structuring their own time, volunteering on their own initiative.

Smith: *Sounds like they're entrepreneurs.*

Crozier: Yes, think of them as running their own show. But they need to learn how to express that in a marketable way. In turn we need to help the employer recognize what the woman returning to the workforce really has to offer.

Leduc: *How does a counsellor encourage that reframing of experience?*

Crozier: That's a good word, "reframing." That is counselling's work, to reframe and refocus. I have some exercises that look at skills in homemaking then do a parallel analysis looking at the skills required in a job. These help women see the value of what they've done at home. In general there's a lot of self-esteem work in the career counselling of women. You validate individuals and help them learn how to validate themselves because often women haven't learned to say, "I'm really good at this or that." Group work is helpful in that process, especially a group that has a variety of ages so you have women who've moved ahead in the career process there to reassure other women that, "Yes, you will have lots of skills to offer as a university student or employee."

The Role of Interest Inventories

Smith: *Where do interest tests fit in all this counselling?*

Crozier: Good old interest inventories. Once again I have mixed feelings. Okay, two things. One, I'm coming around to seeing that women really do have the interests that come out on those inventories, the traditional social, conventional and artistic interests. And I think those are to be validated. We can't say, "Well, those are just good old women's interests and let's ignore them and put you instead into nontraditional categories."

Two, using interest inventories it's important how you interpret them and how much credibility and weight you give them in the counselling process. You need to establish good rapport with your client first and have them do a bit of work ahead of time, such as self assessment and maybe seeking out feedback from family and friends. Women have been told not to trust their intuition, so it's important to take those steps first. Then something like an interest inventory can be introduced because at this point the woman will see it more as a piece of information she can use rather than the answer.

After that, you have to watch for traditional male interests that emerge— investigative, realistic, enterprising and so on—even if they are less prominent than social and artistic, which quite often they are. You help her consider them too. You have to be careful not to pressure her but at the same time realize she may be afraid to look at these because they are nontraditional. You are walking a fine balance, validating women's traditional interests but also highlighting any nontraditional interests, which otherwise can get overlooked in the regular inventory interpretation. I ask the woman to compare all parts of herself, to realize that a portion of her personality lies in those high interest areas, yes, but here's another part in this other area. Then she can try to integrate both into who she is. That is critical.

I use myself as an example, again, because I have both social and investigative interests. I say "I still have an interest in math that shows on the inventory but let's look at how I express it. I could have chosen to follow my investigative interests to engineering and the sciences. But by choosing a counselling career I've integrated my social interests as well. I can still enjoy statistics and analysis and use those skills in my counselling research. That helps a woman see that, given the options of today's work world, she doesn't have to make the either-or split. She can meld diverse interests, whether it's conventional with artistic or social with realistic. I spend a lot of time with clients processing that issue but I must say we are just on the tip of understanding it. However, there are some good books with examples of women in both nontraditional and integrated careers.

Leduc: *From counselling experience I find that one of the first requests a client interested in career change makes is for a test. How do you respond?*

Crozier: I ask them why they want the test and what they expect it to reveal. And often they believe I have one test up my sleeve that can tell them what they should do with the rest of their life. Usually they ask for an aptitude test. For me that's an opener to do two things. First to display myths about career planning. To say, for example, "We don't have magic tests that can give you the answer. I do have tests, yes, but they are only part of the process."

The other thing it helps me with is to educate them in the process of career planning. They're going to do this many times throughout their life although, whether they're 30 or 18, they usually come in thinking it's a once in a lifetime thing. The other myth is, "All I have to do is find the one right career and I'll be set." No such luck! Career choice is complex and dynamic. The world of work changes and you change too. A single answer is only going to last for a while. Then you need another answer. But if you learn the process of career decision-making, that's more helpful in the long run.

Women and Nontraditional Careers

Leduc: *I would like to touch upon nontraditional career choices for women. That's what some people are promoting.*

Crozier: I would be very careful. I would not push the "ought to" at any level. If you look at the literature on women's career issues and limitations, one direction has been the promotion of women into nontraditional careers. Since then, we've stepped back and walked a finer balance. A couple of reasons for that. One, we ran into it naively and full force ahead—and found that it did not fit everyone. If you do a single ten-week long course on women in nontraditional occupations you achieve little change. It has to be a more integrated, long-term approach.

We need to change the social system. And that is a tougher, bigger process than promoting women into nontraditional careers.

At the same time, if we promote nontraditional careers only, the male model, that does not validate women choosing homemaking for a period of their life. It does not validate women choosing the traditional female careers, such as social work and teaching. My hope would be to find some balance between those two that allows women freer choice across the job spectrum.

As we do that, two issues need attention. We still have to tell women about the reality of the world of work. For example, many traditional female careers are lower paying. They don't have the prestige, the perks—so you have to look at that trade-off. And we need a larger role for career counselling advocacy. We need to change the social system. And that is a tougher, bigger process than promoting women into nontraditional careers. It means we have to question things in the work system that aren't just bad for women but men too. Look at the fact that you're supposed to go into work with your whole soul and being. I don't think that's good for anybody's mental health, let alone family relationships. I think we have seen the costs of that in men for years—heart attacks and stress-related diseases.

The other thing we have to understand—and I don't think we are good at this in career counselling—is that economic factors affect the way work is structured. For instance, to make our economic system work, there has to be cheap labor somewhere. Women have been traditionally the cheap labor. One possible solution is more job sharing. What's interesting is that in the developed countries, Canada, North America and so on, we are going to have a shortage of employees and need more women workers.

Smith: *We keep hearing this but now we have high unemployment. Is this really going to happen?*

Crozier: I think so, but maybe in five to ten years, not the immediate term. The workplace is shrinking but due to North America's aging population, we're going to have a lot of retirement soon that will require new workers. We're already importing immigrant workers. Because of this trend the work place should become more flexible, but due to economic factors, not to altruism as companies will try to tell you. If we think strategically, women will be able to use that trend to their advantage, to have a work place that fits better with their values and is more respectful of how they operate. So there is some hope. We're seeing it already in Calgary, with some of the more progressive companies allowing women time out, job sharing, and in-house day care.

Career Education for Younger Women

Leduc: *With the emphasis on women entering nontraditional occupations, are you finding that younger students are more likely to consider nontraditional occupations? Or is it the returning students?*

Crozier: The younger student, I would say.

Leduc: *If younger women are more ready to look at nontraditional careers, do we need more career and life management courses in high schools, to reach girls earlier? I was thinking of courses such as CALM[1].*

Crozier: Well, I'm really pleased that many school systems throughout the States and Canada have career education embedded in their programs. CALM, the Alberta program, in particular involves more than just career planning. What

---

1 Required in Grade 11 for all Alberta high school students since 1989. It can be a semester or a year long program depending on how the school is structured.

students learn in the program is integrated so what they find out about self-esteem or values is applied to careers and vice versa.

Leduc: *Are interest tests a fundamental part of CALM?*

Crozier: No, using interest inventories at the high school level is completely optional. It's very much up to the people teaching the course and also depends somewhat on their access to the counselling services. In the CALM curriculum itself there are more paper and pencil types of self assessment for the students.

Some other very exciting intervention programs involve role modelling—bringing women in nontraditional careers into the elementary schools, taking the kids on field trips to see a woman dentist, a woman scientist and so on. Role models are a critical factor in women's decision-making. That's true with men as well. An example is male nurses, where the numbers are still very small. I might note that more often the issue for men with regard to nontraditional careers is the low prestige and pay of women's occupations. Women shifting to nontraditional careers can look forward at least to more rewards. But one big plus for nontraditional men is that they generally advance a lot quicker into administration.

We've also tried, unsuccessfully as yet, to have a credited career planning course at the University of Calgary. Credit is important otherwise the students are too busy struggling with other requirements to fit the course in. But we've been finding that we have to do more of this earlier, that you cannot just start at university or high school. The world of work is becoming so complex we need to introduce younger students to ideas about work and careers.

Smith: *When you talk about expanding counselling to reach younger students, are you really talking about changing socialization?*

Crozier: I wouldn't even call this counselling. I feel it's education and I see it integrated within existing school programs. That means the shop teacher talking about the sort of work you can do with shop skills, the math teacher with math skills. But CALM as such in the Alberta system is a separate program. Again I have to give the States credit here because, more than Canada, they're moving forward with the integration of career education as part of the existing school coursework. And yes, it is a form of socialization.

Leduc: *Would you and I be talking ourselves out of a job if career education is done effectively at the earlier stages?*

Crozier: No, never. I am not worried at all. As we said earlier, people do levels of career development throughout their lifetime. They can do some in the early school years but they also need to revisit this issue when they're older.

Leduc: *Different developmental issues.*

Crozier: Yes, as individuals change and as the world of work changes, they will still need us in career counselling as another resource in their process. They would just be better at it.

Smith: *Do you know when is the best time for people to seek career counselling?*

Crozier: It's effective whenever people want it.

Training Career Counsellors for Women & Men

Smith: *Given so many changes in people's developmental needs and in the world of work, how should counsellors be trained to provide the best assistance?*

Crozier: Career counsellors need a broad background. First, they need to be good personal counsellors with training in human development, both male and female. They also need excellent communication, interpersonal, and human relationship skills. Then career counselling comes as a later specialization. There, you need a background in career theory and the process of career development plus a great deal of background in handling information sources, because the world of work is so complex.

After that you need further specialization for women's career development, handicapped people's career development, whichever groups you are going to be dealing with. You also have to have some background in lifestyle planning and probably in leisure planning. You need both theoretical and practical courses. You need skills in both individual and group or psycho-educational counselling because a lot of career counselling is with groups and in schools, as noted earlier.

Smith: *To achieve this broad training, are there any changes in counsellor education that have to be made?*

Crozier: My own vision for the future would be a higher level of education for career counsellors. The Canadian situation is such that many people are counselling with limited training and that concerns me for two reasons. I'm concerned for the individual trying to do the counselling because I think they feel over their heads. And I'm concerned for the clients. We've had a history of trying to separate career and vocational counselling from personal counselling and I don't think that can be done. I don't think it serves Super's ideas well at all. Your career is who you are as a person. So if you are going to counsel somebody in their career, you have to be able to deal with their personal issues as they go through that process and struggle. So it's really critical that counsellors put quite a few years into their education.

Choosing a Career Counsellor

Leduc: *Any advice for women choosing a good counsellor?*

Crozier: Given what I just said, a critical issue is credentials. Check to see that they have a solid background in counselling.

Leduc: *And don't be afraid to ask them about their background, just because they have this expert title of "counsellor"?*

Crozier: That's right. The second thing is make sure they have specific background in career counselling including particular courses and practicum, that they keep up in their reading and that it's a true area of interest, not something they do on the side. Personally I would look for a counsellor who says, "I can deal with your career issues and also your personal issues in the process." I don't want a career counsellor who's going to send me out the door to a personal counsellor as soon as I mention I don't have enough self confidence or decision-making skills.

Smith: *Is the best choice someone with either a psychology or an educational psychology background?*

Crozier: Well, there are very good social workers and human resources people, speaking in a broad sense, but I would make sure they have that broad background first, plus a specialization with the career work. The other given is that you feel comfortable with your counsellor and respected. Counsellors can be biased and say, "Those nontraditional careers are going to be too macho for you." Or be biased the other way and say, "Forget that social work and teaching. You should go into math completely." If counsellors aren't respectful of where I am coming from and not helping me explore that openly, they're not giving me what I need.

Smith: *So you're talking about a feminist counsellor?*

Crozier: I think feminist counsellors do that, yes. I think other people do it as well. Feminist counsellors to my mind try to use that approach as the basis from which they work and declare that openly. But there are humanistic counsellors and so on who may not be comfortable with the title of feminist, but who do assume that broad perspective allowing people to move in the direction important to them.

Research in Women's Career Counselling: Future Needs

Smith: *Given all that we've talked about, where are the gaps in our knowledge about counselling women?*

Crozier: Two major areas come to mind. I think people are speculating a lot right now on women's career development and paths, like we did this afternoon. But I don't think we've done enough good longitudinal research. My impression is that career development would be very different for women in their teens and early twenties as compared to those in their thirties or forties. Some of that research could be done retrospectively.

The second area where we need more research involves how women make their career choices—what are the real factors they consider, how do they weigh things out? We've haven't sat down and asked women these questions, like in some other kinds of research, for example, the work of Gilligan and Belenky.

Another thing to recognize is that women are heterogeneous and we have to be careful in saying that anything is true for all women. So a critical factor in all research is being sure you have background information, demographics and so on, to understand how women fit into different groupings. That way you can detect common themes across their choices but also differences.

Smith: *Is there any research that you would like to see done on interest tests to make them more useful?*

Crozier: Yes, there's a real need for ongoing research and clarification of who we are calling "norm" groups. For example, what age cohort are you comparing your client to? We also need more work on using and interpreting interest inventories in a way that makes them fair to apply to women.

Smith: *What about the items themselves. Do they need replacement?*

Crozier: I can't tell you off the top of my head. For me the inventories are only a small part of the whole process so I don't give much credibility to any given item or even in a sense to the whole inventory. I do a lot of work around what people know about their interests before we even look at an inventory.

I also think exciting things are happening in qualitative research methods which could interact with counselling to gather new information. We've done quantitative research with large groups and questionnaires but we haven't tapped into the kind of research that you could do through the counselling process. In qualitative research you have the phenomenological perspective, the significant life events for that person, and you learn how individuals construct their world. Well, we do that very often in counselling too. There are ways we listen and integrate which could contribute to such a research methodology.

Leduc: *How do you find the funds to do it?*

Crozier: If we did that kind of research as part of counselling, it wouldn't be that costly. You don't have to use big samples, you don't have to develop major questionnaires. What costs is the transcribing and analyzing of interviews for themes, and analysis takes time, so there does need to be some funding. But there are good software packages that help do the job.

Leduc: *Once it's funded, how do you get the research results out efficiently to busy counsellor-practitioners for their use?*

Crozier: Two ways. One is in the traditional academic journals, although the journals need to flex a bit in what they take as research. They need to recognize the merit of single case studies and qualitative research, for example. We also need practitioners themselves writing more about case studies so we'd have access to cases of real people in the counselling process with the methodology highlighted for us.

Finally, we need a better understanding of how to deliver career information to the clients themselves, how to offer programs and information and be involved with the individual so that she finds it more meaningful.

References and Recommended Readings

Belenky, M.F., Clinchy, B.M., Goldberger, N.R. & Tarule, J.M. (1986). *Women's ways of knowing: The development of self, voice & mind*. New York: Basic Books, Inc. Publishers.

Bradshaw, B. & Stewart, D. (1990). *Job stories: I like my work, I like the money*. Vancouver, B.C.: Learning Resource Society.

Derr, C.B. (1986). *Managing the new careerists: The diverse career success orientations of today's workers*. San Francisco: Jossey-Bass.

Gilligan, C. (1982). *In a different voice: Psychological theory and women's development*. Cambridge, MA: Harvard University Press.

Halpenny, F.G. (1991) *Claiming the future: The inspiring lives of 12 Canadian women scientists and scholars*. Toronto: Pembroke Publishers Ltd.

Sher, B. (1979). *Wishcraft: How to get what you really want*. New York, NY: Ballantine Books.

Statham, A., Miller, E.M., & Mauksch, H.O. (1988). *The worth of women's work: A qualitative synthesis*. Albany, N.Y.: State University of New York Press.

Super, D.E. (1957). *The psychology of careers*. New York: Harper.

Super, D.E. (1980). A life-span, life-space approach to career development. *Journal of Vocational Behavior, 16*, 282-298.

Super, D.E. (1990). A life-span, life-space approach. In D. Brown, L. Brooks, & Associates, *Career Choice and Development* (Second Edition). San Francisco: Jossey Bass.

Significant Events in the Life of Sharon Crozier

1960	Started school
1972	Encouraged by Math teacher to continue studies in that area. Entered University of Calgary
1973	Married High School Sweetheart
1976	Completed Bachelor of Education, specializing in Secondary Mathematics
1976	First teaching position; High School Biology, Lethbridge, Alberta
1977-78	Moved to Victoria B.C. but unable to find work
1979	Divorced
1980	Taught Family & Life Education
1981	Entered Master's Degree program in Educational Psychology
1981	Remarried a man with three sons, one of whom is disabled
1982	Research work on Computerized Career Guidance Programs. Mentored by two professors
1983	Entered Ph.D. program in Educational Psychology, specializing in Career Counselling Program Evaluation and Group Counselling
1985	Completed Dissertation in the Life Roles of Teachers, reviewing the Career & Life Roles of Male and Female Teachers
1986	Started work at the University of Calgary, University Counselling Services with specific area of specialization in Career Counselling
1986	Developed Career/Life Planning Modules, a series of six career/life planning workshops designed to address the career planning issues of university students
1987-92	Active work in a variety of Women's Organizations, which increased awareness of women's issues
1987	Developed and piloted a week-end workshop, Advanced Career Planning, for University Alumni. Currently offered to 500 Alumni annually
1988	Co-authored the Strategies for Career & Life Management text, used for Alberta High School students in the CALM program
1989	Awarded the Career Development Award for Southern Alberta by the Government of Alberta, Career Development Branch
1990	Awarded the First Outstanding New Professional Award by the Alberta Student Services Association
1991	Published the Student Journal, to accompany the *Strategies for Career and Life Management* text

Conclusions

Distilling the Wisdom +social zation

So what have we learned? Is women's choice of work a matter of chance or real choice? Or simply socialization? Judging from our interviewees' lives and those of the women they have studied, all three factors play a role. But gender socialization, that is, all those messages society passes on to us about what are proper behaviors and even thinking patterns for men and women, is clearly the major influence. Chance is an often critical but supporting player. And, in real life, informed choice, which should be our goal, only becomes important as we gather experience. With age we finally begin to make career decisions based on how our real abilities and interests match up with the full range of job options. ✳

Messages from Women's Lives

Certainly socialization was the dominant force in shaping the early occupational aspirations and decisions of our interviewees. We had expected to hear that the educational accomplishments of such obviously talented women had given them enough confidence and direction to chose an appropriately ambitious career path early in life. But in almost every case it was chance events that later convinced +comp them of their worth. Most, as young women, doubted they had the right stuff to learned be professionals, even though they were the high school "brains." A common self-tendency was to believe in the myths that women did well because they worked esteem harder than boys, not because they were talented.

Where socialization had its most pernicious effect was in the general lack of encouragement that interviewees received to pursue the kinds of careers warranted by their early performance. "It didn't really seem to matter to my family or teachers what I planned to do with my life," was the common theme. Some, such as Betz, Lee, Astin and Crozier, faced negative or puzzled reactions when they expressed interest in a nontraditional career. But only rarely, as in the case of Astin's choice of physics, were they told a particular career was not possible. Instead, for most, the pervasive message they received as young women was that they should marry, ✳ raise children and view their future jobs as only a supplement to family income or a fallback in case something happened to their husbands.

Looking back on their youth, our interviewees described themselves overall as incredibly naive, aware of only a few careers appropriate to them as women. Most essentially stumbled into their original choice of university major. Even Hansen who knew in her teens she wanted a Ph.D. did not know in what field. Almost no one had career counselling, and what counselling they did receive tended to be unrealistic. For example, no one informed Farmer when she aspired to the ministry that a woman would not be allowed a pulpit. Given this lack of strong career direction as young women, by default they were vulnerable to a central message of traditional socialization: "Why should girls even bother to aim high?"

But chance, combined with their real capabilities, planted the seeds of ambition. Many had female role models in their lives who demonstrated that power and achievement were not incompatible with femininity. Some of these models were close female relatives with a career, such as Hollinger's aunt and Betz' and Hansen's mothers. For many it was a case of friendships with other girls in school who were driven to achieve. Doing well in school, even in math and science, therefore seemed normal. And as Farmer, Eccles, Betz and Hollinger reported, they often learned independence and decision making from being treated more like sons than daughters by their parents. In some families, such as Kahn's, advanced education was expected of all the children.

Encouraging comments by a respected older adult could also catalyze ambitions. Eccles and Gottfredson, who joined the Peace Corps, reported their supervisors simply expected them to apply to graduate school. Crozier, Astin and Hollinger noted how encouraged they were by older colleagues or supervisors who recognized their potential and urged them on to a doctorate.

Another common theme of chance was the fact that these women in general did not consider they had a real choice in high school to opt out of advanced training. Good grades automatically put both girls and boys into advanced classes. As well, they all reported enjoying math and science. In Lee's case, despite no encouragement from her family to go to university, her high school enrolled her at a neighboring university as though she had no other option. However, despite Messing's having the top grades in physics she was overlooked as a candidate for physics summer camp.

Unfortunately some reported a price for achieving contrary to the cultural expectations for women. For example, Betz and Gottfredson felt often like social misfits in high school when it came to dating and Lee noted her family thought she was "weird." And as Lee in particular reported, this social cost intensified in university if a girl chose to major in a very nontraditional field like math and ended up as a token female in her classes.

Fortunately the role of informed choice grew more significant as the women grew older and more experienced. In general they worked before going on to graduate school, which gave them a hands-on opportunity to develop and test their skills. For example, Eccles' Peace Corps stint in another culture reassured her it was possible to combine work and family. And working as a university research assistant allowed Gottfredson to compare her abilities with professionals and realize she did have research skills. By teaching high school, Crozier came to realize she was good at and interested in counselling students in life planning. Kahn in turn was motivated to continue in counselling at least partly by her volunteer experience working with other women in the early Women's Movement. Farmer also tried her hand at several jobs while raising her children until she realized she would not be satisfied unless she worked as a professional psychologist. Messing was inspired by reading a feminist book to try a few science courses, just to prove she was not scared of them. That experience helped convince her to make genetics a career.

Overall the interviewees' personal and professional experiences challenged the myth promoted by traditional socialization, which says science/math types of workers (read "men") are distinct from emotive, interpersonal types (read "women"). Given half an opportunity, all the women interviewed excelled in and combined both skill areas in their work. While they reported sensing as they grew up that helping others was an important task for women, their research accomplishments amply demonstrated their analytical skills.

Another repeated theme was that even as adults our interviewees did not escape the pressures created by the effect of gender socialization on society's day-to-day operations. They reported their struggles to raise children while holding down academic postings that presumed the full-time support of a spouse at home. Some talked openly of discrimination on the job. If married, they also faced the nightmare of the dual-career couple: how to find decent jobs for both in the same city. Double standards were rampant. As Astin noted, if her husband switched jobs employers assumed he was in demand; if she switched jobs, she was not committed to her career.

Messages from Research

Discussions of the available research delivered the same messages. Woven through several chapters was the theme that the effect of gender socialization in classrooms and at job sites discourages women's occupational aspirations and choices. Schools, with their sex stereotypic textbooks and teaching methods designed to appeal to men, turn women off science and math. And employers consider women just small men on the job. Even if laws dictate the hiring of more women, employers often fail to adapt procedures, equipment, schedules, uniforms, etc., to women's bodily and social needs. Male employees have difficulty accepting women as colleagues, not as sex objects. The message potential employees receive is clear: "Women are not welcome here and only certain jobs are right for each gender." The result is severe restriction of the job choices considered by young women and men.

Another theme was the clash between young women's expectations that spouses will share domestic responsibilities with the contrasting traditional views of the young men who they'll likely marry. Few men have any perspective of integrating a family with a career. Yet women expect to have it all—a tall order without spousal co-operation.

Despite the demands of this domestic balancing act, the workplace is only slowly adapting to the needs of people with a family, male or female. But for now, given the tenacity of traditional socialization, the responsibilities and their consequences still fall largely on women. The work world follows the male model and does not value balancing nurturing and achievement. Its motto remains "full steam ahead on careers." That forces many women to choose between relationships and achievement. However, as Lee and Messing testified, asking women to mutilate their psyches this way to become more like men is not a solution. Women tend to thrive in settings that allow them to nourish relationships even at work, to co-operate and share with people rather than compete.

Such hostile messages leave women underestimating their abilities and, as Astin found, that underestimation extends far into adult life. Women constantly feel they don't belong, particularly in math and science-related jobs. They drop out and abandon their career dreams. As Hansen in particular noted, women as a whole may never have the same interest patterns as men and the exact same distribution of jobs, no matter how much workplace equality we achieve. But many women are interested in nontraditional careers and should not be pushed out.

For women to seriously consider nontraditional occupations, interviewees agreed the workplace has to change. And that means adapting to individual employee needs, male and female, with caregiving leaves, flextime and on-site daycare, for example. The work place has to satisfy the health and safety needs of women, although first we need to develop the research methodology to find out what these are.

Ultimately the interviewees called for changes to catalyze informed choice at an earlier stage. Society must provide career and life planning education in time to teach children about the full range of job options and to counter socialized gender restrictions. Later, as adults, they have to be given the chance to apply for these jobs. That means changes in hiring and promotion practices, such as Kahn discussed. But the critical message for employers and employees alike is that changes for women benefit men too. It is just that the need for change has not been essential for men to remain on the job whereas it is for women.

In addition, educators need to accept that people are not "brain dead" at thirty. Given the typical life cycle of women, they should be welcomed back to retrain after staying home to raise children. The interviewees sent a strong message that it is never too late to pick up a career.

Another urgent message was the lack of adequate counsellor training in women's occupational issues. Counsellors need to help women learn about real conditions in the work world—it's not all rosy out there—but at the same time, break the association of certain careers with gender. Counsellors must also establish rapport with clients before the use of vocational interest tests, which are only additional pieces of information on which to base a choice. Clients do best if they learn the whole process of career decision making because they will likely have to make such decisions over and over throughout their working lives.

However, the interviewees agreed that we must not devalue traditional careers. Why replace old "shoulds" with new ones? Instead, they called for research to learn why girls do choose the careers they do and stop thinking of traditional choices as indicating some kind of deficit in women. Nurturing others, so associated with being female, is worthwhile and essential to society's survival.

Fortunately, as we heard over and over, simple demographics will likely force change. One of the most consistent predictions was a coming shortage of skilled employees that can only be met by hiring women and minorities. Right now women earn more than half of the undergraduate degrees and an increasing share of graduate degrees. The marketplace cannot afford to waste women, a belief which echoes the United Nations Population Fund Annual Report (published in April 29, 1992) stating that women are the world's wasted asset. Given this trend, there has to be more funding for long-term studies of women's career development, particularly those involving direct interviewing.

Key Messages on Career Choice

For any woman considering a career, the interviewees had invaluable advice. Keep your job options open, get the training, especially all the math and science you can stomach. Take Women's Studies courses for a better idea of the socialization pressures influencing you and your friends. Don't be pushed by others' expectations. Particularly don't expect Prince Charming to come along to take care of you. Statistics suggest this is highly unlikely. And don't be surprised when you find educational and on-the-job conditions difficult, particularly in a nontraditional career. Above all, try not to underestimate yourself and think these difficulties represent some personal failing. As Hansen pointed out, we're facing an economy with too few positions for some job interests. It's going to be very competitive for everyone.

If you decide to seek help from a counsellor, the interviewees urge a careful check of counsellors' credentials How much training in women's career needs have they had? Avoid anyone pushing either nontraditional jobs or the stereotypical view. In addition, recognize there is no magic test to identify your one best career choice.

Final Thoughts

Socialization, it appears, is still so powerful that men and women will probably be brought up in what amounts to separate social ghettos for a good while longer, as noted by John Holland in this book's opening quote. But if we continue with steps to achieve genuine equality of opportunity in the workforce we may see remarkable change in our society. Donald Super described what that future possibly holds:

I'm talking about a much more fundamentally single culture in which men and women will function as equals and there really won't be any differentiation, except obviously when it comes to child bearing and breast feeding. I suspect the time will come when that's about the only real difference between men and women.
—Personal Communication, April 24, 1991, American Association
for Counseling and Development, AGM, Reno, Nevada.